CAMBRIDGE LIBRARY COLLECTION

Books of enduring scholarly value

Travel and Exploration

The history of travel writing dates back to the Bible, Caesar, the Vikings and the Crusaders, and its many themes include war, trade, science and recreation. Explorers from Columbus to Cook charted lands not previously visited by Western travellers, and were followed by merchants, missionaries, and colonists, who wrote accounts of their experiences. The development of steam power in the nineteenth century provided opportunities for increasing numbers of 'ordinary' people to travel further, more economically, and more safely, and resulted in great enthusiasm for travel writing among the reading public. Works included in this series range from first-hand descriptions of previously unrecorded places, to literary accounts of the strange habits of foreigners, to examples of the burgeoning numbers of guidebooks produced to satisfy the needs of a new kind of traveller - the tourist.

Narratives of the Rites and Laws of the Yncas

The publications of the Hakluyt Society (founded in 1846) made available edited (and sometimes translated) early accounts of exploration. The first series, which ran from 1847 to 1899, consists of 100 books containing published or previously unpublished works by authors from Christopher Columbus to Sir Francis Drake, and covering voyages to the New World, to China and Japan, to Russia and to Africa and India. This 1873 volume was the second on the history of Peru to be translated and edited by Clements R. Markham, Secretary of the Society. It contains four manuscript accounts of the rites and laws of the Incas which throw light on many aspects of Inca and pre-Inca society. All were written by people who had lived and worked in Peru in the sixteenth and early seventeenth century and had access to indigenous sources and traditions. The book includes a contextualising introduction and several indexes.

T0381573

Cambridge University Press has long been a pioneer in the reissuing of out-of-print titles from its own backlist, producing digital reprints of books that are still sought after by scholars and students but could not be reprinted economically using traditional technology. The Cambridge Library Collection extends this activity to a wider range of books which are still of importance to researchers and professionals, either for the source material they contain, or as landmarks in the history of their academic discipline.

Drawing from the world-renowned collections in the Cambridge University Library, and guided by the advice of experts in each subject area, Cambridge University Press is using state-of-the-art scanning machines in its own Printing House to capture the content of each book selected for inclusion. The files are processed to give a consistently clear, crisp image, and the books finished to the high quality standard for which the Press is recognised around the world. The latest print-on-demand technology ensures that the books will remain available indefinitely, and that orders for single or multiple copies can quickly be supplied.

The Cambridge Library Collection will bring back to life books of enduring scholarly value (including out-of-copyright works originally issued by other publishers) across a wide range of disciplines in the humanities and social sciences and in science and technology.

Narratives of the Rites and Laws of the Yncas

CLEMENTS R. MARKHAM

CAMBRIDGE
UNIVERSITY PRESS

CAMBRIDGE UNIVERSITY PRESS

Cambridge, New York, Melbourne, Madrid, Cape Town, Singapore,
São Paolo, Delhi, Dubai, Tokyo

Published in the United States of America by Cambridge University Press, New York

www.cambridge.org
Information on this title: www.cambridge.org/9781108010603

© in this compilation Cambridge University Press 2010

This edition first published 1873
This digitally printed version 2010

ISBN 978-1-108-01060-3 Paperback

WORKS ISSUED BY

The Hakluyt Society.

NARRATIVE OF THE RITES AND LAWS OF THE YNCAS.

M.DCCC.LXXIII.

NARRATIVES

OF

THE RITES AND LAWS

OF

THE YNCAS.

TRANSLATED

FROM THE ORIGINAL SPANISH MANUSCRIPTS,

AND EDITED,

With Notes and an Introduction,

BY

CLEMENTS R. MARKHAM, C.B., F.R.S.

LONDON:

PRINTED FOR THE HAKLUYT SOCIETY.

M.DCCC.LXXIII.

COUNCIL

OF

THE HAKLUYT SOCIETY.

CONTENTS.

I.

An Account of the Fables and Rites of the Yncas, by Christoval
de Molina - - - - Page 3

II.

An Account of the Antiquities of Peru, by Juan de Santa Cruz
Pachacuti-yamqui Salcamayhua - - - 67

III.

A Narrative of the errors, false gods, and other superstitions and
diabolical rites in which the Indians of the province of
Huarochiri lived in ancient times, by Dr. Francisco de Avila 123

IV.

Report by Polo de Ondegardo - - - 151

INDEX.

I.—Subjects - - - - - 173

II.—Names of Places - - - - 177

III.—Quichua Words - - - - - 186

IV.—Names of Gods and Huacas - - - - 211

V.—Names of Indian men, women, lineages, and tribes - 214

VI.—Names of Spaniards - - - 219

INTRODUCTION.

MUCH as students would now prize the information that was collected by the Spaniards who first over-ran the New World, they can only obtain a small fraction of it. In these days, when scientific methods are understood, and all evidence can be sifted and receive its relative weight, much of that evidence is lost. Of all the narratives and reports furnished to Herrera, for his history of the Indies, and of which he made such scanty and unintelligent use, very few have been preserved. Diligent search, for which we have to thank Don Pascual de Gayangos, has brought four such documents to light, relating to ancient Peruvian history, translations of which have been selected by the Council of the Hakluyt Society to form a volume of their series. The originals are manuscripts in the National Library at Madrid, marked B 135.

The first of these manuscripts is a report on the fables and rites of the Yncas, addressed by Christoval de Molina, the priest of the hospital for natives, at Cuzco, to Dr. Don Sebastian de Artaun, the bishop of that ancient capital. It must have been written between 1570 and 1584; the period during which Artaun was bishop of Cuzco.

The second is an account of the antiquities of
Peru, by an Indian named Juan de Santa Cruz
Pachacuti-yamqui Salcamayhua.   His great-great
grand parents were living at the time of the Spanish
conquest of Peru ; so that the author may have
written in about 1620.

The third is an account of the religion and tradi-
tions of the Indians of the mountainous province of
Huarochiri, on the Pacific slope of the maritime
Cordillera, near Lima, by a resident priest, named
Dr. Francisco de Avila.   It was written in 1608.

The fourth is a report, written in a memorandum
book, apparently as a rough draft, among the papers
of the Licentiate Polo de Ondegardo, an able and
accomplished statesman, who was Corregidor of
Cuzco, in 1560.

The first of these documents is the most important.
Cristoval de Molina had peculiar opportunities for
collecting accurate information.   He was a master
of the Quichua language ; he examined native chiefs
and learned men who could remember the Ynca empire in the days of its prosperity, and he was intimately acquainted with the native character, from
his position in the hospital at Cuzco.   In his opening address to the bishop, he mentions a previous
account which he had submitted, on the origin, history, and government of the Yncas.   Fortunately
this account has been preserved, by Miguel Cavello
Balboa,[1] who tells us that his history is based on the

[1] A French translation of the work of Balboa was published by
Ternaux Compans, in the second series of his translations, in 1840.

learned writings of Christoval de Molina. The present manuscript shows the importance of Molina as an authority, and a special value is thus given to Balboa's work, which may now be looked upon as the most authentic version of early Yncarial traditions and history.

The report on the fables and rites is supplementary to the history used by Balboa; but which is not now extant as a separate work. It contains a minute and detailed account of the ceremonies performed in the different months throughout the Ynca year, with the prayers used by the priests on each occasion in Quichua and Spanish, the sacrifices, and festivities. There are some very interesting points, which must be noticed in their order, in connection with Molina's account of the Yncas; for they throw fresh light on several doubtful questions.

The first of these points is the position held by the Supreme Being or Creator, in the religion of the Yncas. Our knowledge of this subject has hitherto been derived from Garcilasso de la Vega, who tells us that, besides the Sun, the Yncas worshipped the true supreme God and Creator; that they called him Pachacamac, a name signifying " He who gives animation to the universe," or " He who does to the universe what the soul does to the body;" that they held Him in much greater inward veneration than the Sun; but that they did not build temples to him,

Balboa commenced his work at Quito in 1576, and completed it in 1586; the very period when Molina was prosecuting his researches at Cuzco.

nor offer him sacrifices.[2] He quotes from Blas Valera, that all subjugated tribes were ordered to worship the most powerful god Ticci-Uira-ccocha, otherwise called Pachacamac;[3] and in another place, he says that the temple of Pachacamac, on the sea-coast, was the only one to the Supreme Being throughout the whole of Peru.[4]

I have discussed the questions relating to the temple on the sea coast, in my introduction to the "Reports on the Discovery of Peru" (Hakluyt Society, 1872); and have shown that it was not dedicated to the Supreme Being of the Yncas. Garcilasso de la Vega wrote the particulars touching what he had heard in Peru, after a lapse of many years, but without conscious exaggeration. Indeed his statements, as a rule, are wonderfully accurate, as I shall presently show. But the evidence of Molina is more reliable, because he wrote on the spot, with a full knowledge of the language, and after carefully examining the surviving priests and wise men of the old Ynca court.

The name *Pachacamac* occurs three times in the prayers given by Molina, as an attribute of the Deity; but the term most constantly used was *Pachayachachic*, "the teacher of the universe." Another name was *Tecsi-viracocha*, which Molina interprets, "the incomprehensible God." In the prayers, however, the first word is *Aticsi*, probably from *Atini* (I conquer), and the meaning would rather be the

---

[2] G. de la Vega, i, p. 106.   [3] *Ibid.*, ii, p. 38.
[4] *Ibid.*, ii, p. 186.

conquering *Uiracocha*. Respecting the meaning of
the word *Uira-cocha*, I am at present doubtful; but
Garcilasso has clearly shown that it does not mean,
as has been suggested by writers unacquainted with
the language, "the foam of the sea."[5] The usual
names for the god of the Yncas, and those which
occur in their prayers, are Pachayachachic Aticsi-
Uiracocha. Molina relates that one of the Yncas
erected a temple to the Supreme Being at Cuzco,[6] on
a site now occupied by the Church of the Nazarenes,
and in Molina's days by the house of Hernan Lopez
de Segovia.[7] The Indian Salcamayhua also mentions
this temple, and it is quite true that on the site
indicated, there are the walls of an ancient edifice,
with serpents carved in relief on the stones. Molina
adds, that there was a golden statue to represent the
Creator in this temple, which received honours at all
the periodical festivals.

The sun, moon, and thunder, appear to have been
deities next in importance to Pachayachachic; sacrifices were made to them at all the periodical festivals,
and several of the prayers given by Molina are addressed to them. Another image, called *Huanacauri*,
which is said to have been the most sacred of the
ancestral gods of the Yncas, received equal honours.
In all this we may discern the popular religion of the
Andean people, which consisted in the belief that all
things in nature had an ideal or soul which ruled
and guided them, and to which men might pray for

[5] G. de la Vega, ii, p. 66.   [6] P. 11.
[7] P. 11.

help. This worship of nature was combined with the worship of ancestors; the nature gods being called *huaca*, and the ancestral deities *pacarina* or *pacarisca*. The universal tradition pointed to a place called Paccari-tampu, as the cradle or point of origin of the Yncas. It was, from Cuzco, the nearest point to the sun-rising; and as the sun was chosen as the *pacarisca* of the Yncas, the place of their origin was at first assigned to Paccari-tampu. But when their conquests were extended to the Collao, they could approach nearer to the sun, until they beheld it rising out of lake Titicaca, and hence the inland sea became a second traditional place of royal origin.

The language of the Collas, Pacasas, and Lupacas, the people in the basin of the lake Titicaca (erroneously called Aymara), added very few words to the rich idiom of the Yncas ; but a vast number of Quichua words were adopted by the Collas. Two or three Colla words, however, occur in the manuscripts of Molina and Salcamayhua, which may give rise to speculation. According to Molina, the Ynca name for the sun was *Punchau*,[8] the god of day, and not *Ynti*, as given by Garcilasso. In the prayers, the word used is always *Punchau*. But Salcamayhua records a speech which the chief of the Collas made to the Ynca : "Thou art Lord of Cuzco, I am Lord of the Collas. I have a silver throne, thy throne is of gold. Thou art a worshipper of Uira-ccocha Pa-

---

[8] See also *Arriaga. Extirpacion de la idolatria del Peru.*

chayachachic. I worship Ynti."[9] Further on we are
told that Ynti was the god of the Collas,[1] and that
the Ynca adopted the name when he set up an image
at Titicaca.[2] According to these accounts, Punchau
was the sun-god of the Yncas, and Ynti was that of
the Collas. Yet the modern word for the sun, in the
Collao, is *Lupi*, from the Quichua word *Rupay*,
meaning heat and warmth. The word for the moon
in the Colla dialect (*Pacsa*) also occurs twice in the
manuscript of Molina. He speaks of *Pacsa-mama*,[3]
in one place, as the name of the moon-god, the Quichua word being *Quilla;* and he gives two names for
the month of July.[4] One is *Tarpui-quilla*, composed
of two Qichua words, meaning " the sowing month."
The other is *Moron-pasca*, the last word being the
Colla name for the moon.

A fourth point of interest is the additional proof
furnished in these manuscripts of the antiquity of
the Quichua drama of Ollanta.[5] Hitherto no evidence has been discovered of the word *Ollanta* being
as old as the time of the Yncas ; and the place now
called Ollantay-tampu, the traditionary scene of the
events recorded in the drama, is simply called Tampu
by all other old Spanish writers. But both Molina[6]
and Salcamayhua[7] speak of it as Ollanta-tampu.
This is a proof that the name is not of modern origin.

[9] P. 90.   [1] P. 101.   [2] P. 112.
[3] P. 37.   [4] P. 19.
[5] See " *Ollanta, an ancient Ynca Drama, translated from the
original Quichua, by Clements R. Markham, C.B. (Trübner, 1871.)*
[6] P. 51.   [7] P. 116.

In the introduction to my translation of the Quichua drama,[8] I gave a derivation of the word Ollanta, suggested by Señor Barranca. A more probable etymology has since been given by Dr. Vicente Lopez.[9] *Oll*, he says, should be *Uill* or *Uilla*, a legend, from *Uillani* (I record); and *Anta*, the Andes—*Ollanta*, "a legend of the Andes." So that before the Spanish conquest, as we now learn from Molina and Salcamayhua, there was a place called *Ollanta-tampu*—" the site of the legend, or drama of the Andes." Salcamayhua mentions plays as being enacted at the festivals of the Yncas; one called *Anay-sauca*, which means literally, "How pleasant!" another *Hayachuco*, and others.

The full details of Ynca ceremonies given by Molina furnish incidental evidence of the truthfulness of Garcilasso de la Vega. Thus the account of the feast of *Situa*, in the *Royal Commentaries*,[1] would serve as a very accurate abstract of the fuller and more detailed narrative of Molina.[2] Garcilasso wrote from memory, forty years after he had left Peru, with the aid of letters from correspondents.[3] His main object was to publish a commentary, correcting the errors of Spanish authors who professed to give a history of the Yncas without being acquainted with their language. In doing this, he added much precious information from the storehouse of his own

---

[8] P. 11.

[9] *Les races Aryennes du Pérou*, p. 327.

[1] See my translation, ii, p. 228.   [2] Pp. 20-34.

[3] See my translation of the *Royal Commentaries*, i, p. 76.

memory, and the more his work is sifted and examined, the more clearly does it appear that he was scrupulously truthful, and that, allowing for the disadvantages under which he laboured, his statements are wonderfully accurate. Perhaps the excellence of the Ynca's memory is best shown in his topographical details. He gives the conquests of each successive Ynca, mentioning the places through which the conquerors marched in the gradual acquisition of their vast empire. He enumerates three hundred and twenty places in Peru, yet, in describing the marches, he does not make a single mistake, nor give one of these places out of its order, or in the wrong position. When Garcilasso's routes of each conquering Ynca are placed on a map, they furnish convincing proofs of the remarkable accuracy of the author. The narrative of Molina also supplies more than one incidental corroboration of the correctness of Garcilasso's statements.

The words of the prayers actually offered up by the Ynca Priests to their Deities are the most valuable part of Molina's report. He gives fourteen of these prayers: four to the Supreme Being; two to the Sun; one for fruitful flocks; four for the Yncas; two for or to the other *huacas* or gods, and one to the earth. Unfortunately the Quichua words have, in many instances, been incorrectly transcribed, so that the meaning is not always clear; and the translations in Spanish, which are now given in English, are in some cases far from literal. Under these circumstances I have thought the best course would be to give all the Quichua words in an alphabetical index, with the

English meanings of those which can be recognized.[1]
The translations in the text give the meaning of the
Quichua with general accuracy.

The second Report, entitled " An Account of the
Antiquities of Peru," by an Indian named Salcamayhua,
was written about forty years after the time of Molina.
It is curious and valuable, because it gives the traditions of Ynca history, as they were handed down by
the grandchildren of those who were living at the
time of the Spanish conquest, to their grandchildren.
Salcamayhua gives two prayers which are traditionally
attributed to Manco Ccapac, the first Ynca, in the original Quichua, and two or three other Quichua prayers
and speeches. His narrative of events, and record of
customs and ceremonies, are valuable so long as they
are given their due place. They are entitled to a
certain authority as coming from a recipient of native
tradition, living a generation or two after the death
of the last man who had seen the Ynca empire in the
days of its glory. Salcamayhua, as an authority,
ranks after Cieza de Leon, Polo de Ondegardo, Molina,
Balboa, and Garcilasso de la Vega ; but before Spanish writers who were ignorant of the native language,
though they lived and wrote before his time, such as
Zarate, Fernandez, and Acosta. Montesinos both
wrote after Salcamayhua, and is totally unreliable.
The Indian Salcamayhua was intimately acquainted
with the language, which was his own, and he received
the traditions from his own people. But neither he
nor Molina corroborate one of the fabulous stories

[1] See p. 186.

told by Montesinos ; whose pretensions to having received his list of a hundred kings, and other absurdities, from the Indian *Amautas* or wise men, are discredited by the absence of all corroborative testimony. It is clear that Montesinos was ignorant of the Quichua language, and his work, in my opinion, is quite inadmissible as an authority.

The third document in the present collection is a narrative of the false gods and other superstitions of the Indians of the province of Huarochiri, by the Dr. Francisco de Avila, Priest of the principal village in the province. This is one of the very few fragments from which we can glean some slight knowledge of the mysterious civilized nation which occupied the coast of Peru, before the Ynca conquest. Researches into the history of this coast-people are surrounded by peculiar difficulties. The Yncas conquered the Peruvian coast two or three generations before the arrival of the Spaniards, and used all their influence and power to substitute the Quichua language, and to destroy the separate polity and religion of the conquered race. Hence many Quichua words appear in their traditions, as told by Father Avila, and the student must carefully eliminate them, before forming any conclusions respecting the intellectual position of the original people of the Pacific coast. For instance, the god of the Huarochiri is said to be *Coniraya Uiracocha*, the former word being indigenous, and the latter a foreign term introduced by the Yncas; just as we should say the *God Vishnu*, combining an English and a Hindu word. The root *Con*, in the words *Coniraya* and

b

Conopa, is the term for the deity, or for anything sacred in the language of the coast, and has nothing to do with Quichua.

The province of Huarochiri, of which a map is given to illustrate the curious narrative of Avila, is very mountainous. It occupies the western slopes of the maritime cordillera of the Andes, overhanging the coast plain from the latitude of Lima to that of Pachacamac. Avila unconsciously furnishes evidence that the inhabitants of Huarochiri originally came from the coast. " They declare," he says, " that in the days of Coniraya their country was *yunca*,"[5] " and that the crops ripened in five days." Avila enters into an elaborate explanation to prove that this is impossible. But obviously the tradition referred to the time when the ancestors of the Huarochiri people inhabited the *yuncas* of the coast.

The sources of information respecting the civilized race of the Peruvian coast are very scanty, and consequently very precious. We have the silent testimony of the grand ruins of Chimu near Truxillo,[6] and in other coast valleys, of the great mounds, and of the works of irrigation. There is a grammar and vocabulary of their language, written by Fernando de la Carrera in 1644 ; and the Lord's Prayer in *Mochica*, one of their dialects, preserved by Bishop Orè, and published at Naples in 1602. Cieza de Leon[7] travelled through the coast valleys in the early

---

[5] *Yunca* is a warm tropical plain or valley.

[6] Described by Rivero, and photographed, in detail, by Mr. Squier.   [7] See my translation, pp. 233-63.

days of the Spanish conquest, and gave an interesting
account of what he saw, to which Garcilasso de la
Vega[8] has added some additional particulars. Balboa[9]
relates the legends of the coast Indians of Lambayeque
respecting their first arrival by sea ; and the curious
report of Arriaga[1] on the destruction of idols in the
provinces of Yauyos and Conchucos, has some bearing
on the people of the coast. But here again great care
must be taken to eliminate all Ynca words and ideas,
before use can be made of the report, in an inquiry
as to the Yuncas of the sea board. A still more
remarkable report was made by an Augustin[2] friar,
in 1555, on the idolatry and superstitions of the
inhabitants of the province of Huamachuco, which,
like Conchucos, Yauyos, and Huarochiri, overhangs
the coast valleys. It is from these scanty materials
that some knowledge can be acquired, after careful
study, of the civilized race on the coast, and of the
extent to which branches from it had spread over the
mountainous districts of the maritime cordillera. The
most curious of these sources of information, is, I
think, the narrative of Father Avila, which has never
been printed in Spanish, and a translation of which is
now printed for the first time.

[8] See my translation, ii, pp. 147, 154, 185, 193, 195, 424, 428,
460.   [9] P. 89 (Ternaux Compans' ed.)

[1] *Extirpacion de la idolatria del Peru, dirigido al Rey N.S.*, *en
su real Consejo de Indias : por el Padre Pablo Joseph de Arriaga
de la Compania de Jesus* (*Lima*, 1621.)

[2] Translated into French by M. Ternaux Compans, in his *Re-
cueil de Documents et Mémoires originaux sur l'Histoire des Possessions
Espagnoles dans l'Amérique* (*Paris*, 1840), p. 85.

The last document in this volume is a Report by
Polo de Ondegardo, an accomplished lawyer and
statesman who came to Peru with the President
Gasca. He was Corregidor of Charcas, and afterwards of Cuzco, and studied the language and laws
of the Yncas with minute care, in order that he might
be better able to conduct the administration of the
provinces under his charge. The document is in the
form of a rough draft or set of notes, apparently
intended as material for a more finished report. He
describes the principle on which the Ynca conquests
were made, the division and tenure of land, the system
of tribute, the regulations for preserving game and
for forest conservancy, and other administrative details; and he points out, here and there, the way in
which the wise legislation of the Yncas ought to be
utilized and imitated by their conquerors.

These four curious papers, which have never been
printed in the language in which they were written,
are now translated for the first time ; and it is
believed that they will form an important addition to
the sources of knowledge respecting the early civilization of the American races.

AN ACCOUNT

OF

THE FABLES AND RITES OF

THE YNCAS.

THE FABLES AND RITES OF THE YNCAS,

BY

CHRISTOVAL DE MOLINA,

Priest of the Parish of Our Lady of Healing of the Hospital for Natives in the City of Cuzco :[1]

Addressed to the Most Reverend LORD BISHOP DON SEBASTIAN DE ARTAUN,[2] of the Council of His Majesty.

———————

As in the account which I submitted to your most illustrious Lordship of the origin, lives, and customs of the Yncas, Lords of this land, of the names and number of their wives, of the laws they gave and the wars they waged, and of the tribes and nations they conquered ; I also treated, in some places, of the ceremonies and worship they established, though not very fully ; I now propose, chiefly by reason of the wish expressed by your reverend Lordship, to take similar pains to describe the ceremonies, worship, and idolatries of these Indians. For this purpose I assembled a number of aged persons who had seen and participated in them in the days of Huayna Ccapac, of Huascar Ynca, and of Manco Ynca, as well as some leaders and priests of those days.

———

[1] For an account of the origin of this hospital, see my translation of *G. de la Vega*, ii, p. 258.

[2] *Bishops of Cuzco—*

    1534. Fray Vicente de Valverde.

    1543. Fray Juan Solano, to 1550.

    1570. SEBASTIAN DE ARTAUN. Died at Lima 1584, at a Provincial Council.

    1584-93. Fray Gregorio de Montalvo.

And first with regard to the origin of their idolatries, it is so that these people had no knowledge of writing. But, in a house of the Sun called Poquen Cancha, which is near Cuzco, they had the life of each one of the Yncas, with the lands they conquered, painted with figures on certain boards, and also their origin. Among these paintings the following fable was represented.

In the life of Manco Ccapac, who was the first Ynca, and from whom they began to be called children of the Sun, and to worship the Sun, they had a full account of the deluge. They say that all people and all created things perished in it, insomuch that the water rose above all the highest mountains in the world. No living things survived except a man and a woman who remained in a box, and when the waters subsided, the wind carried them to Huanaco,[3] which will be over seventy leagues from Cuzco, a little more or less. The Creator of all things commanded them to remain there as *mitimas* ;[4] and there, in Tiahuanaco, the Creator began to raise up the people and nations that are in that region, making one of each nation of clay, and painting the dresses that each one was to wear. Those that were to wear their hair, with hair ; and those that were to be shorn, with hair cut ; and to each nation was given the language that was to be spoken, and the songs to be sung, and the seeds and food that they were to sow. When the Creator had finished painting and making the said nations and figures of clay, he gave life and soul to each one, as well men as women, and ordered that they should pass under the earth. Thence each nation came up in the places to which he ordered them to go. Thus they say that some came out of caves, others issued from hills, others from fountains, others from the trunks of trees. From this cause, and owing to having come forth and commenced to multiply,

[3] Tia-huanacu.
[4] Mitimac, a colonist or settler.—See *G. de la Vega*, I, lib. iii, cap. 19.

from those places, and to having had the beginning of their
lineage in them, they made *huacas* and places of worship
of them in memory of the origin of their lineage which
proceeded from them. Thus each nation uses the dress with
which they invest their *huaca*; and they say that the first
that was born from that place was there turned into stones,
others say the first of their lineages were turned into falcons,
condors, and other animals and birds. Hence the *huacas*
they use and worship are in different shapes.

There are other nations which say that when the deluge
came, all people were destroyed except a few who escaped on
hills, in caves, or trees, and that these were very few, but
that they began to multiply, and that, in memory of the first
of their race who escaped in such places, they made idols of
stone, giving the name of him who had thus escaped to each
huaca. Thus each nation worshipped and offered sacrifices
of such things as they used. There were, however, some
nations who had a tradition of a Creator of all things. They
made some sacrifices to him, but not in such quantity, or
with so much veneration as to their idols or *huacas*. But to
return to the fable. They say that the Creator was in
Tiahuanaco, and that there was his chief abode, hence the
superb edifices, worthy of admiration, in that place. On these
edifices were painted many dresses of Indians, and there
were many stones in the shape of men and women, who had
been changed into stone for not obeying the commands of
the Creator. They say that it was dark, and that there he
made the sun, moon, and stars, and that he ordered the sun,
moon, and stars to go to the island of Titicaca, which is near
at hand, and thence to rise to heaven. They also declare
that when the sun, in the form of a man, was ascending
into heaven, very brilliant, it called to the Yncas and to
Manco Ccapac, as their chief, and said :—" Thou and thy
descendants are to be Lords, and are to subjugate many
nations. Look upon me as thy father, and thou shalt be my

children, and thou shalt worship me as thy father." And
with these words it gave to Manco Ccapac, for his insignia
and arms, the *suntur-paucar*[5] and the *champi*,[6] and the other
ensigns that are used by the Yncas, like sceptres. And at
that point the sun, moon, and stars were commanded to
ascend to heaven, and to fix themselves in their places, and
they did so. At the same instant Manco Ccapac and his
brothers and sisters, by command of the Creator, descended
under the earth and came out again in the cave of Paccari-
tambo,[7] though they say that other nations also came out
of the same cave, at the point where the Sun rose on the
first day after the Creator had divided the night from the
day. Thus it was that they were called children of the Sun,
and that the Sun was worshipped and revered as a father.

They also have another fable, in which they say that the
Creator had two sons, the one called Ymaymana Viracocha,
and the other Tocapo Viracocha. Having completed the
tribes and nations, and assigned dresses and languages to
them, the Creator sent the sun up to heaven, with the moon
and stars, each one in its place. The Creator, who in the
language of the Indians is called Pachayachachi[8] and
Tecsiviracocha, which means the incomprehensible God,
then went by the road of the mountains, from Tiahuanaco,
visiting and beholding all the nations, and examining how
they had begun to multiply, and how to comply with his commands. He found that some nations had rebelled and had
not obeyed his commands; so he turned a large number of
them into stones of the shape of men and women, with the
same dress that they had worn. These conversions into
stone were made at the following places : in Tiahuanaco,
and in Pucara, and Xauxa, where they say that he turned

---

⁵ One name for the Ynca's head-dress. The " brilliant circle".

⁶ The battle-axe used with one hand.—*G. de la Vega*, I, lib. 9, cap. 31.

⁷ Near Cuzco. From *Paccari*, the dawn, and *tompu*, an inn.

⁸ " Teacher of the World."

the *huaca* called Huarivilca into stone, and in Pachacamac and Cajarmarca, and in other parts. In truth there are great blocks of stone in those places, some of which are nearly the size of giants. They must have been made by human hands in very ancient times; and, by reason of the loss of memory, and the absence of writing, they invented this fable, saying that people had been turned into stones for their disobedience, by command of the Creator. They also relate that in Pucara, which is forty leagues from the city of Cuzco on the Collao road, fire came down from heaven and destroyed a great part of the people, while those who were taking to flight were turned into stones.

The Creator, who is said to be the father of Ymaymana Viracocha, and of Tocapo[9] Viracocha, commanded that the elder, named Ymaymana Viracocha, in whose power all things were placed, should set out from this point, and go by the way of the mountains and forests through all the land, giving names to the large and small trees, and to the flowers and fruits that they bear, and teaching the people which were good for food or for medicine, and which should be avoided. He also gave names to all the herbs, and explained which had healing virtues and which were poisonous. The other son, named Tocapo Viracocha, which means in their language " the maker," was ordered to go by the way of the plains, visiting the people, and giving names to the rivers and trees, and instruction respecting the fruits and flowers. Thus they went until they reached the sea, whence they ascended to heaven, after having accomplished all they had to do in this world.

They also relate, in this same fable, that at Tiahuanaco, where all mankind was created, all the different kinds of birds were made, male and female, and that each was given the songs they were to sing; those that were to live in the

[9] The " Tocay" of the tradition given by *G. de la Vega*, I, lib. i, cap. 18.

forest being sent there, and each kind to its respective
place. In like manner all the different beasts were created,
male and female, and all the serpents and lizards that are
met with in the land; and the people were taught the
names and qualities of each of these birds, beasts, and
reptiles.

These Indians believed for a certainty that neither the
Creator nor his sons were born of woman, that they were
unchangeable and eternal. The tribes have many other
fables teaching their origin, insomuch that if all were to be
told, there would be no end. I will, therefore, only insert
some of these fables.

In the kingdom of Quito, there is a province called
Cañaribamba, and the Cañaris Indians are so named from
their province.[1] These Cañaris say that, at the time of the
deluge, two brothers escaped to a very high mountain called
Huaca-ÿnan. As the waters rose the hill also increased in
height, so that the waters never reached them. After the
flood had subsided, their store of provisions being ended,
they came forth and sought for food in the hills and valleys.
They built a very small house in which they dwelt, living on
herbs and roots, and suffering much from hunger and
fatigue. One day, after going out in search of food, they
returned to their little house, and found food to eat and
chicha to drink, without knowing who could have prepared
or brought it. This happened for ten days, at the end of
which time they consulted how they should see and know the
being who did them so much good in their great need. So
the elder of the two agreed to remain concealed. Presently
he saw two birds, of the kind called *agua*, and by another
name *torito*. In our language they are called *guacamayos*.[2]
They came dressed as Cañaris, with hair on their heads
fastened in front as they now wear it. The concealed

---

[1] See my translation of *G. de la Vega*, ii, pp. 241, 335, 527.

[2] A macaw.

Indian saw them begin to prepare the food they brought
with them, as soon as they came to the house, the larger
one taking off the *lliclla* or mantle worn by the Indians.
When the concealed man saw that they were beautiful, and
that they had the faces of women, he came forth ; but as
soon as they saw him, they were enraged and flew away
without leaving anything to eat on that day. When the
younger brother came home from searching for food, and
found nothing cooked and ready as on former days, he asked
his brother the reason, who told him, and they were very
angry. On the next day the younger brother resolved to
remain in concealment, and to watch whether the birds
returned. At the end of three days the two *guacamayos*
came back, and began to prepare the food. The men
watched for an opportune time when they had finished
cooking, and shutting the door, enclosed them inside. The
birds showed great anger; but while they were holding the
smaller one, the larger went away. Then they had carnal
knowledge of the smaller one, and had by it six sons and
daughters. It lived with them for a long time on that hill,
and they subsisted on the seeds they sowed, which were
brought by the *guacamayo*. And they say that from these
brothers and sisters, children of the *guacamayo*, all the
Cañaris proceed. Hence they look upon the hill *Huaca
yñan* as a *huaca*, and they hold the *guacamayos* in great
veneration, and value their feathers very highly, for use at
their festivals.

In the province of Ancasmarca, which is five leagues from
Cuzco, in the Anti-suyu division, the Indians have the
following fable.

They say that a month before the flood came, their sheep
displayed much sadness, eating no food in the day-time, and
watching the stars at night. At last the shepherd, who had
charge of them, asked what ailed them, and they said that
the conjunction of stars showed that the world would be

destroyed by water. When he heard this, the shepherd consulted with his six children, and they agreed to collect all the food and sheep they could, and to go to the top of a very high mountain, called Ancasmarca. They say that as the waters rose, the hill grew higher, so that it was never covered by the flood ; and when the waters subsided, the hill also grew smaller. Thus, the six children of that shepherd returned to people the province. These and other tales are told, which I do not insert, to avoid prolixity. The chief cause of the invention of these fables, was the ignorance of God, and the abandonment of these people to idolatries and vices. If they had known the use of writing they would not have been so dull and blind. Nevertheless, they had a very cunning method of counting by strings of wool and knots, the wool being of different colours. They call them *quipus*, and they are able to understand so much by their means, that they can give an account of all the events that have happened in their land for more than five hundred years. They had expert Indians who were masters in the art of reading the *quipus*, and the knowledge was handed down from generation to generation, so that the smallest thing was not forgotten. By the *quipus*, which are like these strings that old women use for praying in Spain, only with ends hanging from them, they keep such an account of the years and months, that no error is committed in the record. The system became more complete under the Ynca Yupanqui, who first began to conquer this land, for before his time the Yncas had not advanced beyond the vicinity of Cuzco, as appears from the account now in the hands of your Reverence. This Ynca appears to have been the first to order and settle ceremonies and religions. He it was who established the twelve months of the year, giving a name to each, and ordaining the ceremonies that were to be observed in each. For although his ancestors used months and years counted by the *quipus*, yet they were never pre-

viously regulated in such order until the time of this Lord.
He was of such clear understanding, that he reflected upon
the respect and reverence shown by his ancestors to the
Sun, who worshipped it as God. He observed that it never
had any rest, and that it daily journeyed round the earth ;
and he said to those of his council that it was not possible
that the Sun could be the God who created all things, for if
he was he would not permit a small cloud to obscure his
splendour; and that if he was creator of all things he would
sometimes rest, and light up the whole world from one
spot. Thus, it cannot be otherwise but that there is some-
one who directs him, and this is the Pacha-Yachachi or
creator. Influenced by this reasoning and knowledge, he
ordered the houses and temple of Quisuar-cancha[3] to be
made, which are above the houses of Diego Ortiz de Guzman,[4] coming towards the great square of Cuzco, where
Hernan Lopez de Segovia now lives. Here he raised a
statue of gold to the creator, of the size of a boy of ten
years of age. It was in the shape of a man standing up,
the right arm raised and the hand almost closed, the fingers
and thumb raised as one who was giving an order.
Although the Yncas had a knowledge of a creator of all
things from the first, whom they reverenced and to whom
they offered sacrifices; yet he never was held in such
great veneration as from the time of this Ynca, who gave
orders to the heads of provinces throughout his dominions
that temples should be erected to him, and that he should
have flocks, servants, farms, and estates, out of which the
sacrifices should be provided. This also was the Ynca who
so sumptuously erected the house of the Sun at Cuzco : for

[3] *Quisuar* is the name of a tree (*Buddleia Incana*). *Cancha*, a
place.

[4] See *G. de la Vega*, i, p. 295, and ii, p. 243, of my translation ; and
the plan of Cuzco. There is still an ancient wall, with serpents carved
on it, at this spot.

before his time it was very small and poor. The cause of this is related in the following fable.

They say that, before he succeeded, he went one day to visit his father Viracocha Ynca, who was in Sacsahuana, five leagues from Cuzco. As he came up to a fountain called Susur-puquio,[5] he saw a piece of crystal fall into it, within which he beheld the figure of an Indian in the following shape. Out of the back of his head there issued three very brilliant rays like those of the Sun. Serpents were twined round his arms, and on his head there was a *llautu*[6] like that of the Ynca. His ears were bored, and ear-pieces, like those used by the Yncas, were inserted. He was also dressed like the Ynca. The head of a lion came out from between his legs, and on his shoulders there was another lion whose legs appeared to join over the shoulders of the man ; while a sort of serpent also twined over the shoulders. On seeing this figure the Ynca Yupanqui fled, but the figure of the apparition called him by his name from within the fountain, saying :—" Come hither, my son, and fear not, for I am the Sun thy father. Thou shalt conquer many nations : therefore be careful to pay great reverence to me, and remember me in thy sacrifices." The apparition then vanished, while the piece of crystal remained. The Ynca took care of it, and they say that he afterwards saw everything he wanted in it. As soon as he was Lord, he ordered a statue of the Sun to be made, as nearly as possible resembling the figure he had seen in the crystal. He gave orders to the heads of the provinces in all the lands he had conquered, that they should make grand temples richly endowed, and he commanded all his subjects to adore and reverence the new Deity, as they had heretofore worshipped the Creator. In the narrative of his life, which your Lordship has, it is related that all his conquests

---

[5] *Puquio*, a spring or source.
[6] The royal fringe, worn across the forehead.

were made in the name of the Sun his Father, and of the
Creator. It was this Ynca, also, who commanded all the
nations he conquered to hold their *huacas* in great veneration, and to propitiate them by sacrifices, saying that thus
they would not be enraged at not receiving their due quantity of reverence and worship. He also caused worship to
be offered to the thunder, and he had a statue of a man
erected in gold, in a temple in the city of Cuzco. This
huaca also had a temple, near that of the Sun, in all the
provinces, with estates, flocks, and servants for the celebra-
tion of sacrifices. But as my intention is to touch upon
worship and ceremonies, and not to treat of laws and customs, I will pass on to the other points of my present treatise.

They also had, in some nations, many huacas and temples
where the devil gave answers; and in the city of Cuzco
there was the huaca of Huanacauri.[7] There were many kinds
of wizards in the provinces, with names and attributes differ-
ing one from the other. The names and offices were as
follows :—

Calparicu, which means those who bring luck and success, and were expected to obtain the things that were
desired. With this object they killed birds, lambs, and
sheep, and, inflating the lungs, through a certain vein, they
discerned certain signs, by which they declared what was
about to happen.

There were others called *Virapiricuc,* who burnt the
breasts of sheep and coca in the fire, and foretold what
would occur from certain signs at the time the things were
burning. Those who consulted them said that they were
the least to be relied on, because they always lied.

---

[7] Mentioned four times by *Garcilasso de la Vega*, i, pp. 65, 66, and ii,
pp. 169 and 230. He says that the first settlement, made in the valley
of Cuzco, was on the hill called Huanacauri, and that a temple was
built there. It was looked upon as very sacred, and was the spot
whence races were run.

Others were called *Achicoc,* who were the sorcerers that told fortunes by maize and the dung of sheep. They gave their replies to those who consulted them, according as the things came out in odd or even numbers.

Others were called *Camascas,* who declared that their grace and virtue was derived from the thunder; saying that, when a thunder-bolt fell, and one of them was struck with terror, after he came to himself he proclaimed how the thunder had revealed to him the art of curing by herbs, and how to give replies to those who consulted them. In like manner, when one escaped from some great danger, they said that the devil had appeared ; and those who wished to be cured by herbs were also said to be instructed. Hence many Indians are great herbalists. Others were shown the poisonous herbs, and these were called *Camascas.*

Others were called *Yacarcaes,* and these were natives of Huaro. They had mighty pacts with the devil, as appears from the ceremony they performed, which was as follows :— They took certain tubes of copper mixed with silver, about the length of an ordinary arquebus ; and some brass vessels in which they light fires with charcoal, which they blew and made to blaze up by means of the tubes. It was in these fires that the devils delivered their replies, and the sorcerers said that it was concerning the soul of such a man or woman that they were making inquiry, who might be in Quito or in any other part of the empire which the Yncas had conquered. The principal questions they asked were whether such an one was against the Sun his father, or whether such others were thieves, murderers, or adulterers. By means of this invocation the Ynca knew all that passed in his dominions, with the help of the devil. These *Yacarcaes* were much feared, as well by the Ynca as by the people, and he took them with him wherever he went.

There were other sorcerers who had charge of the huacas, among whom there were some who conferred with the devil, and received his replies, telling the people what they wished to know, but they very seldom gave correct answers. According to the accounts they give, all the people of the land confessed to the sorcerers who had charge of the huacas ; and these confessions were made publicly. In order to test the truth of the confessions, the sorcerers tried them by consulting signs, and in this way, with the aid of the devil, they discovered who had confessed falsely, and upon these they inflicted severe punishments. Those who had grave crimes to confess, which merited death, confessed them in secret to the sorcerer.

The Yncas, and the people of Cuzco, always made their confessions in secret, and generally they confessed to those Indian sorcerers of Huaro who were employed for this office. In their confessions they accused themselves of not having reverenced the sun, the moon, and the huacas, with not having celebrated the feasts of the Raymis, which are those in each month of the year, with all their hearts; with having committed fornication against the law of the Ynca not to touch a strange woman or to seduce a virgin unless given by the Ynca, and not because fornication was a sin. For they did not understand this. They also accused themselves of any murder or theft, which we hold to be grave sins, as also were murmurs, especially if they had been against the Ynca or against the Sun.

They also confess, O most reverend Sir, that the people before the flood were made, with all other things, by the Creator ; but they are ignorant of the order in which they were made, nor how, beyond what has already been said concerning Tiahuanaco. This is what I have been able to learn, touching their fables and their origin, from all the old men with whom I have conversed on this subject. The form of the worship and sacrifices that they established for each month, was as follows :—

MAY.

They commenced to count the year in the middle of May, a few days more or less, on the first day of the moon; which month, being the first of their year, was called *Hauca* and *Llusque*, and in it they performed the following ceremonies, called *Yutip-Raymi*, or the festivals of the Sun. In this month they sacrificed to the Sun a great quantity of sheep of all colours. Those called *huacar-paña* were white and woolly. Others were called *huanacos;* and others, also white and woolly, were called *pacos-cuyllos*. Others, which were females with a reddish woolly fleece, were called *paucar-paco*. Other pacos were called *uqui-paco*. Other large sheep were called *chumpi*, which was their colour, being almost that of a lion's coat. Other sheep were called *llanca-llama*, which were black and woolly. At this season they also sacrificed lambs of the same colours. The sacrifices were performed in the following order :—

They went to Curicancha[8] in the morning, at noon, and at night, bringing the sheep that were to be sacrificed on that day, which they carried round the idols and huacas called *Punchao Ynca,*[9] which means the Sun ; and *Pachaya-chachi,*[1] another idol in the shape of a man. The word means a Creator ; and *Chuqui yllayllapa,*[2] which was the huaca of lightning and thunder, and thunderbolt. It also was in the form of a person, though the face could not be seen, and it had a *llautu* of gold, and ear-rings of gold, and medals of gold called *canipo*. These huacas were placed on a bench, and the live sheep were taken round them, while the Priests said :—

" O Creator, and Sun, and Thunder, be for ever young ! do not grow old. Let all things be at peace ! let the people

---

[8] " Place of gold." The temple of the Sun at Cuzco.
[9] *Punchau,* " day". A name for the Sun.
[1] " Teacher of the World."   [2] Thunder and lightning.

multiply, and their food, and let all other things continue to increase."

These sayings were addressed to the Creator, and to the Sun they prayed that he might always be young, and continue to give light and splendour. They did not know the Sun as their Creator, but as created by the Creator. To the thunder and lightning they prayed that it might rain, in order that they might have food. They also knew that the rain came with thunder and lightning, by command of the Creator.

Then, in the morning, they sent a sheep to Huanacauri, which is their principal huaca, where it was killed and burnt by the *tarpuntaes*,[3] who were those that had the duty of supplying food to the huacas. While the sacrifice was burning, at the rising of the Sun, many Yncas and Caciques came, and, pulling the wool off the sacrifice before it was consumed, walked round it with the wool in their hands, crying out and saying:—

" O Creator, O Sun, and O Thunder, be for ever young, multiply the people, and let them always be at peace."

At noon, in the same order, they burnt another in the court of the Coricancha or house of the Sun, which is now the cloister of the Friars of the Lord St. Domingo: and in the evening they took another to the hill called *Achpiran*, because there the Sun sets, which they sacrificed with the same ceremonies. They also offered up to the same huacas, certain *cestos*[4] of coca, called *paucar-runcu*, and others called *paucar-quintu* like coca, and some toasted maize, and red and yellow sea shells called *mullu*, in the shape of maize. In addition to these ceremonies, on every other day of this month, they went to burn sheep and the other offerings at the following places: on a hill called *Succanca*, on another called *Omoto-yanacauri*, on another called *Ccapac-uilca*, which

---

[3] Priests. The word does not occur in Garcilasso de la Vega. *Tarpuni* is the verb " to sow".   [4] Baskets.

is three leagues from Huanacauri, and on others called
Queros-huanacauri, Rontoca which is in the Quehuares,[5]
Collapata in Pumacancha, fourteen leagues from the city, on
a plain called *Yana-yana,* on another hill called *Cuti* in the
puna of Pumacancha, and continuing along the same road
they came on the next day to Vilcañota, which is twenty-six
leagues from Cuzco. The reason for taking this direction
in this month is because they say that the Sun was born in
that part,[6] and thus they went on that road, performing
the sacrifices. On a plain near Rurucache they made the
same offering, as well as on another hill called *Suntu,* near
to *Sihuana* in Cacha, in another hill called *Cacha-Uiracocha,*
in another called *Yacalla-huaca,* and in another called
Rurama, on the plain of Quiquijana.[7] The same was done
in *Mullipampa,* in *Urcos,* on a hill called *Urcos Uiracocha,*
on a plain called *Anta-huaylla,*[8] on another plain near Anta-
huayla, called *Pati,* on another called *Acahuara,* on a hill in
Quispicancha, and on another called *Sulcanca.* The Tarpuntaes went by one road and came back by another. The
Ynca, with all his lords, went to Mantucalla, and there
remained to drink and enjoy himself in revelry and *taquis.*[9]
They called this taqui *Huallina,*[1] and it was a dance with
singing, which was performed four times in the day. The
Yncas alone celebrated this feast; and the mama-cunas,
women of the Sun, gave drink to those who performed it;
their own wives did not enter the place where the Yncas
were, but remained outside in a court. All the vases and
utensils from which they ate and drank, and with which
they cooked the food were of gold. Thus they performed the

---

[5] A tribe south of Cuzco.

[6] On leaving Cuzco, this road is nearly east.

[7] All these places are in the vale of Vilca-mayu, up which the road
passes from Cuzco to lake Titicaca.

[8] Not Andahuaylas, but a village near Cuzco, now called Andahuaylillas.   [9] Music.

[1] More correctly *Huayllina,* a song.

taqui called *Huayllina,* and in it they worshipped the Creator. At this festival they brought out the two female figures called *Pallasillu* and *Ynca uillu,* covered with very rich clothes and small plates of gold, called *llancapata, colcapata* and *paucaruncu.* In front they bore the *suntur-paucar* and certain great figures of the size of sheep, two of gold and two of silver, with cloths placed over the loins in the fashion of horse cloths. They were carried on litters, and this was done in memory of the sheep which, they say, came forth from the tambo with them. The Indians who carried them were principal lords, dressed in very rich clothes, and they call the figures of gold and silver sheep *corinapa collque-napa.*[2] The Ynca remained at Mantucalla until the end of the month, and when that time arrived he went to the square in front of the church of Cuzco, called *uacay-pata,* the path by which he came being strewn with plumes of bird's feathers of all colours. There he drank during the remainder of the day, and at night he went to his house. Thus this month was ended.

JUNE.

The month of June was called *Canay,* and by another name *Chahuarhuay.* The people were entirely occupied in irrigating their fields, and in arranging the distribution of water from the channels.

JULY.

They called the month of July *Moronpassa tarpuiquilla,*[3] and in it they celebrated the festivals called *yahuayra,* when they besought the Creator to grant them a full harvest in that year, for this was the month for sowing the seeds. The following ceremonies were then performed.

The *Tarpuntaes,* who are a sort of priests, were careful

---

[2] *Ccuri,* gold; *Collque,* silver; *Napa,* salutation.
[3] *Tarpuy-quilla,* the sowing month.

to fast from the time the maize was sown until it was a finger's length out of the ground. Their wives and children also fasted, eating nothing during that time but boiled maize and herbs. They drank no chicha, but only muddy stuff called *concho*, and they chewed no coca. In this season they carried a little row of maize in their *chuspas*, which they put in their mouths. All the common people celebrated a feast called *yahuayra*, from the name of the song they chaunted in which they besought the Creator to grant them a prosperous year. They sang it dressed in red shirts reaching to the feet, and no mantles. Then they came out to sing and dance in the place now called by the Spaniards Limapampa,[4] which is beyond the square of San Domingo. Here the Priests of the Creator sacrificed a white sheep, maize, coca, plumes of coloured feathers, and sea shells called *mullu*, in the morning; beseeching the Creator to grant a prosperous year, and that, as He had made all things out of nothing and given them being, so he would be pleased to comply with their prayer. The Priests of the Sun, called *Tarpuntaes*, and the Priests of the Thunder also offered up sacrifices, praying the Sun to give warmth that so their food might be produced, and the Thunder, called *Chuqui Yllapa*, to send its waters to assist in the production, and not to bring down hail. As soon as the sacrifices were completed, the labourers went to their work, and the nobles to the house of the lord Ynca, until the month, which in their language was called *quispe*,[5] was ended.

August.

The month of August was called *Coya-raymi*; and in it they celebrated the *Situa*. In order to perform the ceremonies of this festival, they brought the figures of their huacas from all parts of the land, from Quito to Chile, and placed them in the houses they had in Cuzco, for the pur-

---

[4] Rimac-pampa.— *G. de la Vega*, ii, p. 239.   [5] *Quespi*, crystal.

pose which we shall presently explain. The reason for celebrating the feast called *Situa*, in this month, was, because the rains commenced, and with the first rains there was generally much sickness. They besought the Creator that, during the year, he would be pleased to shield them from sickness, as well in Cuzco, as throughout the territory conquered by the Yncas. On the day of the conjunction of the moon, at noon the Ynca, with all the chiefs of his council, and the other principal lords who were in Cuzco, went to the Ccuricancha, which is the house and temple of the Sun, where they agreed together on the way in which the festival should be celebrated; for in one year they added, and in another they reduced the number of ceremonies, according to circumstances.

All things having been arranged, the High Priest addressed the assembly, and said that the ceremonies of the *Situa* should be performed, that the Creator might drive all the diseases and evils from the land. A great number of armed men, accoutred for war, with their lances, then came to the square in front of the temple. The figures called *Chuquilla*[6] and *Uiracocha*[7] were brought to the temple of the Sun from their own special temples in *Puca-marca* and *Quihuar-cancha*, which are now the houses of Doña Ysabel de Bobadilla. The priests of these huacas joined the assembly, and, with the concurrence of all present, the priest of the Sun proclaimed the feast. First, all strangers, all whose ears were broken, and all deformed persons were sent out of the city, it being said that they should take no part in the ceremony, because they were in that state as a punishment for some fault. Unfortunate people ought not to be present, it was believed, because their ill-luck might drive away some piece of good fortune. They also drove out the dogs, that they might not howl. Then the people, who were armed as if for war, went to the square of Cuzco,

---

[6] Thunder.   [7] The Creator.

crying out: "O sicknesses, disasters, misfortunes, and dangers, go forth from the land." In the middle of the square, where stood the urn of gold which was like a fountain, that was used at the sacrifice of *chicha*, four hundred men of war assembled. One hundred faced towards Colla-suyu, which is the direction of the Sun-rising. One hundred faced to the westward, which is the direction of Chinchasuyu. Another hundred looked towards Antisuyu, which is the north, and the last hundred turned towards the south. They had with them all the arms that are used in their wars. As soon as those who came from the temple of the Sun arrived in the square, they cried out and said: "Go forth all evils." Then all the four parties went forth to their appointed places. Those for Collasuyu set out with great speed, and ran to Augostura de Acoya-puncu, which is two short leagues from Cuzco, crying out as they ran "Go forth all evils." The people of Huvin-Cuzco carried these cries, and there they delivered them over to the mitimaes of Huayparya, who in their turn passed them to the mitimaes of Antahuaylla, and thus they were passed to the mitimaes of Huaray-pacha, who continued them as far as the river at Quiquisana, where they bathed themselves and their arms. Thus was the shouting ended in that direction. The Indians who passed the shouting along the Colla-suyu road from Cuzco, were of the lineage of Usca Mayta Ayllu,[8] Yapomayu Ayllu, Yahuaymin Ayllu Sutic, and Marasaylla Cuynissa Ayllu.

Those who went out to the west, which is towards Chinchasuyu, shouting in the same manner, were of the lineage of Ccapac Ayllu,[9] and Hatun Ayllu, Vicaquirau[1] and Chamin-Cuzco Ayllu, and Yaraycu Ayllu. These went shouting as far as Satpina, which will be a little more than a league

---

[8] Descendants of Ynca Mayta Ccapac.
[9] Descendants of Tupac Ynca Yupanqui.
[1] Vicaquirau. Descendants of Ynca Rocca.

from Cuzco. There they passed the cries on to the mitimaes of Jaquijahuana,[2] and these delivered them to the
mitimaes of Tilca, which is above Marca-huasi, about ten
leagues from Cuzco, who carried them on to the river Apurimac, where they bathed and washed their clothes and
arms.

Those who carried the cries in the direction of Anti-suyu
were of the following lineages, Usca-panaca Ayllu, Aucaylli
Ayllu, Tarpuntay Ayllu, and Sañu Ayllu. They ran as far as
Chita, which is a league and a half from Cuzco, and handed
them to the mitimaes of Pisac, who are those of the Coya
and Paullu,[3] and these carried them forward to the river at
Pisac, and there bathed and washed their arms.

Those who went towards Cunti-suyu were of the following
lineages. Yaura-panaca[4] Ayllu, and China-panaca Ayllu,
and Masca-panaca Ayllu, and Quesco Ayllu. They ran as
far as Churicalla, which is two leagues from Cuzco, and there
they delivered them to the mitimaes of Yaurisquis, which
will be about three leagues from Cuzco. These passed them
on to those of Tautar, which is four leagues from Cuzco, who
carried them on to the river of Cusipampa, where the Friars
of La Merced have a vineyard. This is seven leagues from
Cuzco, and there they bathed and washed their arms.[5]

Such was the ceremony for driving the sicknesses out of
Cuzco. Their reason for bathing in these rivers was because
they were rivers of great volume, and were supposed to
empty themselves into the sea, and to carry the evils with
them. When the ceremony commenced in Cuzco, all the
people, great and small, came to their doors, crying out,

---

[2] Sacsahuana or Xaquixaquana.

[3] Ccoya, the Princess, and Paullu, a son of the Ynca Huayna Ccapac.
They were the lords of the Pisac vassals when Molina was writing.

[4] *Panaca* is a term for lineage.—See *G. de la Vega*, ii, p. 531. Perhaps from *Pana*, sister of a brother.

[5] See the account of the ceremonies in *G. de la Vega*, ii.

shaking their mantles and *llicllas,* and shouting, " Let the evils be gone. How greatly desired has this festival been by us. O Creator of all things, permit us to reach another year, that we may see another feast like this." They all danced, including the Ynca, and in the morning twilight they went to the rivers and fountains to bathe, saying that their maladies would come out of them. Having finished bathing, they took great torches of straw, bound round with cords, which they lighted and continued to play with them, passing them from one to the other. They called these torches of straw *pancurcu.* At the end of their feast they returned to their houses, and by that time a pudding of coarsely ground maize had been prepared, called *sancu* and *elba.* This they applied to their faces, to the lintels of their doors, and to the places where they kept their food and clothes. Then they took the *sancu* to the fountains, and threw it in, saying, " May we be free from sickness, and may no maladies enter this house." They also sent this *sancu* to their relations and friends for the same purpose, and they put it on the bodies of their dead that they also might enjoy the benefits of the feast. Afterwards the women ate and drank their food with much enjoyment; and on this day each person, how poor soever he might be, was to eat and drink, for they said that on this day they should enjoy themselves, if they had to pass all the rest of the year in labour and sorrow. On this day no man scolded his neighbour, nor did any word pass in anger, nor did any-one claim what was owing to him from another. They said that there would be trouble and strife throughout the year, if any was commenced on the day of the festival.

In the night, the statues of the Sun, of the Creator, and of the Thunder, were brought out, and the priests of each of these statues warmed it with the before mentioned *sancu.* In the morning they brought the best food they could pre-pare to present at the temples of the Creator, of the Sun, and of the Thunder; which the priests of those *huacas* received and consumed. They also brought out the bodies of the dead lords and ladies which were embalmed, each one being brought out by the person of the same lineage who had charge of it. During the night these bodies were washed in the baths which belonged to them when they were alive. They were then brought back to their houses, and warmed with the same coarse pudding called *çancu;* and the food they had been most fond of when they were alive was placed before them, and afterwards the persons who were in charge of the bodies consumed the food.

The persons who had charge of the huaca called *Guana-caucique*,[6] which is a great figure of a man, washed it and warmed it with the *sancu;* and the principal Ynca lord and his wife, after they had finished their bath, put the same *sancu* in their house, and on their hands. Afterwards, they placed certain plumes on their heads, of a bird called *pialco,* which are of a changing colour. The same was done with the figure of the Creator, and those who had charge of it called this ceremony *Pilcoyacu*. At about eight or nine in the morning the principal lord Ynca, with his wife, and the lords of the council who were in his house, came forth into the great square of Cuzco, richly dressed. They also brought out the image of the Sun called *Apupunchau*,[7] which was the principal image among those in the temple. They were accompanied by all the priests of the Sun, who brought the two figures of gold, and their women called Ynca-Ocllo and Palla-Ocllo. There also came forth the woman called Coya-facssa, who was dedicated to the Sun. She was either the sister or the daughter of the ruler. The priests carried the image of the Sun, and placed it on a bench prepared for it in the square. The priests of the Creator likewise brought forth his image, and deposited it in its place. So also did the priests of the Thunder, called

---

[6] *Huanacauri.*   [7] *Apu-ppunchau.* The lord of day.

Chuqui-ylla, bring forth his image. Each had its bench of gold, and before them were borne *yauris*, which were made like sceptres of gold. The priests of these *huacas* came in very rich dresses, to celebrate this feast. Those who had charge of the huaca called Huanacauri, also brought its figure into the square. They say that a woman was never assigned to the *huaca* of the Creator. It was believed that the Creator did not need women, because, as he created them, they all belonged to him. In all their sacrifices, the first was offered to the Creator. At this feast they brought out all the embalmed bodies of their lords and ladies, very richly adorned. The bodies were carried by the descendants of the respective lineages, and were deposited in the square on seats of gold, according to the order in which they lived.

All the people of Cuzco came out, according to their tribes and lineages, as richly dressed as their means would allow; and, having made reverences to the Creator, the Sun, and the lord Ynca, they sat down on their benches, each man according to the rank he held, the Hanan-Cuzcos being on one side, and the Hurin-Cuzcos[8] on the other. They passed the day in eating and drinking, and enjoying themselves; and they performed the *tauqi* called *alançitua saqui*, in red shirts down to their feet, and garlands called *pilco-casa* on their heads; accompanied with large or small tubes of canes, which made a kind of music called *tica-tica*. They gave thanks to the Creator for having spared them to see that day, and prayed that they might pass another year without sickness; and they did the same to the Sun and to the Thunder. The Ynca came with them, having the Sun before him. He had a great vase of gold containing chicha. It was received by the priest, who emptied it into the urn, which, as has been said, is like a stone fountain plated with gold. This urn had a hole made in such a way, that the chicha could enter a pipe or sewer passing under the ground

[8] Upper and Lower Cuzco.

to the houses of the Sun,[9] the Thunder, and the Creator.
The priests came in procession, and the families of Hurin
and Hanan Cuzco, each with the embalmed bodies of their
ancestors. They passed that day in the manner already
described, and in the evening they took back the Sun and
the other *huacas* to their temples, and the embalmed bodies
to their houses. The Yncas, and the rest of the people also
returned to their homes.

The next day they all came to the great square in the
same order, placing the *huacas* on their benches as before.
The Ynca and the people brought with them a very great
quantity of flocks from all the four quarters of Colla-suyu,
chinchay-suyu, Antis-suyu, and Cunti-suyu. The number of
animals was so great, according to those who made this de-
claration, that they amounted to more than one hundred thousand, and it was necessary that all should be without spot or
blemish, and with fleeces that had never been shorn. Presently the priest of the Sun selected four of the most perfect,
and sacrificed them in the following order: one was offered to
the Creator, another to the Thunder, another to the Sun, and
another to Huanacauri. When this sacrifice was offered up,
the priest had the *sancu* on great plates of gold, and he
sprinkled it with the blood of the sheep. The white fleece-
bearing sheep were called *cuyllu*; and the plates containing
sanco were in front of the bench of the Sun. The high priest
then said in a loud voice so that all might hear: "Take heed
how you eat this *sancu* ; for he who eats it in sin, and with
a double will and heart, is seen by our father, the Sun, who
will punish him with grievous troubles. But he who with
a single heart partakes of it, to him the Sun and the Thunder will show favour, and will grant children and happy
years, and abundance, and all that he requires." Then they
all rose up to partake, first making a solemn vow before
eating the *yahuar-sancu*,[1] in which they promised never to

---

[9] See also G. de la Vega.   [1] *Yahuar*, blood ; *Sancu*, pudding.

murmur against the Creator, the Sun, or the Thunder; never
to be traitors to their lord the Ynca, on pain of receiving
condemnation and trouble. The priest of the Sun then
took what he could hold on three fingers, put it into his
mouth, and returned to his seat. In this order, and in this
manner of taking the oath, all the tribes rose up, and thus
all partook down to the little children. They all kept some
of the *yahuar-sancu* for those who were absent, and sent some
to those who were confined to their beds by sickness; for
they believed it to be very unlucky for any one not to partake of the *yahuar-sancu* on that day. They took it with such
care that no particle was allowed to fall to the ground, this
being looked upon as a great sin. When they killed the
sacrificial sheep, they took out the lungs and inflated them,
and the priests judged, from certain signs on them, whether
all things would turn out prosperously in the coming year
or not. Afterwards, they burnt them before the Creator,
the Sun, and the Thunder. The bodies of the sheep were
divided and distributed, as very sacred things, a very small
piece to each person. The rest was given to the people of
Cuzco to eat, and each man, as he entered the square,
pulled off a piece of the wool, with which he sacrificed to
the Sun. When they distributed the sheep, the priests
offered up the following prayers.

Prayer to the Creator.

Aticsi-Uiracochan[caylla] caylla-Uiracochan tocapo ac nupo
viracochan camachurac carica-
chun huarmicachun ñis pallurac
rurac camas cayqui churascai-
qui casilla quespilla canca musac maipimcanqui ahuapichu
ucupichu pusupichu llantupichu
huyarihuay hayniquay yuihuay
ymaypachacama haycaypacha-

O Creator ! [O conquering
Uirachocha ! Ever present Uiracocha !] Thou who art without equal unto the ends of
the earth ! Thou who givest
life and strength to mankind,
saying, let this be a man and
let this be a woman : And as
thou sayest, so thou givest life,
and vouchsafest that men shall

cama canca chihuay marcari-
huay hatallihuay caycustayri
chasquihuay may piscapapas
Uiracochaya.

live in health and peace, and
free from danger :—Thou who
dwellest in the heights of heaven,
in the thunder, and in the storm
clouds, hear us ! and grant us
eternal life. Have us in thy
keeping, and receive this our
offering, as it shall please thee,
O Creator !

Another Prayer for Fruitful Flocks.

Uiracochan apacochan titu-Ui-
racochan hualpai huana-Uiraco-
chan topapo acnupo Uiracochan
runayachachachuchun hucerma-
yachachacbun mirachun llacta-
pachacasilla quispillacachun ca-
mas-cayqui taquacaycha yatalliymay Pachacama haycay Pachacama.

O Creator ! who doest won-
ders and marvels. O most
merciful and almighty Creator !
multiply our flocks and cause
them to bring forth young, let
the land continue in peace and
free from danger, and these
whom thou hast made, hold
them in thy hand.

To the Huacas.

Coy [caylla] Uiracochan ticçi
Uiracochan hapacochan hualpai
huanaUiracochan chanca-Uiraco-
chan acsa-Uiracochan atun-Uiracochan caylla-Uiracochan tacancuna hunichic llaularuna y achacuc ccapac hahuay pihucupi
Puris papas.

O Creator, thou who art co-
eval with the world ! O Chanca-
Uiracocha ! O Atun-Uiracocha !
grant our prayer, that thou
wilt, with the Creator, give
health and prosperity to the
people.

Chanca-Uiracocha was a *huaca* in Chuqui-chaca, where
was Manco Ynca. Atun-Uiracocha is in the *huaca* of Urcos;
where there was an eagle and a falcon carved in stone at
the entrance of the *huaca*. and an image of a man with a
white robe reaching to his feet, and coming down to his
waist. Apotin-Uiracocha is in Amaybamba, beyond Tampu.
Urusayna-Uiracocha is in the same place. Chuqui-chanca-
Uiracocha is in Huaypau.

Another Prayer.

O Uiracochan cusiussapochay lipo-Uiracochaya runacay amaycay miruna yana huaccha quisaruna yquicauras cayquichuras cayquicasiquis-pilla camachun huarmay huanchurin huanchin canta amaquaquinta huarya yaichichuruay huasa causachun mana alleas pamana pitispa mucumuchun. Upia muchun.

O most fortunate and propitious Creator, have pity and mercy upon all men whom thou hast made. Keep thy poor servants in health. Make them and their children to walk in a straight road, without thinking any evil. Grant that they may have a long life, and not die in their youth, and that they may live and feed in peace.

Another Prayer.

O Uiracochay [atic]a ticçi-Uiracochaya hualparillac camacchurac cay hurin pacha pimicuchun upiachun ñispachurascay quictacamascay quita micuynin yachachun papacara ymaymana micuncancachun ñis-cayqui tacamachic michachic mana muchuncunpac mana muchuspacau yñincampac amacaçachunchu amachupichupichichunchu casilla huacaychamuy.

O Creator! Lord of the ends of the earth! O most merciful! Thou who givest life to all things, and hast made men that they may live, and eat, and multiply. Multiply also the fruits of the earth, the *papas* and other food that thou hast made, that men may not suffer from hunger and misery. O preserve the fruits of the earth from frost, and keep us in peace and safety.

Prayer to the Sun.

Uiracocha yapunchau cachuntu tacachun ñispac nicpacarichun yllarichun ñispac nicpunchaochuri yquicta casillacta quispillacta purichic runarunascay quicta cauchay uncancampac Uiracochaya casilla quispilla punchau yncarunayanani uhiscayquita quillari canchari amahuncochispa amananu chispa cacicta quispicha huacus-chaspa.

O Creator! Thou who gavest being to the Sun, and afterwards said let there be day and night. Raise it and cause it to shine, and preserve that which thou hast created, that it may give light to men. Grant this, O Creator!

O Sun! Thou who art in peace and safety, shine upon us, keep us from sickness, and keep us in health and safety.

Prayer for the Ynca.

A - Uiracochan ticçi - Uiracochan hualpa y huana - Uiracochan atun-Uiracochan Tarapaca-Uiracochan capaccachun Yncacachun nispachucapac churaspac quicta Ynca camascayquita casillacta quispullacta Huacaychamuy runan yananya chachuchun accari punari usachun ymaypacha cama ama allcachispa churinta mitanta quanpas huacay chay chaycaçillacta uiracu-chaya.

O pious Creator, who ordered and saw fit that there should be a Lord Ynca, grant to the Ynca that he may be kept in peace, with his servants and vassals, that he may obtain the victory over his enemies and always be a conqueror. Cut not short his days, nor the days of his children, and give them peace, O Creator!

Another Prayer.

Uiracochaya qualpay huana-Uiracochaya ninacta casi quispillacta capac Ynca-churi yquiguarmayqui pacamascayqui huacay chamuchun hatallimuchun pachachacara runa llama micuy paycaptin yacachun ccapac Ynca camascayquita Uiracochaya ayni huni marcari hatalli ymaypachacama.

O Creator! Vouchsafe that the subjects of the Ynca may have peace while thy son the Ynca lives, to whom thou hast said: Be thou Lord! Grant that they may multiply. Keep them in peace, let their days be prosperous, let their farms yield increase; and keep this Lord Ynca in thy hand for ever, O Creator!

Another Prayer.

Pachacama casillacta quispillacta Ccapac Ynca huahuay quicta marcari atalli.

O Creator of the world, keep thy child the Ynca in peace and security upon it.

Prayer for all the Yncas.

Apunchau Ynca Yutiryayay Cuzco tampu cachun aticoclla saccoccachun ñispa churac camac muchas-cay quicusiquispu cachun amatisca amalla sasca

O Sun! Thou who hast said, let there be Cuzcos and Tampus, grant that these thy children may conquer all other people. We beseech thee that thy child-

cachunchu aticuc paclla sacapac camascayqui churascayqui.

ren the Yncas may be conquerors always, for this hast thou created them.

Prayer for all the Huacas.

O pachachulla Uiracochan ucuhulla Uiracochan huaca-vilcacachun nispacamacatu napahuay pihuana tayna allastu Uiracochaya hurinpacha anacpacha cachun nispa nicocupa chapipuca umacta churachay nihuay hunihuay quispicasica musac Uiracochaya micuy niocmin cacyoc curayoc llamayoc ymayna yochaycaymayoc amacacharihuay cuchuy maymana aycay mana chiquimanta catuiman manta nacasca hustusca amusca manta.

O sacred Huacas, ancestors, grandsires, and parents! O Hatun-apu! O Hualpa-huanatayua! O Apu Allastu! bring us near to the Creator, us thy sons, and our children, that they may be fortunate and near the Creator, as thou art.

When they had distributed the flocks, the sheep were killed in great numbers, to be eaten on that day. Then a vast quantity of chicha was brought into the square, from the store houses where it was kept. It was made of boiled white maize, in the valley of Cuzco. The flocks that were used at this festival, were the property of the Creator, the Sun, and the Thunder, from their estates set apart in all the provinces of Peru. Having finished eating with much rejoicing, they performed their *taquis*, and drank in the same order as on the day before. This continued for four days. The first day of the festival was called *Citua*, and it was then that they ate the *sancu* called *yahuar-sancu*. The second day was dedicated to the Creator, the Sun, and the Thunder, when they performed sacrifices, and a prayer was offered up for the Ynca. The fourth day was for the Moon and the Earth, when the accustomed sacrifices and prayers were offered up. On a subsequent day people of all the

nations, that had been subdued by the Yncas, came with
their *huacas* and in the richest costumes, peculiar to their
respective countries, that they could procure. The priests,
who had charge of the *huacas*, carried them on litters.
When they entered the square, coming from the direction
of the four *Suyus* already mentioned, they made reverences
to the Creator, the Sun, and the Thunder, and to the Huanacauri, a *huaca* of the Yncas, and then they did the same
to the Ynca, who was in the square on that occasion.
Having made these obeisances, they proceeded to the places
assigned to them, and, in order to make more room, the
families of Hanan-Cuzco and Hurin-Cuzco formed themselves into one, and thus left more space in the square. As
soon as all the people were in their places, the High Priest
of the Sun sprinkled a large quantity of *sancu* with blood,
and the Caciques rose up in their order, and repeated the
following :—

Prayer to the Creator.

Aticçi Uiracochan caylla Uiracochan tocapu acnupu Uiracochan camac churac carica chuyu-
armicachun nispallutac rurac
camascay quichuras cayquica-
silla quispilla causamus ay may-
pincanqui ahuapichu ucupichu
llantupichu uyarihua ayrihuay
ynihuay ymay pachacamac cançachihuay marcallihuay attolli-
huay caycoscay tarichasquihuay
may picaspapas Uiracochaya.

O Creator ! ? [O conquering
Viracocha! Ever present (*caylla*)
Viracocha !] Thou who art in
the ends of the earth without
equal ! Thou who gavest life
and valour to men, saying, Let
this be a man ! and to women,
saying, Let this be a woman !
Thou who madest them and
gave them being ! Watch over
them that they may live in
health and peace. Thou who
art in the high heavens, and
among the clouds of the tempest,
grant this with long life, and
accept this sacrifice, O Creator !

Then the Priest of the Sun distributed the *sancu*, and
afterwards the people ate the flesh of the sheep which had
been sacrificed to the Creator, the Sun, and the Thunder.

D

Each nation passed the rest of the day in performing the *taqui* and in singing and dancing, according to the custom of their respective countries before they were subdued by the Yncas. On this day all the deformed persons, who had previously been expelled from Cuzco, were allowed to join the feast. This part of the feast lasted for two days, and at its conclusion, in the evening, they burnt in sacrifice a sheep, and a vast quantity of clothes of many colours. Then those who had to return to their homes, sought permission from the Creator, the Sun, the Thunder, and the Ynca, which was granted, and they left at Cuzco the *huacas* they had brought there in that year. They returned to their homes with the *huacas* they had brought for the festival of the previous year, and, as a recompense for their trouble in having come from such great distances, their chiefs were given gold and silver and clothes and servants, and permission to travel in litters. Their *huacas* were also granted estates and attendants to wait on them, and so they returned to their homes.

The inventor of this feast was Ynca Yupanqui, at least he established the above ceremonies, for though it was celebrated from the time that there ever were Yncas, it was not performed in the order described above. The rest of the month was passed as each man found it convenient, or as suited him best. The same feast, called *Situa*, was celebrated at the chief places in all the provinces, by the Ynca governors, wherever they might be: and, although the ceremonies were less grand, and the sacrifices fewer, no part of the festival was omitted.

SEPTEMBER.

They call the month of September *Uma-Raymi*, because the Indians of Uma, which is two leagues from Cuzco, celebrated the feast of *Hurachillo*.[2] This was the occasion

---

[2] Huarachicu.

when the youths were admitted to knighthood, and when their ears were pierced, as we shall mention in its place. The women of Cuzco, whose sons were to have their ears bored, and to perform the huarachicu, employed their time in sewing the cloths in which their sons were to be dressed on the day of the feast of the huarachicu. Several relations assembled to help them to sew, and to rejoice and drink for some days in their houses: and so the month ended.

OCTOBER.

They called the month of October *Aya Marca Raymi*, because the Indians of the village of Ayamarca performed the feasts of huarachicu, and the youths of that tribe had their ears bored, and were admitted to knighthood, with the ceremonies we shall presently describe. In Cuzco, the people were employed in preparing a great quantity of chicha, for the feast called *Ocapac Raymi*. This way of making chicha was called *cantoray*. The youths who were about to receive their arms, went to the huaca called *Huanacauri*, to offer sacrifice, and to ask permission to receive knighthood. For this was their principal *huaca*, the brother, as was said, of Manco Ccapac, whence they descend. But, to avoid prolixity, I will not here give the tradition respecting this huaca, referring for an account of it, to the history of the Yncas which I have written. The youths who were to be armed as knights, passed that night on the hill of *Huanacauri*, where the huaca was kept, in memory of the journey which their ancestors commenced from that spot. On the next day they returned in the afternoon, bringing with them loads of straw, on which their parents and relations might sit. On this day the youths fasted; and the month was passed in preparing many kinds of chicha for the festival. At this time, and indeed throughout the year, the priests of the Creator, of the Sun, and of Thunder, and those who had charge of the *huaca* of

Huanacauri, made three daily sacrifices; offering up three
sheep, one in the morning, one at noon, and a third at
night, with other food that was dedicated to these deities.
The *huacas* were supposed to consume it where they were;
but they carried the food to the hills in the feast of Yntic-
raymi. The persons also, who had charge of the embalmed
bodies, never came forth to offer up the food, and pour out
the chicha that was dedicated to them, such as they used
when they were alive. These they consumed, because they
held for very truth, the doctrine of the immortality of the
soul, and they said that wherever the soul might be, it would
receive the food and eat as when alive. Thus ended this
month.

November.

The month of November was called Ccapac Raymi, which
means the Feast of the Lord Ynca. It was one of the three
principal feasts of the year. In this month they gave arms
to the youths, pierced their ears, and gave them breeches,
which in their language are called *huara*. For the said
feast, and for the arming of the knights, during the eight
first days of the month, all the parents and relations of
those who were to receive knighthood were engaged in the
preparation of the *usutas*, which were their shoes made of
very fine reeds, almost of the colour of gold; and of the
huaracas from the sinews of sheep; and in broidering the
trimmings of the shirts in which they were to appear, when
they went to the huaca called Huanacauri Chumpicasico.
The shirts were made of fine yellow wool, with the borders
of fine black wool like silk, a little more than a *palmo* and
a half in width. They also wore mantles called *supayacolla*,
which were of white wool, long and narrow, not being more
than two *palmos* in width, but reaching to the knees. They
were fastened round the neck by a knot, whence hung a
woollen cord, at the end of which there was a red tassel.
The *llautus*, that were put on them on that day, were black.

On the ninth day they all proceeded to the square in the morning, as well the parents of those who were to receive knighthood, as the relations. The parents and relations were attired in certain dresses called *collca-uncu*. There was a special dress for each festival. On this occasian the mantles were yellow, and the plumes on their heads were black, being taken from a bird called *quito*. Hence the plumes were called *quito-tica*. Those who were to be armed as knights were shorn, and after the shearing they were clothed in the dress already described. Many maidens, who were selected to give their services at this feast, then came to the square, dressed in a costume called *Cuzco asu ycochilli-quilla*. Their ages were from eleven to twelve or fourteen years, and they were of the best families. They were called *Ñusta-calli-sapa*.[3] Their duty was to carry small vases of chicha, as we shall relate further on. Being all clothed in these costumes, they proceeded to the house of the Sun and of the Thunder, and brought the images to the square. Then the Ynca came forth, and took his place near the statue of the Sun. The youths, who were to receive knighthood, rose up in their order, and made their *mucha*,[4] which was their manner of worshipping the huacas. They also brought out the figure of a woman, which was the huaca of the moon, and was called *Passa*[5]-*mama*. It was in charge of women; and when it was brought from the house of the Sun, where it had a special place on the site of the *mirador* of Santo Domingo, they carried it on their shoulders. The reason for giving it in charge to women was that they said it was a woman, and the figure resembled one.

After making their reverence, the youths waited until the hour of noon, when they again made reverences to the

---

[3] *Ñusta*, princess; *Calli*, valorous; *Sapa*, alone, unrivalled.

[4] *Muchani*, the verb to adore, to kiss.

[5] *Pacsa* is the word for the moon, in the Collao dialects. In the Ynca language it is *Quilla*.

huacas; and sought permission from the Ynca to make their
sacrifices, which were offered up in the following way.

Each of the youths who were about to be armed had
a sheep prepared for sacrifice. They all went, with their
relations, to the hill called Huanacauri. That night they
slept at the foot of the hill, at a place called Matahua, and
at sunrise of the tenth day, all fasting, for they had fasted
on the previous day, they ascended the hill until they came
to the huaca *Huanacauri*. They left the sheep for sacrifice
at the foot of the hill in Matahua, the Tarpuntays pulling
out a small handful of wool from each. These Tarpuntays
are the priests who make the sacrifices. When they reached
the top of the hill, the Tarpuntays took five lambs and
sacrificed them before the huaca. They then divided the
wool they held in their hands among the youths who were
about to be made knights, and the chiefs who came with
them. The youths and chiefs then blew the wool into the
air, while the sacrifices were being consumed, with these
words " O Huanacauri ! our father, may the Creator, the
Sun, and the Thunder ever remain young, and never become
old. May thy son the Ynca always retain his youth, and
grant that he may prosper in all he undertakes. And to us,
thy sons and descendants who now celebrate this festival,
grant that we may ever be in the hands of the Creator, of
the Sun, of the Thunder, and in thy hands." After the
sacrifices, at the ninth hour of the day, they put *huaracas*,[6]
and bags called *chuspas* into the hands of the youths, and
on presenting them with the *huaracas*, they said: "Now
that our father *Huanacauri* has given the *huaracas* as a sign
of valour, live henceforth as brave men." The High Priest
of the huaca used these words when the *huaracas* were given
to the youths. They were made of aloe fibre and the sinews
of sheep, the aloe fibre being like flax. It was said that
their ancestors, when they came forth from Paccari-tampu,

[6] Slings.

wore them. They then walked on, until they came to a
ravine called Quiras-manta, where they were met by the
uncles and parents, and by the chiefs, who whipped them on
the arms and legs, saying, "Be brave as I have been, and
receive these gifts that you may imitate me." Then they
chaunted a song called *Huari*, the armed knights standing
up with the handfuls of straw in their hands, and all the rest
of the people being seated. As soon as the *taqui* was ended,
they rose up and went to Cuzco, whence a shepherd came,
who was one of those in charge of the flock called *Raymi-
napa*, which was dedicated for this feast. They brought a
sheep called *napa*, which was covered with a red cloth
having ear holes of gold. Those who came with it, blew
upon sea shells bored through, called *hayllayquipac*. An
Indian also brought the *suntur-paucar*, which is one of the
insignia of the Lord. When they arrived at the *plaza* where
the people were assembled, they performed a dance, and
then led the sheep and the *suntur-paucar* in front of them.
The people returned to Cuzco, marching according to their
families and tribes, those who had received knighthood
carrying the *huaracas* on their heads, and the bundles of
straw in their hands. When they reached the square they
worshipped the *huacas*. The fathers, uncles, and relations
then whipped them on the arms and legs, and afterwards
all the people made the music *(taqui)* called *huari*, and the
youths gave drinks to the fathers, uncles, and relations who
had flogged them. By that time it was nearly night, and
they went to their houses and ate the sacrificial sheep. The
Priests took the *huacas* back to their temples.

In the subsequent days the people remained in their
houses, and the youths who had received knighthood
rested from their labours. But on the 14th day of the
month they all came forth into the square of Cuzco, called
Huacay-pata. Each came with his father and relations;
and it must be known that all the youths who received arms

were obliged to be descendants and relations of the Lord
Yncas by direct line, for no others were admitted. In the
same month the Ynca Governors of Provinces who had sons
of the proper age, performed the ceremonies in the provinces, boring the ears of the boys, and arming them as
knights.

On the 14th day they brought into the square the huacas
of the Creator, of the Sun, of the Moon, and of the Thunder,
which were placed together near the Ynca, the Priests being
stationed near their huacas. Dresses were given to the
youths who had been armed as knights, called *umisca-uncu*,
which were shirts striped red and white, and a white mantle
with a blue cord and red tassel. All the people of the land
had to make these dresses, as a tribute; and the relations
provided the *usutas*, made of a straw which was highly
prized among them, called *ychu*. The Priest of the Sun,
whose duty it was to give these dresses in the name of the
Sun, caused all the maidens to be brought before him, and
to each he gave a dress, which was red and white, and called
uncallu; the *lliclla* being the same; together with a cloth
in the shape of a bag, with both ends open, of the same
colour. Then they put staves into the hands of the youths,
to the upper part of which a knife was attached, which they
called *yauri*. Then the breeches were given, called *huaraca*,
made of sinews and red cloth, with a little *chahuar*.[7] After
receiving the clothes they went, in their order, to worship
the images of the Creator, the Sun, the Moon, and the
Thunder, and they bowed reverently to the Ynca. Before
this the uncles and relations had flogged them on the arms
and legs, exhorting them to be valiant, and ever to pay
attention to the worship of the Huacas and the Ynca. At
the end of these ceremonies they went out of the square, in
the order of their tribes, each one with those of his family;

---

[7] Aloe fibre.

and went to sleep in a desert called *Rauranu,* which is about
a league from Cuzco.

Each of those who had been armed as knights brought a
tent in which to sleep, for himself and his relations. There
went with them all the maidens who had received the
dresses which the Sun had given. They were called *Ñusta-
callisapa.* They brought with them small jars of chicha, to
give drink to the relations of the knights, and to offer as
sacrifice, as well as to give drink to the youths who were
armed as knights. On this day they brought with them
the sheep called *tupa-huanacu* or *raymi-napa ;*[8] with a red
shirt placed over it, having golden ears, as before described.
They also carried the *suntur-paucar* or insignia of royalty.
When the people had all departed from the square, they
carried each huaca back to its temple, and the Ynca returned
to his palace. Next day they rose up and went to a ravine
in a mountain called *Quilli-yacolca ;* which is not more than
half a league from the place where they slept. Here they
had breakfast, and after their meal they fastened a little
white wool to the ends of their staves, and to the handles
of the said *topa-yauri* they secured some *ychu.* Then they
continued to advance until they came to a hill called Anahuarqui, which is two leagues from Cuzco, to the huaca of
the same name on the top of the hill, which was the huaca
of the Indians of the villages of Choco and Cachona. The
reason why they went to this huaca to perform a sacrifice
was that, on this day, they had to run a race, to try which
was the best runner. The tradition had been handed down,
from the time of the deluge, that this huaca ran like a lion.
On coming before the huaca, the youths offered a little wool
which they held in their hands. The priests of the Sun (not
the High Priest) and those of the other huacas, called *Tarpuntays,* then sacrificed five lambs, burning them in the
name of the Creator, the Sun, the Moon, and the Thunder.

[8] Raymi-napa.

Then the relations once more flogged the youths who were
now knighted, urging them to set great store by the valour,
and endurance of their persons.   After this the people sat
down and performed the *taqui* called *haurita*[9] with the
huayllaquipas and shells; the knights remaining on their
feet, holding in their hands the staves called *yauri*.   Some
were headed with gold, others with copper, each according
to the means of the owner.   At the end of the *taqui* all the
maidens called *Ñusta calli-sapa* rose up, and each ran as
fast as she could to the place where they had slept; and
there waited for those who had been armed as knights,
with the chicha to give them to drink.   The girls cried out,
and said :—" Come quickly, youths, for here we are waiting
for you."   Then the youthful knights stood in a row before
the huaca of Anahuarqui, and behind them there was a
second row of men, who served as arm bearers.   These
carried the *yauris* and sticks in their hands; and in their
rear was yet a third row, whose duty it was to aid those who
fell.   In front of all these was an Indian, very gaily dressed,
who gave the word.   On hearing it they all began to run at
full speed and with all their force.   Those who fell or fainted,
were assisted by the men in the rear, but some died of the
falls.   Those who reached the goal received drink from the
maidens, and they drank as they ran.   The object of this
race was to prove who was the best of those who had received knighthood.

On each occasion they armed eight hundred knights and
upwards.   When they were all assembled on the hill called
Raurana, they again performed the *taqui* called *huari* ; after
which they took the *huaracas* and the *yauris,* and again began to flog the knights upon the arms and legs.   By this
time it was the hour of vespers, and they all rose up in their
order, to return to Cuzco, bearing in front the *suntur-pancar*
and the sheep called *raymi-napa.*   They marched to the

[9] *Huari.*

square called *Huacay-pata* in Cuzco, where were the statues
of the Creator, the Sun, the Thunder, and the Moon ; and
where the Ynca was seated near the statue of the Sun, with
his courtiers. As they entered they performed *mucha* to
the huacas and the Ynca. The tribes of Hanan Cuzco and
Hurin Cuzco then sat down in the places assigned to them,
while the youths remained standing for a short time. They
again performed the *taqui* called *huari*, and once more
flogged the youths. Afterwards the Ynca and his court
went to his house, and the youths, with their fathers and
relations, went to the hill called *Raurana*. They passed
the night at the foot of the hill, in a place called *Huaman-
cancha*.[1] At dawn they arose and ascended the hill *Raurana*,
which is half a league from Cuzco. The Lord Ynca came
here on this day, to grant favours to those who had been
armed as knights, giving them ear-pieces of gold, red
mantles, with blue tassels, and other marks of distinction.
The huaca of *Raurana* consisted of two falcons in stone,
placed upon an altar on the summit of the hill. It was instituted by Pachacutec Ynca Yupanqui, as the place where
they should receive the breeches which they call *huara*.
This huaca was at first the idol of the Indians of Maras,
and Huascar Ynca caused the falcons to be brought here,
to beautify it. The sacrifice that was performed on this
occasion was to burn five lambs, and to pour out chicha,
beseeching the Creator, the Sun, the Moon, and the
Thunder, that the youths who had been armed, might become valiant and enterprising warriors, that all they put
their hands to might prosper, and that they might never
suffer defeat. The sacrifice was performed by the Priest of
the huaca *Raurana ;* who also besought the huaca that the
youths might be fortunate. As soon as the sacrifices were
consumed, the *Huaca-camayoc,* who was the Priest, gave to
each of the youths a pair of breeches called *huarayarus,* and

---

[1] *Huaman*, a falcon ; *Cancha*, place.

a red shirt with a blue binding, which clothes were brought
by order of the Ynca, as the tribute paid throughout the
land on this occasion.   The youths were given ear-pieces of
gold, which were then fastened in their ears, and diadems
with plumes called *pilcocassa*, and small pieces of gold and
silver to hang round their necks.   After those things had
been distributed, they had breakfast, and performed the
taqui called *huari* for the space of an hour.   Then the
fathers and parents again flogged the youths, reminding
them of the prayers just offered up, urging them to emulate
the deeds of their ancestors, and to be valiant warriors,
never turning their backs on the foe.

   With reference to the *taqui* so often repeated in the ceremony, they say that, in the time of Manco Ccapac, the first
Ynca from whom they are all descended, when he came
forth from the Cave of Tampu, it was given to him by the
Creator with a command that it should be sung at this
festival, and at no other.

   After the *taqui*, they drank in their order, and marched
back to Cuzco, the *suntur-paucar* being borne before them
as a banner, and the sheep dressed as on former occasions.
Manco Ccapac instituted this feast, and caused these ceremonies to be observed in the case of his son Sinchi Rocca,
as we have related in the history of the Yncas.[2]   On reaching the square of Cuzco, they performed the *mucha* or
adoration before the Huacas which the Priests had brought
out, and they also made obeisances to all the embalmed
bodies of the dead Lord and Ladies which had been brought
into the square by those who had charge of them ; to drink
with them as if they had been alive, and that the young
knights might beseech them to make their descendants as
fortunate and brave as they had been themselves.

   Then all the people sat down, those of Hanan and Hurin

   [2] G. de la Vega says that the lineage of the Ynca Sinchi Rocca was
called *Raurana Panaca.*

Cuzco in their respective places. The skins of lions, with the heads, had been prepared, with gold ear-pieces in the ears, and golden teeth in place of the real teeth which had been pulled out. In the paws were certain *ajorcas* of gold, called *chipanas*. They called these lions *hillacunya chuqui-cunya*. Those who dressed in the skins, put on the head and neck of the lion so as to cover their own, and the skin of the body of the lion hung from the shoulders. Those who had to take part in the *taqui* wore red shirts, with red and white fringes, reaching to the feet. They called these shirts *puca-caychu-uncu*. The *taqui* was called *coyo*. It was first introduced by the Ynca Pachacutec Yupanqui, and was performed with drums, two from Hanan Cuzco, and two from Hurin Cuzco. They performed this *taqui* twice a day for six days, and during these six days each person offered sacrifices to the Creator, the Sun, the Moon, and the Thunder; for the Ynca and for those who had been armed as knights. These sacrifices consisted of a quantity of sheep, cloth, gold, silver, and other things. It was offered up that those who were armed as knights might be fortunate in war, and in everything they undertook.

On the 21st day of this month all the youths who had been armed as knights, went to bathe in a fountain called Calli-puquio, in a ravine about a quarter of a league to the rear of the fortress of Cuzco. They then took off the clothes in which they had been armed as knights, and dressed themselves in others called *nanaclla,* coloured black and yellow, and in the centre a red cross. Thence they returned to the square, where they found all the huacas. They made the usual obeisances. They were placed according to the families to which they belonged; and the principal uncle presented each knight with a shield, a sling, and a club with a metal knob at the end, with which to go to the wars. The other relations and chiefs then offered up cloth, sheep, gold, silver, and other things, with a prayer that the youths might always be rich and fortunate. Each relation that offered sacrifice, flogged a youth and delivered a discourse to him, exhorting him to be valiant and never to be a traitor to the Sun and the Ynca, but to be diligent in devotion to the huacas, and to imitate the bravery and prowess of his ancestors. When the principal Lord Ynca was armed as a knight, all the chiefs and great lords, who were present from all parts of the land, made great offerings in addition to those usually supplied. At the end of the sacrifices, the Priests of the Sun and of the Creator brought a great quantity of fuel tied together in handfuls, and dressed in the clothes of a man and a woman. The faggots, thus dressed up, were offered to the Creator, the Sun, and the Ynca, and were burnt in their clothes, together with a sheep. They also burnt certain birds called *pilcopichio*[7] and *camantera-pichio*; and this sacrifice was performed for the youths who had been armed as knights; with a prayer that they might always be fortunate in war.

On the 22nd of the month the knights were taken to the houses of their relations, and their ears were pierced, which was the last ceremony in arming the knights. Among these people they thought so much of this boring the ears, that, if the orifice was broken through by any accident, the man to whom it happened was looked upon as unfortunate. They stuff pieces of cotton into the orifice of the ear, and each day they put in more in order to enlarge it. On the same day the priests of the Creator and the Sun, of Thunder and the Moon, and the shepherds of the Ynca counted the flocks of the huacas and of the Ynca. Then commenced the feasts that were celebrated for the flocks of the huacas, that they might multiply; for which sacrifices were made throughout the kingdom. The shepherds whose flocks increased most rapidly were rewarded, and those whose flocks failed to multiply were punished.

[3] *Pichio* for *piscu*, a bird.

On the 23rd day of the month they carried the statue of the Sun called *Huayna punchao*, to the houses of the Sun called *Puquinque*, which are on a high hill, a little more than three arquebus shots from Cuzco. Here they sacrificed to the Creator, the Sun, the Thunder, and the Moon, for all nations, that they might prosper and multiply. The statue of the Sun was then brought back, preceded by the *suntur-paucar* and two sheep, one of gold and the other of silver, called *cullque-napa ccuri-napa* ; which were the insignia borne before the statue of the Sun, wheresoever it was taken. Thus ended this festival and month called *Ccapac-raymi.*

DECEMBER.

The name they gave to the month of December was *Camay-quilla.* On the first day of the month, those who had been armed as knights, as well those of the lineage of Hanan Cuzco as of Hurin Cuzco, came out into the square, with slings in their hands called *huaraca,* and the youths of Hanan Cuzco hurled against those of Hurin Cuzco; their missiles were called *coco,* which are found on certain thistles. At times they came to close quarters, to prove the muscles of their arms; until the Ynca, who was present, rose up and restored order. They called this *chocanaco,* and it was a trial of strength, to see who were the strongest and bravest. Afterwards, they all sat down according to their lineages, the new knights being dressed in black shirts, and mantles of a lion colour. They also wore plumes of white feathers on their heads, from a bird called *tocto.*[4] On this day the new knights began to eat salt and other luxuries, for during the ceremonies they fasted, and were not allowed to touch either salt or *aji.* The youths ate their first meal after the fast with great relish. For this feast they brought all the huacas into the square, as well as the bodies of the dead Yncas, to drink with them; placing those who had belonged

[4] *Toctu* is honey.

to the Hanan Cuzco on the side where that lineage was
stationed, and the same with those of Hurin Cuzco. Then
they brought food and drink to the dead bodies, as if they
were alive, saying : " When you were alive you used to eat
and drink of this ; may your soul now receive it and feed on
it, wheresoever you may be." For they believed and held
it for certain that souls did not die, but that those of good
men went to rest with the Creator. When they died they
declared this belief, and charged their families and relations
to perform all that they had left them to do, and that they
would see them from heaven. They also believed that there
was a place of punishment for bad men, where they were tor-
mented by demons called Supay. They said that those who
went there, suffered much hunger and thirst, and that their
food was charcoal, snakes, toads, and other things of that
kind. Those who went to heaven, on the other hand, eat
and drank the best that the Creator had, and they also
received the food and liquor which their relations offered up.

Thus all with great joy passed this day, on which they
began to dance and sing. Afterwards, they all went forth
to plough their fields, which they called *chacra*. This lasted
for twelve days. On the 15th day of the month, at the full
of the moon, all returned from their estates to Cuzco ; and on
that night they performed the dance and *taqui*, called
yahuayra, through all the streets and squares of the city,
from nightfall until dawn. In the morning the priests brought
out the huacas of the Creator, the Sun, the Moon, and the
Thunder, and the dead bodies, and placed them in the square.
The Ynca also came forth, and took his place near the Sun.
The rest of the people had gone to a house called *Moro-urco*,
near the houses of the Sun, to take out a very long cable
which was kept there, woven in four colours, black, white,
red, and yellow, at the end of which there was a stout ball
of red wool. Every one took hold of it, the men on one
side, and the women on the other, performing the *taqui* called

yaqauyra. When they came to the square, after making reverences to the huacas and the Ynca, they kept going round and round until they were the shape of a spiral shell. Then they dropped the *huascar* on the ground, and left it coiled up like a snake. They called this cable *Moro-urco.* The people returned to their places, and those who had charge of the cable took it back to its house. When they celebrated this feast, they were dressed in clothes called *pucay-urco;* a black shirt with a white band, and white fringes at the edges. They also wore white plumes from a bird called *tocto.* Presently, they brought a lamb to be sacrificed for the cable, and for rain, and the winter time, saying to the winter : " Why hast thou rained ?"

From noon to sunset was passed in rejoicings, and in drinking with the huacas and dead bodies. As, in my account of the *Yntic-Raymi,* which is the month of May, I described the manner of their drinking to the Sun, and to the other huacas, pouring the chicha down certain pipes, I will not repeat the description here. In all the festivals the manner of drinking to the huacas was the same. Half-an-hour before sunset they took the huacas back to their temples, and the Ynca returned to his house. The performing of this *taqui,* with the sacrifices and drinking, lasted for two days. On the 18th of the said month, they came out in the square, clothed in very gay dresses called *sanca-sonco-quila pionco;* and in small mantles, and with plumes called *cupaticas* on their heads, being the tails of macaws and pilos called *gualanpapi,* made of feathers. On reaching the square they made their obeisances to the huacas in the usual order, and took their places. A priest then rose up and burnt a lamb as a sacrifice, praying to the winter ever to send its waters so that, through its means, they might eat and drink.

They preserved the cinders and ashes, not only of this sacrifice, but of all others that were made throughout the year, in order to throw them into the river.

E

On this day they performed the *taqui chapay quenalo,* — which, with all the other ceremonies that were performed in the course of the year, was invented by Pachacutec Ynca Yupanqui; excepting those of the *huarachico* when they armed the knights, and those of *quicochico* and *rutuchico yayascay*, which are festivals invented by the first Ynca, as will presently be mentioned.

On the following day, which was the 19th of the said month, they went to the square of Cuzco, called *Huacay-pata,* both the Ynca and all the people, and they brought out the huacas and the embalmed bodies of the dead. Having made the usual obeisances, they began to offer up the sacrifice called *mojocati*, in the following order.

A small river flows through the centre of Cuzco called Capi-mayu and Huaca-puncu-mayu. It comes down from some ravines in the heights above the town. In these ravines they constructed dams to confine the water, although it was winter, in order that it might bear away the sacrifices that were about to be offered in it, with greater force. On this day they collected all kinds and sorts of food, all the different sorts of *ajis,* great quantities of bags of coca, all kinds of cloths of different colours and shoes, *llautus* and plumes worn as head dresses, sheep, flowers, gold and silver, and every other sort of thing that they used, as well as all the ashes and cinders of all the sacrifices, that had been preserved throughout the year.

All these things were thrown into the river, the first dam was thrown down, and the water rushed out with such fury that it carried the other dams away with it, and all the sacrifices. A lamb had been sacrificed on this day, and its ashes, with the cinders, were thrown into the river with the rest.

Many people were assembled on both sides of the river, outside the city of Cuzco, at a place called *Pumap-chupa,* where the sacrifices were offered up. They were made at a little less than an hour before sunset, and the Indians who were on both sides of the river, were commanded by the Lord Ynca, who was present, to go with the sacrifices to Ollantay-tampu. By the round they had to make the distance was ten leagues from Cuzco. Indians of the villages by which they had to pass, were stationed at intervals, with torches, in order to give light during the night, and no part of the sacrifices was allowed to remain in the river. When they reached the bridge of Ollantay-tampu, which is over a great river flowing to the North Sea, they threw two bags of coca, called *pilculuncu paucar uncu*, from the bridge, as the sacrifices flowed past, and afterwards they were allowed to pass on by themselves.

During that day and the next, those who had passed on the sacrifices were dancing and rejoicing, and performing the *taqui chupay huayllu*. The reason for throwing these sacrifices into the river was as follows. They said that, as the Creator of all things had granted them a good year, it seemed well that, out of the things that he had given them, they should offer these sacrifices, that they might not appear ungrateful, beseeching him to receive them, wheresoever he might please to be. At the end of two days, those who had followed the sacrifices as far as the bridge, returned to Cuzco. Those who had gone furthest, carried in their hands lances and falcons made of salt; while those who lagged behind had toads made of salt, as a sign that they had gone slowly, which made the people laugh at them. During the rest of the month every man attended to his farm.

The Month of January.

They called the month of January *Atun-pucuy*, and they had no special festival in it, the people merely attending to their work.

FEBRUARY.

The name for the month of February was *Pacha pucuy,*
and neither in this month did they do anything but attend
to their farms.

MARCH.

The month of March was called *Paucar-huara.* No festival was celebrated of any kind in this month.

APRIL.

The month of April was called *Ayrihuay.* In it they
reaped the crops and got in the harvests, and hence they call
it *Ayrihuay.* Those who had received arms as knights,
went to the farm of *Sausiru,* to fetch the maize that had
been reaped there; which is beneath the *citadel.* It is here
they say that Mama-huaca, the sister of Manco Ccapac,
sowed the first maize. They cultivated this farm every
year, for the body of this Mama-huaca, making from the
crop the chicha that was necessary for the service of the
body, and delivering this chicha to those who had charge
of the body, which was embalmed. Then, in their order,
they brought the maize of the harvests of the Creator, the
Sun, the Moon, the Thunder, the Ynca, and Huanacauri,
and of all the dead lords. They brought it in small baskets,
singing a chaunt called *yaravi,* and dressed in gay clothes.
All the rest of the people of Cuzco went to bring in this
maize, except on the first day, when it was brought by
the youths who had received knighthood. The priests,
called *Tarpuntays,* offered up a lamb in sacrifice, beseeching the Creator ever to grant them good harvests. This
lasted for four days, after which they went back to their
farms; and so the year ended, and the month of May returned.

Besides the ceremonies peculiar to each of these months, they performed others called *ayuscay rutu-chica-quicu-chicu.* The *ayuscay* was when a women conceived. On the fourth day they put the babies into a cradle called *quirau,* and they invited the uncles and other relations to see it; but no other ceremony of any kind was performed in consequence of this event.

The *rutuchico* is when the child attains the age of one year. Then, whether it be a boy or a girl, they give it the name that it is to have until it is of age. In the case of a boy, this is when he is armed as a knight, and receives the *huaraca.* He is then given the name that he is to bear until death. In the case of a girl it is when she attains the age of puberty, when she also receives the name she is to bear until death. The child was then shorn, and to perform the ceremony, the eldest uncle was called, who cut the first hair. Then the other relations did the same, and afterwards the friends of the parents. They all drank, and the principal uncle gave the child the name it was to bear until it came of age.

The *quicuchica* is when girls reach the age of puberty : from the first day until the last, which was three days more or less. They fasted during the two first days, without eating anything at all, and on the third day they were given a little raw maize, that they might not die of hunger. They were confined in a place within the house, and on the fourth day they were washed, and dressed in clothes called *ancalluasu,* with shoes of white wool. Their hair was plaited, and a sort of bag was placed on their heads. On this day the principal relations came, and the girl came forth to set food before them, and to give them to drink. This lasted for two days, and the principal relation gave her the name she was to bear from thenceforth, and taught her how she should behave, and how she should obey her parents. They then offered gifts according to their means, without any idolatrous practice whatever; and this custom was ordained by Ynca Yupanqui.

When the Ynca gave women as wives, they were received because it was the command of the Ynca. The man went to the house of the girl's father, not to say that the Ynca had given her, but that he desired to serve for her, and so the relations of the girl were assembled, and their consent was obtained. The youth remained in the house of his father and mother-in-law for a space of four or five days, and carried in fuel and straw for them. Thus the agreement was made, and he took the girl for his wife; and because the Ynca had given her, it was considered that she was taken until death, and she was received on this understanding, and never deserted.

The *Ccapac-cocha* was instituted by Pachacutec Ynca Yupanqui, and was as follows. The provinces of Colla-suyu, Chincha-suyu, Anti-suyu, and Cunti-suyu brought to this city, from each lineage or tribe, one or two male and female children aged about ten years. They also brought cloth and flocks, gold and silver. Then the Ynca seated himself in the Huacay-pata, or great square of Cuzco. The children and the other sacrifices walked round the statues of the Creator, the Sun, the Thunder, and the Moon, which were placed in the square, taking two turns. The Ynca then called to the Priests of the provinces, and commanded them to divide the sacrifices into four parts, in token of the four provinces, Colla-suyu, Chincha-suyu, Anti-suyu, and Cunti-suyu, which are the four divisions into which the land is divided. He told them, "Take, each one of you, his part of these offerings and sacrifices, and offer them to your principal *huacas*." So the children were strangled and buried with the silver figures of sheep, and the gold and silver figures of men and sheep, and they burnt the cloth, with some bags of coca. The people of Cuzco carried these sacrifices as far as Sacalpiña, about a league from Cuzco, where they were received by the Indians of Anta, and in this way they were passed on until they were delivered at the places where they were to be offered up. In the same way, they were passed on to the other provinces. The Lord Ynca offered these sacrifices when he began to reign, that the *huacas* might give him health, and preserve his dominions in peace. No *huaca* or place of worship, how small soever, was left out in the distribution of the sacrifices, for the things that were to be sacrificed at each place were all set apart. The reason why all the *huacas*, whether they were sacred trees, fountains, or hills, or lakes, received part of the sacrifice, was because it was held to be an evil omen if any were left out, and because it was feared that if any were omitted they would be enraged, and would punish the Ynca. If any of the hills were very steep and could not be ascended, the sacrifices were hurled to the summits from slings. Thus, at all the principal *huacas* throughout the provinces, these sacrifices were offered up; and afterwards at all the smaller sacred places. At each place was offered up the portion that was assigned for it at Cuzco; for in Cuzco there was the *Quipucamayu*, or accountant, who took an account of each portion of the sacrifice, and of the province to which each was to be sent.

They began to make the sacrifices in Cuzco, in the following order. The first was offered to the Creator, and was received by the priest who had charge of its image, and they prayed for long life and health, and for victory against the enemies of the Yncas, also that while this Ynca was Lord all the provinces might remain at peace, and be prosperous. After this prayer they strangled the children, first giving them to eat and drink, that they might not enter the presence of the Creator discontented and hungry. From others they took out the hearts while yet alive, and offered them to the *huacas* while yet palpitating. They anointed the *huaca* with the blood from ear to ear, and they called this *pirac*. To others they gave the body with the blood, and finally they interred the bodies with the other sacrifices, in a place called Chuquicancha, which is a small hill above San Sebastian, about half a league from the town. Then the Priests of the Sun, in the same order, received what was assigned to their Deity, and in the same place they performed the sacrifice to the Sun, with the following prayer:—

Prayer for the Sun.

Uiracochaya punchau cachan tutacachannas pacnicpacarichun yllarichun nispac nicpunchac churi yquicta carillacta quispillacta purichuruna rurascayquictacancharin yampac quillarincanpac Uiracochaya casilla quispilla punchau Ynca runayanani chisca yquicta quillari canchari ama un cochispa amananachispa caçista quispicta huacaychaspa.

O Creator! Thou who saidest, let there be night and day, dawn and twilight, grant to thy child the Sun that when he rises he may come forth in peace. Preserve him that he may give light to men whom thou hast created. O Creator! O Sun! thou who art in peace and safety, shine down upon these people, and keep them in health and peace.

In like manner, the priests of the Thunder, which was called *Chuqui-ylla*, received the children and other sacrifices which were assigned to it, and buried them in the same place, called *Chuqui-cancha;* and the same order was observed with the sacrifices to the Moon; prayers being offered up on each occasion that the Ynca might always be granted health and prosperity; and that he might always be victorious over his enemies. Afterwards the whole of the priests together offered to Heaven the sacrifices that were set apart for that purpose, and also to the earth; repeating the following prayer:—

Pachacmama! cuyrumama casillacta quispillacta Ccapac Ynca huahuay yquctamacari hatalli.

O mother earth! preserve the Lord Ynca, thy son, who stands upon thee, in peace and safety.

All the above sacrifices were placed in the *Chuqui-cancha.*
Then the priests who had charge of the huaca *Yanacauri*
offered their sacrifice.   This huaca was of Ayar-cachi,[5] one
of the four brothers who were said to have come out of the
cave at Tampu ; but, as I have treated of this fable in the
beginning of the history which your most illustrious Lordship possesses, I will not dwell upon it here.   As this was
the principal *huaca,* besides those already mentioned, the
priest who had charge of it, with his comrades, received the
children and other things that were dedicated to it, and
sacrificed them on the hill called Huanacauri, which is two
leagues and a half from Cuzco, a little more or less.   They
offered up a prayer at the time of making the sacrifice, beseeching the huaca that the Ynca, its descendant, might
ever be youthful and victorious, and that ever, during the
life of the reigning Ynca, the country might be at peace.
Afterwards sacrifices were performed at all the fountains,
hills, and other places in Cuzco that were held to be sacred ;
but no child was killed for these sacrifices.   These places
were so numerous in Cuzco, that it would be tedious to
enumerate them here, and I will not do so because they are
given in the account of the *huacas* which I have presented
to your most reverend Lordship.   As soon as they had concluded the sacrificial ceremonies in Cuzco, the Priests brought
out those which had to be sent to other parts, in the way
that has already been described.   The order of marching
with the sacrifices was that all the people who went with
the *Ccapac-cocha* (also called *Cachahuaca*) took ways apart
from each other.   They did not follow the royal road, but
traversed the ravines and hills in a straight line, until each
reached the places where the sacrifices were to be made.
They ran, and as they went they raised cries and shouts
which were commenced by an Indian who was deputed to
perform this duty.   Having given the word, all the others

[5] See *G. de la Vega,* i, p. 73.

continued the same cries. The cries were to beseech the
Creator that the Ynca might ever be victorious, and be
granted health and peace. They carried on their shoulders
the sacrifices and the lumps of gold and silver, and the
other things destined to be offered up. The children that
could walk went on foot, and others were carried in their
mothers' arms. When they reached their destinations, the
Huacacamayoc, who had charge of the *huacas*, received those
that were intended for their *huacas*, and sacrificed them,
bringing the gold and silver and other things; and the
children, having first been strangled, were burnt in sacrifice,
with the sheep, lambs, and cloth.

It is worthy of remark that children were not sacrificed
at all the *huacas*, but only at the chief *huaca* of each lineage
or province. In this way they travelled over all the
dominions of the Ynca, with these sacrifices, until each one
reached the extreme point of the empire, in the direction in
which he travelled. The journeys were so well ordered and
arranged, and they were so well equipped when they started
from Cuzco that, although the sacrifices and the places at
which they were to be delivered were numerous, they never
made a mistake. For this service the Ynca had Indians in
Cuzco, who were natives of the four *Suyus* or provinces.
Each one had a knowledge of all the *huacas*, how small soever they might be, that were in the province over which
he was *Quipucamayoc* or Accountant. They were called *Vil-
cacamayoc*. Each Indian had charge of nearly five hundred
leagues of country, and he had an account of the things that
were to be sacrificed at every huaca within his district.
Those who had to set out from Cuzco received their destined
sacrifices from the *Vilca-camayocs*, with instructions as to
whom they were to deliver them. In the chief places of
each province there were also Indians with the same duties,
who kept an account of the sacrifices; nevertheless, as the
sacrifices were increased or augmented according to the will

of the Ynca, the instructions were sent from Cuzco as regarded what was to be done at each place.

They held this sacrifice, called *Ccapacocha* or *Cachahuaca*, in such veneration that, when those who were making journeys over uninhabited tracts with the sacrifices met other travellers, they did not raise their eyes to look at them, and the travellers prostrated themselves on the ground until the sacrifice-bearers had passed. When those bearing sacrifices passed through a village, the inhabitants did not come out of their houses, but remained, with deep humility and reverence, until the said *Ccapac-cocha* had passed onwards.

They also had a custom, when they conquered and subjugated any nations, of selecting some of the handsomest of the conquered people and sending them to Cuzco, where they were sacrificed to the Sun who, as they said, had given them the victory.

It was also their custom that, whenever anything excelled all the rest of its kind in beauty, they worshipped it, and made it *huaca* or sacred.

They worshipped the summits of all peaks and mountain passes, and offered maize and other things; for they said that, when they ascended any pass and reached the top, they could there rest from the labour of the ascent. This they called *chupasitas*.

About ten years ago there was a joke among the Indians. They had a kind of song called *taqui uncu*; and, as one Luis de Olivera, a Priest in the province of Parinacochas, in the bishopric of Cuzco, was the first who described this idolatrous pleasantry, I will here insert his account of it.

In the province of Parinacochas, in the diocese of Cuzco, the said Luis de Olivera learnt, that not only in that province, but in all the other provinces and cities of Chuquisaca, La Paz, Cuzco, Guamanga, and even Lima and Arequipa, most of the Indians had fallen into the greatest apostasy, departing from the Catholic Faith, which they had received, and returning to the idolatries which they practised in the time of their infidelity. It was not understood how this had come to pass; but it was suspected that the wizards, whom the Yncas kept in Uiscacabamba, were at the bottom of it. For in the year 1560, and not before, it was held and believed by the Indians, that an ointment from the bodies of the Indians had been sent for from Spain to cure a disease for which there was no medicine there. Hence it was that the Indians, at that time, were very shy of the Spaniards, and they would not bring fuel or grass or anything else to the house of a Spaniard, lest they should be taken in and killed, in order to extract this ointment. All this had originated from that villainy, with the object of causing enmity between the Indians and Spaniards. The Indians of the land had much respect for the things of the Ynca, until the Lord Viceroy, Don Francisco de Toledo, abolished and put an end to them, in which he greatly served God our Lord. The deception by which the Devil deceived these poor people was the belief that all the huacas which the Christians had burnt and destroyed had been brought to life again; and that they had been divided into two parts, one of which was united with the huaca *Pachacama*, and the other with the huaca *Titicaca*. The story went on that they had formed in the air, in order of battle against God, and that they had conquered Him. But when the Marquis[6] entered this land, it was held that God had conquered the huacas, as the Spaniards had overcome the Indians. Now, however, it was believed that things were changed, that God and the Spaniards were conquered, all the Spaniards killed, and their cities destroyed, and that the sea would rise to drink them up, that they might be remembered no more. In this apostacy they believed that God our Lord had made the Spaniards, and Castille, and

---

[6] Pizarro.

the animals and provisions of Castille ; but that the huacas had made the Indians, and this land, and all the things they possessed before the Spaniards came. Thus they stripped our Lord of his omnipotence. Many preachers went forth from among the Indians, who preached as well in the desert places as in the villages, declaring the resurrection of the huacas, and saying that they now wandered in the air, thirsty and dying of hunger, because the Indians no longer sacrificed nor poured out chicha to them. They declared that many fields were sown with worms, to be planted in the hearts of the Spaniards, and of the Spanish sheep, and of the horses, and also in the hearts of those Indians who remained Christians. The huacas, it was announced, were enraged with all those who had been baptized, and it was declared that they would all be killed unless they returned to the old belief and renounced the Christain faith. Those who sought the friendship and grace of the huacas would, it was urged, pass a life of prosperity and health. Those who would return to the love of the huacas and live, were to fast for some days, not eating salt nor *aji*, nor coloured maize, nor any Spanish thing, nor entering churches, nor obeying the call of the priests, nor using their christian names. Henceforth the times of the Yncas would be restored, and the huacas would not enter into stones or fountains to speak, but would be incorporated in men whom they would cause to speak : therefore the people were to have their houses prepared and ready, in case any huaca should desire to lodge in one of them. Thus it was that many Indians trembled and fell to the ground, and others tore themselves as if they were possessed, making faces ; and when they presently became quiet, they said, when they were asked what they had felt, that such and such a huaca had entered into their bodies. Then the people took such an one in their arms, and carried him to a chosen spot, and there they made a lodging with straw and cloaks ; and began to worship the huaca, offering sheep, *colla-chicha*, *llipta*, *mollo*, and other things. Then they made a festival for two or three days, dancing and drinking, and invoking the huaca that was represented by the possessed man. Such persons, from time to time, preached to the people, threatening them, and telling them not to serve God, but the huacas; and to renounce all christianity, with all christian names, and the shirts, hats, and shoes of Christians. These possessed persons asked the people if they had any relics of the burnt huacas, and when they brought some piece of stone they covered their heads with a mantle before the people, and poured chicha, and the flour of white maize on the fragment. Then the possessed shouted and invoked the huaca; and rose up with the fragment in his hands, thus addressing the people. " You see here your support. You see here that which can give you health, and children, and food. Put it in its place, where it was in the days of the Yncas;" and this was done with many sacrifices. The wizards who in those times were detected and punished, had freely performed their offices, returning to them, and not leaving the Indians who were possessed by huacas, but receiving the sheep and *coys* offered as sacrifices.

This evil was so widely credited that not only the Indians on the *Repartimientos* but those who lived in the cities, among Spaniards, believed and performed the prescribed fasts. At last the said priest, Luis de Olivera, began to punish the people of that province and of Acari, and reported the matter to the Royal Audience of Lima and to the Lord Archbishop, and the Bishop of Charcas, and to Friar Pedro de Toro, the steward of the Bishop of Cuzco. At last the apostacy began to wane, but altogether it lasted for seven years.

As they believed that God and the Spaniards were conquered, the Indians began to rise, as happened in the year 1565, when the Licentiate Castro was Governor of these kingdoms, who received reports from the Corregidors of Cuzco, Guamanga, and Huanuco. These cities were prepared for war during some time.

There were several forms of apostacy in the different provinces. Some danced and gave out that they had the huaca in their bodies. Others trembled for the same reason. Others shut themselves up in their houses and shouted. Others flung themselves from rocks and were killed. Others jumped into the rivers, thus offering themselves to the huacas. At last our Lord, in his mercy, was pleased to enlighten these miserable people; and those who were left were led to see the nonsense that they had believed, that the Ynca was dead or at Vilcapampa, and that nothing of what had been predicted had taken place, but the very opposite.

By reason of this devilish teaching, there are still some Indian sorcerers and witches, though their number is small. When any Indian is sick, these witches are called in to cure him, and to say whether he will live or die. Having pronounced upon the case, they order the sick man to take white maize called *colli sara*, red and yellow maize called *cuma-sara*, yellow maize called *paro-sara*, sea shells called *mullu mullu*, of all the colours they can collect, which they call *ymaymana mullu*. When these things are collected, the wizard grinds the maize with the shell, and gives it ground to the sick man that, breathing on it, he may offer it to the *huacas* and *vilcas*; with these words :—" O all the *huacas* and *vilcas* of the four provinces of the land, my grandfathers and ancestors, receive this sacrifice, wheresoever you may be, and give me health." They also make him breathe on a little coca, and offer it to the Sun, praying for health; and the same to the Moon and Stars. Then, with a little gold and silver of little value in his hand, the sick man offers sacrifice to the Créator. Then the wizard commands him to give food to the dead, placing it on their tombs, and pouring out chicha; if he is in the part of the country where this can be done, and if not in a corner of his house. For the wizard gives the patient to understand that he is visited with this sickness because the dead are starving. If he is able to go on foot to some junction of two rivers, the wizard makes him go there and wash his body with water and flour of white maize, saying that he will there leave his illness. At the end of this ceremony the wizard tells him that, if he would free himself from his sickness, he must confess all his sins, without concealing any. They call this *hichoco*. These Indians are so simple that some of them readily, and with little persuasion, fall into this apostacy and error, though some afterwards repent and confess their sins.

There are also a very great number of Indian men and women who, understanding the offence against our Lord that they commit in doing this, will not permit any such acts, but rather accuse those who do them before the Cura, that they may be punished. If some exemplary punishment was inflicted on the wizards, I believe that this great evil would soon disappear, although, as I have said, there are now few wizards.

In this land there are different nations and provinces, and each one had its own rites and ceremonies, before it was conquered by the Yncas. The Yncas abolished some of the rites, and introduced others. Thus it is no less desirable to know the rites and ceremonies which existed in each of the provinces, other than those of the Yncas, of which I have here written. The means will be acquired, by this knowledge, of rooting out these idolatries and follies; and mean while, with the help of our Lord, the visit I have made through the parishes and valley of this city called Cuzco, is now concluded.

(THE MANUSCRIPT HERE ENDS ABRUPTLY.)

AN ACCOUNT

OF THE

ANTIQUITIES OF PERU.

AN ACCOUNT

OF

THE ANTIQUITIES OF PERU.

JESUS MARIA.

I, DON JUAN DE SANTA CRUZ PACHACUTI-YAMQUI SALCAMAYHUA, a Christian by the grace of God our Lord, am native of the towns of Santiago[1] of Hanalucayhua and Hurinhuayhua-canchi of Urco-suyu,[2] between Canas and Canches of Colla-suyu,[3] legitimate son of Don Diego Felipe Coudorcanqui and of Doña Maria Huayrotari, legitimate grandson of Don Baltasar Cacyaquivi and of Don Francisco Yamquihuanacu (whose wives, my grandmothers, are alive), great grandson of Don Gaspar Apuquiricanqui and of General Don Juan Apu Ynca Mayhua, great great grandson of Don Bernabe Apu-hilas Urcuni the less, and of Don Gonzalo Pizarro Tintaya, and of Don Carlos Anco, all once principal chiefs in the said province, and professed Christians in the things of our holy Catholic faith. They were the first chiefs who came to the tambo of Caxamarca to be made Christians,[4] renouncing all the errors, rites, and ceremonies of the time of heathenry, which were devised by the ancient enemies of the human race, namely the demons and devils. In the

[1] I do not find this Santiago in Alcedo.

[2] Urco-suyu, "the hill country".

[3] That is to say, in the valley of the Vilcamayu, south and east of Cuzco, on the road to the Collao. The Canas and Canches were tribes on either side of the valley.

[4] That is, the last three, his great great grandfathers.

F 2

general language they are called *hapiñuñu*[5] *achacalla.*[6]
When the first Apostolic Priests entered this most noble
province of Ttahuantin-suyu, inspired by the holy zeal of
gaining a soul for God our Lord, like good fishers, with
their loving words, preaching and catechising on the mystery
of our holy Catholic Faith, then my ancestors, after having
been well instructed, were baptized. They renounced the
Devil and all his followers and his false promises, and all
his rites. Thus they became Christians, adopted sons of
Jesus Christ our Lord, and enemies of all the ancient
customs and idolatries. As such they persecuted the wizards,
destroyed and pulled down all the *huacas* and idols, denounced idolaters, and punished those who were their own
servants and vassals throughout all that province. Therefore our Lord God preserved these my ancestors; and to
their grandchildren and descendants, male and female, He
has given his holy benediction. Finally I am, through the
mercy of his divine majesty, and by his divine grace, a
believer in his holy Catholic faith, as I ought to believe.
All my paternal and maternal ancestors were baptized by
the mercy of God, and freed from the servitude of the
infernal yoke under which they were enthralled in the
times of idolatry, with great risk and peril, on whose souls
may our Lord have pity; and pardon all the offences committed in times past by those souls who were made in His
image and likeness. I myself, as the grandchild and legitimate descendant of these ancestors, have, ever since I have
reached manhood, continued firm and established in the
mystery of our holy Catholic faith, exhorting my family to
be good Christians, keeping the ten commandments of the
law of God, believing in our Lord Jesus Christ, in obedience
to our holy Mother Church of Rome. Thus the holy Roman
Mother Church believes what I, Don Juan de Santa Cruz,

---

[5] *Hapini* is the verb "I seize". *Ñuñu* is a woman's bosom.
[6] *Achalla* is an exclamation of admiration.

believe, and in her I desire to live and die in the fear of
God three and one, who lives and reigns for ever without end, as I declare. I believe in God three and one, who
is the powerful God that created heaven and earth and all
things that are therein, the sun, the moon, the stars, the
day star, thunder and lightning, and all the elements. I
also believe that he created Adam, the first man, in his
image and likeness, progenitor of all mankind, whose descendants we, the natives of Ttahuantin-suyu, are, as well as
the other nations throughout the whole world, as well
white as black. I believe that, for their sakes, the living
son of God, our Lord Jesus Christ, by the work of the
Holy Ghost, became incarnate in the womb of the holy
Virgin Mary, coming down from heaven alone to free the
human race from the infernal thraldom of the Devil in
which they were kept. I believe that our Lord Christ,
living among men during thirty-three years, and being
true God and Man, afterwards suffered death on the cross
at Jerusalem to redeem the human race, and died and was
buried, and entered the infernal regions to free the souls of
the holy fathers. I believe that he rose from the dead on
the third day, and was in the body for forty days, and
ascended into Heaven, where he sits in the great power of
the Almighty God, and whence he sent the gift of the
Holy Spirit to his apostles and disciples, that they might
be more powerful in the spiritual things of God. God is
the true God above all other Gods, the powerful God our
Creator, and he it is who, by his order, rules the heavens
throughout all ages, as supreme Lord and Judge and merciful Lord.

I affirm that I have heard, from a child, the most ancient
traditions and histories, the fables and barbarisms of the
heathen times, which are as follows ; according to the constant testimony of the natives touching the events of past
times.

They say that, in the time of *Purun[7]-pacha*, all the nations of Ttahuantin-suyu came from beyond Potosi in four or five armies arrayed for war. They settled in the different districts as they advanced. This period was called *Ccallac-pacha*[8] or *Tutayac-pacha*.[9] As each company selected suitable places for their homes and lands, they called this *Purunpacharacyaptin*.[1] This period lasted for a vast number of years. After the country was peopled, there was a great want of space, and, as the land was insufficient, there were wars and quarrels, and all the nations occupied themselves in making fortresses, and every day there were encounters and battles, and there was no rest from these tumults, insomuch that the people never enjoyed any peace. Then, in the middle of the night, they heard the *Hapi-ñuños* disappearing, with mournful complaints, and crying out— "We are conquered, we are conquered, alas that we should lose our bands!" By this it must be understood that the devils were conquered by Jesus Christ our Lord on the cross on Mount Calvary. For in ancient times, in the days of *Purun-pacha*, they say that the *Hapi-ñuñus* walked visibly over all the land, and it was unsafe to go out at night, for they violently carried off men, women, and children, like infernal tyrants and enemies of the human race as they are.

Some years after the devils called *Hapi-ñuñus Achacallas* had been driven out of the land, there arrived, in these kingdoms of *Ttahuantin-suyu*[2] a bearded man, of middle

---

[7] *Purum* means wild, savage, untamed. *Purum aucca*, unconquered enemy. *Purum soncco*, hardened heart. *Purum allpa*, fallow land. *Purum-purum*, uninhabited wilds. *Purum-pacha*, heathen times.

[8] *Ccallani*, to break down a wall, to destroy by making holes. *Ccallarichini*, to begin. *Ccallariynin-manta*, "from the beginning." "*Ccallac-pacha*," "beginning of time."

[9] "Time of night." Dark Ages.

[1] *Purun*, "savage." *Pacha*, "time." *Racya*, "before." *Ntin*, Plural of multitude. "The people before the savage time."

[2] The four provinces in one. The empire.

height, with long hair, and in a rather long shirt. They
say that he was somewhat past his prime, for he already had
grey hairs, and he was lean. He travelled with his staff,
teaching the natives with much love, and calling them all
his sons and daughters. As he went through all the land,
he performed many miracles. The sick were healed by his
touch. He spoke· all languages better than the natives.
They called him *Tonapa* or *Tarapaca* (*Tarapaca* means an
eagle) *Uiracocharapacha yachipachan* or *Pachaccan*.[3] This
means the servant, and *Uicchaycamayoc*[4] means a preacher,
and *vicchaycamayoc cunacuycamayoc*.[5] Although he
preached the people did not listen, for they thought little
of him. He was called *Tonapa Uiracocha nipacachan*; but
was he not the glorious apostle St. Thomas ?

They say that this man came to the village of a chief
called Apo-tampu (this Apo-tampu is Paccari-tampu[6]) very
tired. It was at a time when they were celebrating a marriage feast. His doctrines were listened to by the chief with
friendly feelings, but his vassals heard them unwillingly.
From that day the wanderer was a guest of Apo-tampu, to
whom it is said that he gave a stick from his own staff, and
through this Apo-tampu, the people listened with attention
to the words of the stranger, receiving the stick from his
hands. Thus they received what he preached in a stick,
marking and scoring on it each chapter of his precepts.
The old men of the days of my father, Don Diego Felipe,
used to say that *Caçi-caçi* were the commandments of God,
and especially the seven precepts; so that they only wanted
the names of our Lord God and of his son Jesus Christ our
Lord; and the punishments for those who broke the com-

---

[3] A steward or head servant. Chamberlain of the Ynca.

[4] *Huichay* (not *Uicchay*) is "up." *Huicharini*, "I ascend." *Cuma-
yoc*, "one who has charge of anything."

[5] *Cunacuni*, "I advise or preach."

[6] The fabled cradle of the Ynca race, near Cuzco.

mandments were severe. This worthy, named *Thonapa*, is said
to have visited all the provinces of the Colla-suyu, preaching to the people without cessation, until one day he entered
the town of *Yamquesupa*. There he was treated with great
insolence and contempt, and driven away. They say that he
often slept in the fields, without other covering than the
long shirt he wore, a mantle, and a book. They say that
Thonapa cursed that village, so that it was covered with
water. The site is now called *Yamquisupaloiga*.[7] It is a
lake, and nearly all the Indians of that time knew that it
was once a village, and was then a lake. They say that, on
a very high hill called *Cacha-pucara*,[8] there was an idol in
the form of a woman,[9] and that *Tonapa* was inspired with
a great hatred against it, and afterwards burnt it, and destroyed it with the hill on which it stood. They say that to
this day there are signs of that awful miracle, the most fearful that was ever heard of in the world.

On another occasion they say that he began to preach
with loving words, in a town where they were holding a
great festival and banquet to celebrate a wedding, and they
would not listen to the preaching of *Tonapa*. For this
they were cursed and turned into stones, which may be
seen to this day. The same thing happened in Pucara and
other places.[1] They further say that this *Tonapa*, in his
wanderings, came to the mountains of Caravaya, where
he erected a very large cross, and he carried it on his
shoulders to the mountain of *Carapucu*, where he preached
in a loud voice, and shed tears. And they say that a
daughter of a chief of that province was sprinkled on the
head with water, and the Indians, seeing this, understood

---

[7] I cannot identify it.

[8] *Cacha*, in the valley of the Vilcamayu. *Pucara*, a fortress. See the
account of the famous temple at Cacha in *G. de la Vega*, i, p. 159; ii,
p. 69.

[9] To this idol they offered human sacrifices.

[1] See *ante*, *Molina*, p. 6.

that he was washing his head. So, afterwards, *Tonapa* was taken prisoner and shorn, near the great lake of *Carapucu*. The meaning of Carapucu is when a bird called *pucu-pucu* sings four times, at early dawn.[2] They say that, when day broke, when Tunapa was a prisoner, a very beautiful youth came to him, and said :—" Do not fear ; for I come to call you in the name of the matron, who alone watches over you, and who is about to go to the place of rest." So saying, he touched the cords, by which *Tonapa* was tied hand and foot, with his fingers. There were many guards, for *Tonapa* had been condemned to a cruel death. But at dawn, being five in the morning, he entered the lake with the youth, his mantle bearing him up on the water and serving in the place of a boat. On his arrival in the town and province of Carapuco, the chiefs and principal men were disturbed at having seen their idol thrown down and destroyed. They say that this idol flew like the wind to a desert place, which was never visited by men. Here the idol or *huaca* was mourning and lamenting with its head down ; and in this plight it was found by an Indian, whose report caused the chiefs to be excited at the arrival of *Tonapa*, who had been imprisoned. They say that *Tonapa*, after he had been freed from the hands of those savages, remained for a long time on a rock called *Titicaca*, and afterwards he passed by Tiquina to Chacamarca, where he came to a town called Tiyahuanacu. They say that the people of that town were engaged in drinking and dancing when *Tonapa* came to preach to them, and they did not listen to him. Then, out of pure anger, he denounced them in the language of the land ; and, when he departed from that place, all the people who were dancing were turned into stones, and they may be seen to this day.[3] *Tonapa* then followed the course of the river Chacamarca until he came to the sea. This is reported by those most ancient Yncas.

[2] See *Mossi*, p. 207.   [3] See *ante, Molina*, p. 6.

They say that the staff which *Tonapa* delivered into the
hands of *Apu-tampu* was turned into fine gold on the birth
of his son named Manco Ccapac Ynca, who had seven
brothers and sisters. Their names were *Ayar-cachi, Ayar-
uchu, Aya-raeca,* etc. The said Apu Manco Ccapac, after
the death of his father and mother, named *Apu Tampu
Pacha* and *Mama Achi,* being now an orphan, but grown to
man's estate, assembled his people to see what power he
had to prosecute the new conquests which he meditated.
Finding some difficulties, he agreed with his brothers to
seek new lands, taking his rich clothes and arms, and the
staff which had been left by *Tonapa.* This staff was called
Tupac-yauri.[4] He also had two golden cups from which
Tonapa had drunk, called *Tupac-usi.* Thus he set out,
with his brothers, towards the hill over which the sun rose.
They say that, marching in this direction, he arrived at the
hill which was the highest point in that land. Then, over
Apu Manco Ccapac arose a very beautiful rainbow, and over
the rainbow appeared another, so that Apu Manco Ccapac
seemed to be in the midst of the rainbows. He exclaimed:
"We have a good sign. We shall have great prosperity and
gain many victories, and we shall obtain all that we desire."
After saying this, he joyfully advanced, singing the song of
Chamay[5] *huarisca* from mere delight. Then he descended
to Collcapampa with his brothers, and from the town of
Sañuc he saw, afar off, the form of a man. One of his
brothers ran towards it, thinking that it was some Indian.
They say that when he came up to it, he saw one like an
Indian, looking most fierce and cruel with bloodshot eyes.
He who went to look at him was the youngest brother, and
when he approached the form raised its head, and said: "It
is well that you have come in search of me; for you will find

---

[4] *Tupac,* royal or splendid. *Yauri,* a sceptre.
[5] *Chamani,* "I am satisfied." *Chamay,* "satisfaction, joy."

that I am looking for you, and now you are in my power." When Manco Ccapac saw that his brother was so long in returning, he sent one of his sisters to call him. But she also remained away, and both were kept at the *huaca* of Sañuc. Seeing that both one and the other did not return, Manco Ccapac went himself in great wrath, and found them both nearly dead. He asked them why they stayed away so long, and they answered by complaining of a stone which was between the two. Then Apu Manco Ccapac struck the stone or *huaca* with much fury, giving it blows with his *tupac-yauri* on the head. Then words came from the midst of the stone, as if it was alive, saying, that if he had not got that staff, it would also do to him as it pleased. " Go on," it added; "for you have attained to great honour. But these, your brother and sister, have sinned, and it is therefore right that they should be where I am," meaning the infernal regions. This is called *pitusiray sanasiray*, which means one person fastened on the top of another. When Manco Ccapac saw his brother and sister in such fearful danger, he shed tears of natural grief and sorrow, and he went thence to the place where he had first seen the rainbow, the names of which are *cuchi*, and *turumanya* and *yayacarui*. He bemoaned the loss of his brother and sister, and exclaimed that he was the most unfortunate of orphans. But the rainbow strengthened him, and removed all his sorrows and afflictions.[6] " *Huaynacaptiy* " or " *Huaynacaptiyllapun chica chiqui unachayamoran Huanacauri*." From that time the place was called *Huaynacaptiy*. Thence he went to Collcapampa[7] with the *tupac-yauri* in his hand, and with a sister named *Ypa mama huaco*, and with another sister and a brother. They arrived at Collcapampa, where they were for

---

[6] Afterwards later Yncas placed a very well-carved stone in the form of a vulture, which means the good omen, and which is called *Yncap huaynacanim*, and the Indians began to treat it with idolatrous worship.   [7] Or *Collcampata*, above Cuzco.

some days. Thence they went to *Huamantiana*,[8] where they remained some time, and thence they marched to *Coricancha*,[9] where they found a place suitable for a settlement. There was good water from *Hurinchacan* and *Hananchacan* (whence the names of Hurin-Cuzco and Hanan-Cuzco), which are two springs. A rock was called by the natives (who are the *Allcayriesas*, the *Cullinchinas*, and the *Cayaucachis*) by the name of *Cuzco-cara-urumi*, whence the place came to be called Cuzco-pampa and Cuzco-llacta; and the Yncas were afterwards called Cuzco-Ccapac and Cuzco-Ynca. This Ynca Apu Manco Ccapac married one of his own sisters named Mama Ocllo, and this marriage was celebrated that they might have no equal, and that they might not lose the caste. Then they began to enact good laws for the government of their people, conquering many provinces and nations of those that were disobedient. The *Ttahuantinsuyus*[1] came with a good grace and with rich presents. The tidings of a new Ynca had spread widely. Some were joyful, others were afflicted; when they heard that the Ynca was the most powerful chief, the most valiant, and the most fortunate in arms, that his captains and men of valour were better armed than other men; and that all his affairs were prosperous.

This Ynca ordered the smiths to make a flat plate of fine gold; which signified that there was a Creator of heaven and earth; and it was of this shape. He caused it to be fixed in a great house called *Ccuricancha pachaya-chachipac huasin*.[2] This Ynca Manco Ccapac was an enemy to the huacas,[3] and, as such, he destroyed the Curaca Pinao Ccapac

---

[8] Or *Sacsahuaman*, the site of the fortress of Cuzco. *Huaman*, "a falcon." *Tiana*, "a throne."

[9] The site of the temple of the Sun. *Ccuri*, "gold;" *Cancha*, "a place."

[1] People of the four provinces.

[2] "The golden place, the house of the teacher of the world."

[3] Idols.

with all his idols. He also conquered Tocay Ccapac, a great idolater.

Afterwards he ordered works to be executed at the place of his birth ; consisting of a masonry wall with three windows, which were emblems of the house of his fathers whence he descended. The first window was called *Tampu-toco*,[4] the second *Maras*[5]*-toco*, and the third *Sutic*[6]*-toco* : referring to his uncles and paternal and maternal grandparents.

These two trees typified his father and mother *Apu-tampu* and *Apachamama-achi*, and he ordered that they should be adorned with roots of gold and silver, and with golden fruit. Hence they were called *Ccurichachac collquechachac tampu-yracan*, which means that the two trees typified the parents, and that the Yncas proceeded from them, like fruit from the trees, and that the two trees were as the roots and stems of the Yncas. All these things were executed to record their greatness.

He ordered that the dresses of each village should be different, that the people might be known, for down to this time there were no means of knowing to what village or tribe an Indian belonged. He also ordered, with a view to each tribe being clearly distinguished, that they should choose whence they were descended and from whence they came, and, as the Indians generally were very dull and stupid,

---

[4] *Toco*, " a window."   [5] *Maras*, " mill-stone."
[6] *Sutini*, " I name." *Sutic*, " name."

some chose, for their *pacarisca*[7] or *pacarimusca*, a lake, others
a spring, others a rock, others the hills or ravines; but every
lineage selected some object for its *pacarisca*. The devils,
or *hapi-ñuñus*, deceived those stupid people with little difficulty, entering into the false *pacariscas*, and thence uttering
deceitful promises. Every day these *pacariscas* continued
to increase, the origin or *pacarinim* being the *Pacari-tampu*.
All the provinces and tribes said *Pacariscanchic huccsiscan-
chic umachun chicpa-pacariscan*.

The leading cause of the invention of the *pacarinim*, was,
that the Ynca Manco Ccapac was often at a loss to know to
what village an Indian belonged. This Ynca also ordered
the heads of infants to be pressed, that they might grow up
foolish and without energy; for he thought that Indians
with large round heads, being audacious in any enterprise,
might also be disobedient.

His legitimate son was Sinchi Ruca Ynca, and he inherited
all the dominions of his father. The other younger sons,
whether legitimate or illegitimate, were called *Chima-
panaca-ayllu*.

Sinchi Ruca Ynca began to rule over all the territory of
his father, and was a great patron of agriculture, of weaving
cloth, and of mining. He was not much addicted to warlike affairs, for, being a very proud man, and of haughty
disposition, he seldom went abroad. All the provinces from
Chacamarca aud Angaraes sent him presents. When he
desired to make conquests he sent his captains and their
men. In each ravine they had to take stones to make *usnus*,
which are certain stones arranged in heaps. They say that
an Indian wizard appeared to one of the officers of war, and
told him that the heaps must be called *apachitas*. A rite
was established, which was that every passer by should bring
a great stone; and the wizard also told the officer of the

---

[7] *Paccari*, "morning, dawn." *Paccarisca*, "birth, origin." *Pacca-
rimuni*, "I am born." *Paccarimusca*, "being born."

Ynca that all the soldiers must throw their coca pallets on the heap as they passed, saying :—*Saycoyñiycaypitac quipasiyon coyñiypashinatac.* From that time they began to bring stones and to throw coca, because the wizard had so ordered it.[8]

They say that when the Ynca Manco Ccapac was very old, he went down on his knees, and prayed for the prosperity of his son in these words :—

A Uiracochantic çicapac caycaricachun cay raimicachun ñeca apa hinamtima chiccha camac maypin canqui manachurycayquiman hanampichun hurimpichun quinrayñimpichun capac usnoyqui hayñillalay, hanan cochaman tarayac hurincocha, tiyancay, camacpacha runarallpac, apoyunay, quicuna camman allcañancyran riaiytam munayqui ricaptiy yachaptiy unanchaptiy hamuttaptiy ricunanquim yacharanquira, yntic quillaca punchaoca, tutaca, pocoyca, chiraoca, manamyancacho, camachiscan purin unanchascaman tupuscamanmi chayan, maycanmi, ttopayaricta apachinarcanqui hayñillaray uyarillaray manaracpas, saycaptiy rañuptiy.

After this he always remembered *Tonapa,* saying :—

Runa rallcapacpalhacan yananssi cahuac, ari, chayariyuya llanay coscocapac churatamuquiy apo, Tarapaca Tonapa pacta varoytiypas capacparatamus cayquicta concaraca rañoytayri yuyayronayta callpanchan quistacmi payllanquitacmi recsichillaran quimampichun carcan achus, camchomcanquiman papi-ñuñu llasac atic manchachic ricsi ayman yacha llayman, allpamantaca maquiylluttaquey riculla raypancanqueña allparnumachun cani.

Having said this he watched to see if he might have a sign from the Creator. He offered a very white lamb upon an altar, which sacrifice is called *arpay.* When no answer was given, he ordered the most beautiful of his sons, aged about eight years, to be offered up, cutting off his head, and sprinkling the blood over the fire, that the smoke might reach the Maker of heaven and earth. To all these offerings no answer was ever given in Coricancha.

[8] The practice is continued to this day.

Afterwards, in the visit of *Ituripanaca* to the people, he admitted a great number of youths aged from seventeen to eighteen, among the number of men and soldiers, giving them white breeches. He marked out a line to a high and very distant hill, called *Huanacauri*, and he ordered to be placed on the hill a falcon, a humming bird, a vulture, an ostrich *(suri)*, a vicuña, an *anatuya* (fox), a serpent, a toad. It was announced that these birds and animals had been placed there that these boys and youths might run to them and show the qualities of their swiftness or sluggishness. The swift received as rewards the *huarachicuy* and *ccamantiras* (*ccamantira* are the small bright feathers that birds have under the beak), and the sluggish were given black breeches. After the breeches and other clothes had been distributed, the youths were made to sit down with the men, and from that time they were called men, and their parents came to them with many presents as a reward for their good deeds. Manco Ccapac, seeing that the fathers and mothers of the youths were so well satisfied, ordered them to be given to eat and drink plentifully, that they might remain his vassals, and the vassals of his son, Sinchi Ruca. Besides this he ordered that the girls of sixteen years should comb and plait their hair. This is called *quicuchicuy* (when they plait the hair to come forth from among young girls). Then he ordered them to be shod with *llanquisi*, which are a kind of shoes. All this was done in order that henceforth they might be known as women or *tasqui huarmi*. Afterwards all the young men of thirty years were ordered to take wives, arms being given to the men, cooking and spinning gear to the women. This was called *huarmi hapiypacha carichasquiy pacha*. Then certain men of holy lives were selected, as priests, to call upon the name of the Creator of heaven and earth, and to these chosen men the Ynca spoke as follows :—

Cusisimirac cusi callurac cayhuacyanquital sasicuspa suyanqui,
ychastalpas cusinchicpi quillpunchicpi maymantapas runahualpac
apu, ticcicapac uyari sunquichay nisunqui camtaca, mayñic mantapas
hinatac viñaypas caycama yocllamunqui.

These chosen men always held the office of priests during
the life of Manco Ccapac.

On the death of the old Ynca, the sovereignty descended
to his son Sinchi Rocca Ynca, who was a very proud man.
In his time it fell out that there were youths and maidens
who loved each other excessively, and, in answer to questions
put to them by the Ynca, they publicly confessed that they
could not live apart. It was found that these lovers had certain small stones, perfectly round, and they said that these
stones were called *soncoapa chinacoc huacca chinacoc.* They
say that a poor boy in rags, a shepherd *(llama-michec)*, entered the house of the Ynca Sinchi Rocca, and that a virgin
who was very dear to the Ynca went away with that boy. A
search was made until they were found, and orders were
given that they should be tortured. The girl confessed that
the *llama-michec* had stolen away her love, after having
made a *huacanqui*[9] to appear, given to him by a demon. The
boy had made a pact with the devil in a certain cave; but the
Ynca did not understand that this was the work of the old
enemy, and that he had succeeded with the boy and girl
because they had become his subjects, and held the
huacanquis in their hands. They say that from that time
many huacas appeared on the hills and in the streams
without shame, and it was ordered that there should be
sacrifices in each village.

In those days they began to sacrifice with human blood,
white lambs, guinea pigs, coca, shells, grease and *sancu.*[1]
This unfortunate Sinchi Rocca passed all his time in
sensuality, and he ordered search to be made for *chutarpu*

[9] *Mossi* (113). Herbs given by sorcerers, as love philtres.
[1] Maize pudding.

and *huanarpu*,[2] to make fornication a custom, and thus
there were so many *huacanquis* that the Indians gave them
as presents.

They say that this ill-fated Ynca had a son named Ynca
Lloque Yupanqui, whom he left as his successor when
he died. This heir was a great proficient at fasting, and
had never chosen to know a woman till he was very old.
He prohibited fornication and drunkenness, and was a great
patron of agriculture. He did not undertake conquests like
his grandfather, though occasionally he assembled an army,
in order to strike terror among his enemies. They also say
that he ordered all his men to pull out their beards and
appear without hair.[3] He also ordered that all the people
in his dominions should flatten the heads of their children,
so that they might be long and sloping from the front; and
this was done to make them obedient. He also commanded
houses to be made for the virgins, and these houses were
divided into four classes :—*yurac-aclla, huayru-aclla, pacu-
aclla*, and *yana-aclla*.[4] The first for the Creator, called
Uiracocha-pacha-yachachi; the *huayru-aclla* for the virgins
of the Ynca, the *pacu-aclla* for the women of the *Apu-curacas*,[5] and the *yana-aclla* for the common people. Many
youths were also reared who were not to know women, who
afterwards became soldiers.

They say that when the Ynca Lloque Yupanqui was very
old, he had a son by a woman named Mama Tancarayacchi
Chimpu Cuca, daughter of a *huaca* in the village of Tancar.
She bore the Ynca Mayta Ccapac[6] at the end of a year, and

---

[2] The *chutarpu* is the male form of committing fornication, and
the *huanarpu* the opposite.

[3] The beardless chin is called *pachacaqui*, and the tweezers with which
they pull out the hairs *canipachi*.

[4] See *Historia de Copacabana*, by Ramos. *Aclla*, " chosen, set apart."
Yurac, " white." *Yana*, " black."

[5] Great Lords.

[6] Mayta Ccapac was so called because, as a child, he used to say *May-*

they say that he cried out many times while he was yet in the womb of his mother. A few months after his birth he began to talk, and at ten years of age he fought valiantly and defeated his enemies. He governed very well, making moral laws, and forbidding evil customs. They say that this Ynca Mayta Ccapac foretold the coming of the holy gospel. While he was a boy he ordered all the *huacas* and idols to be brought to the city of Cuzco, promising to hold a great festival; but he caused trouble to the worshippers of these *huacas* by setting them on fire. They say that many escaped in the form of fire and wind, and as birds. There were *Aysso-uilca, Chinchay-cocha*, and the *huaca* of the Cañaris, and *Uilcañota, Putina, Coropuna, Antapuca, Cho-quiracra*, and *Chuquipillu*.[7]

They say that this Ynca was a great enemy of the idols, and as such he ordered his people to pay no honours to the sun and moon, declaring that the sun and moon and all the elements were made for the service of men. He was also a severe judge of those who practised forbidden things, such as enchanters, *canchus, umus,*[8] *layccas,*[9] *huaca-muchas,*[1] and those who worked on the chief day of the festival of *Ccapac-raymi*. He gave thanks on that day to the Creator *Tica-ccapac* (called also *Caprichay*), and chastised those who were undutiful to himself or to their parents, liars, adulterers, fornicators, evil livers, thieves, murderers, drunkards. He commanded that there should be no unjust wars, and that all men should be employed in tilling the ground and building. He caused landmarks to be set up in every village, and those who moved them were punished. In his reign there was universal peace.

---

tac Ccapac, " O Lord, where art Thou?" and he repeated this thought by reason of his longing to know his Creator.

 [7] Names of the *places* where these Huacas were worshipped.

 [8] Priests.   [9] Sorcerers.

 [1] Idol worshippers. *Huaca,* " an idol," and *Muchani,* " I worship."

They say that, in appearance, this Ynca was more noble
than the others. He caused the plate to be renewed, which
his great-grandfather had put up, fixing it afresh in the
place where it had been before. He rebuilt the house of
Ccuricancha; and they say that he caused things to be placed
round the plate, which I have shown, that it may be seen
what these heathens thought. The Ynca also instituted
new songs, and caused very large drums to be made for the
feast of Ccapac Raymi. But he only held this feast in honour
of the Lord and Creator, despising all the created things,
even the highest, such as men, and the sun and moon.
Here I will show how they were depicted until the arrival of
the holy gospel, except that then the plate was missing, because Huascar Ynca had removed it, and had substituted
another round plate, like the sun with rays. Nevertheless,
some say that they were placed on each side of the plate of
Mayta Ccapac.

Although Huascar Ynca had placed an image of the sun
in the place where that of the Creator had been, yet it shall
not be omitted here; for there was an image of the sun and
moon on either side of it.

Sun.   Moon.

Plate of fine gold; image of the Creator and of the
true Sun of the Sun, called Uiracocha-pachaya-
chachic.

They say that a Spaniard gambled for this plate of gold
in Cuzco,[2] as I shall presently mention in its place, for now
I want to proceed with the lives of other Yncas.

[2] See *G. de la Vega*, i, p. 272.

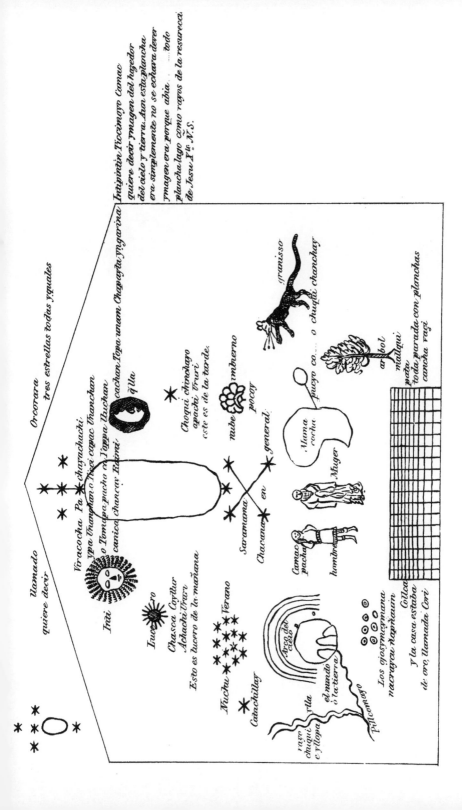

They say that Mayta Ccapac Ynca was very wise, that he knew all the medicines, and could foresee future events. On occasion of the Ccapac Raymi, in honour of Uiracocha Pachayachachi, they held a solemn festival, which lasted for a whole month. The Ynca said many times, in the evenings after the days of festivity, that the feast will soon be over, and then comes death, as the night follows the day, and as sleep is the image of death. The festival, he would say, is the type of the true festival, and fortunate are those reasoning creatures who shall attain to the true feast of eternity, and know the name of the Creator; for men do not die like beasts. In consequence of these reflections he kept a fast in *Toco-cachi*,[3] with great mourning, only eating one row of grains from a mazorca of maize, each day, and so he passed a whole month.

This Mayta Ccapac had a son named Ccapac Yupanqui[4] by Mama Tancapay-yacchi. He had another son *Apu Urco Huaman Ynti Cunti Mayta*, and another *Urco Huaranca*. Their descendants multiplied so as to form the *Usca Mayta Ayllu* and *Huañayñin Ayllu*;[5] though Ccapac Yupanqui was the heir, who was most successful in arms.

After the death of Mayta Ccapac, many great Curacas and chiefs of this kingdom submitted to his son Ccapac Yupanqui. They say that, in his time, they invented the sacrifices of *capaucha-cocuy*, burying virgin boys with silver and gold; and of the *arpac* with human blood, or with white lambs called *uracarpaña, cuyes*,[6] and grease. It happened one day that the same Ynca Ccapac Yupanqui wished to witness how the *huacas* conversed with their friends, so he entered the place selected, which was in a village of the

---

[3] A suburb of Cuzco. See *G. de la Vega*, ii, p. 249.

[4] This son of Mayta Ccapac was called Ccapac Yupanqui because, when he was a child, his father said, " *Ccapacta tacmi yupanqui*", " Thou also shalt count as one rich in all virtues."

[5] See *G. de la Vega*, ii. p. 531. *Huañayñin* is, I think, a clerical error for *Huahuanina*. [6] Guinea pigs.

Andes called Capacuyo. When the young Ynca entered among these idolaters, he asked why they closed the doors and windows so as to leave them in the dark, and they all replied that in this way they could make the *huaca* come, who was the enemy to the name of God Almighty, and that there must be silence. When they had made an end of calling the Devil, he entered with a rush of wind that made them all in a cold sweat of horror. Then the young Ynca ordered the doors and windows to be opened, that he might know the shape of that thing for which they had waited with such veneration. But as soon as it was light the Devil hid its face, and knew not how to answer. The dauntless Ynca Ccapac Yupanqui said—"Tell me what you are called"; and, with much shame, it replied that its name was *Cana-chuap yauirca*. The Ynca then said—"Why are you so frightened and ashamed? If you can grant children, long life, good fortune, *coycollas* and *huacanquis*, why do you stand there like a criminal without raising your eyes? I tell you that you are some false deceiver; for if you were powerful you would not be afraid nor hang down your head. I now feel that there is another Creator of all things, as my father Mayta Ccapac Ynca has told me." The figure of this devil was ugly, with a foul smell, and coarse matted hair. It fled out of the house, raising shouts like thunder; and they say that from that time all the *huacas* feared the Yncas; and the Yncas also used the *yacarcay*, in the name of the Creator, as follows:—

Hurinapachap hicrinpachap, cochamantarayocpa camaquimpa tocuya pacopa sinchiñauiyocpa manchaysimiyocpa caycasicachun cayhuarmicachun ñispacamacpa sutinrammica machiyqui pincanqui maycanmicanqui y mactamñinqui rimayñi.

With these words the Yncas made all the *huacas* tremble; although they had not left off performing *capacochacocuy*. If these Yncas had heard the gospel, with what love and joy would they have believed in God! They say that this Ynca

Ccapac Yupanqui had a son, by his wife *Mama Corillpay-cahua*, named Ynca Ruca, at whose birth there was much festivity. But the Ynca did not entirely separate himself from idolaters, as he allowed the *huacas* of each village to be worshipped. It is said that the Ynca sent men to search for the place called Titicaca, where the great *Tonapa* had arrived, and that they brought water thence to pour over the infant Ynca Ruca, while they celebrated the praises of *Tonapa*. In the spring on the top of the rocks, the water was in a basin called *ccapacchama quispisutuc unu*.[7] Future Yncas caused this water to be brought in a bowl called *curi-ccacca*,[8] and placed before them in the middle of the square of Cuzco, called Huacay-pata : Cusi-pata : where they did honour to the water that had been touched by *Tonapa*.

In those days the Curacas of Asillu and Hucuru told the Ynca how, in ancient times, a poor thin old man, with a beard and long hair, had come to them in a long shirt, and that he was a wise councillor in affairs of state, and that his name was *Tonapa Vihinquira*. They said that he had banished all the idols and *hapi-ñuñu* demons to the snowy mountains. All the Curacas and chroniclers also said that this *Tonapa* had banished all the *huacas* and idols to the mountains of Asancata, Quiyancatay, Sallcatay, and Apitosiray. When all the Curacas of the provinces of Ttahuantin-suyu were assembled in the Huacay-pata, each in his place, those of the Huancas said that this *Tonapa Varivillca* had also been in their land, and that he had made a house to live in, and had banished all the *huacas* and *hapi-ñuñus* in the province of *Hatun Sausa Huanca* to the snowy mountains in Pariacaca and Vallollo. Before their banishment these idols had done much harm to the people, menacing the Curacas to make them offer human sacrifices. The

---

[7] *Ccapac*, " rich." *Chama*, " joy." *Quispisutu*, " crystal drops".
Unu, " water."   [8] " Golden Rock."

Ynca ordered that the house of *Tonapa* should be preserved. It was at the foot of a small hill near the river as you enter Xauxa from the Cuzco road, and before coming to it there are two stones where Tonapa had turned a female *huaca* into stone for having fornicated with a man of the Huancas. It was called *Atapymapuranutapya*, and afterwards, in the time of Huayna Ccapac Ynca, the two stones declared to the people that they were *huacanqui coycoylla*. In those days there were also *huacanquis* in the wilderness of Xauxa, and before coming to Pachacamac, and in a nest of the *suyuntuy* (turkey buzzard) and stones in Chincha-yunca.

The Ynca Ccapac Yupanqui commenced the building of the fortress of Sacsahuaman. He extended his territory to Vilcañota, where he found a *huaca* called *Rurucachi*, and in returning he found another *huaca* in the village of Huaruc called *Uiracochamparaca* besides the *huacas* of Yanacocha, Yacachacota, Yayanacota de Lanquisupa, Achuy Tupiya, and Atantacopap. Ccapac Yupanqui exclaimed :—"How many false gods are there in the land, to my sorrow and the misfortune of my vassals! When shall these evils be remedied?" But he returned to Cuzco without doing more harm to the *huacas;* for in those days there were very few Apu Curacas who had not their *huacas*, and they were all deceived by false gods.

When the Ynca died, he was succeeded by his son the Ynca Ruca, who received the *tupac-yauri, tupac-cusi,* and *tupac-pichuc-llautu*. This Ynca Ruca understood the making of cloth of *cumpis*,[9] and he was a great patron of dancing, so that in his time nothing was done but dancing, eating, drinking, and other enjoyment. Idolatrous rites increased, and people devoted themselves to the worship of *huacas;* for the chiefs and people always follow the example that is set them by their sovereign.

They say that the eldest son of this Ynca Ruca was named

[9] Fine cloth. See *G. de la Vega*, ii, p. 324.

Yahuar-huaccac[1] Ynca Yupanqui. His mother was Mamicay-chimpu; and at his birth there was a grand feast. The square and all the streets were filled with arches of feathers, and the house of Curicancha was entirely covered with rich plumes, both within and without. They played on eight drums, and sang the *ayma, torca, cayo,* and *huallma cha-mayuricssa,* and *haylli,* and *cachra,* giving thanks to the Creator, and saying.—

Hananhamuyrac chiccha hurinchiccha apu hinantima lluttactic-cicapac runahuallpac llaychunca muchay cuscayqui allcañañiy huan chipicñispa hullpaycuscayqui riacllahuay mayucuna pachacunaripis cucunari callapallatichinay hanantarac cahariusinay llapan concay-qui raurac manayllay quihuanpas ynya y cuspalla rochocallasun cusicullasun ancha hinalla tachca nispañicusun.

While they were all singing in the Huacay-pata, they say that the infant wept blood, an unheard of miracle, which caused much alarm, and hence the name Yahuar-huaccac Ynca. His father the Ynca diligently searched for some one who could interpret the meaning of this incident. In those days the *hualla-huisas, cunti-huisas, cana-huisas* were great sorcerers; and there assembled such a vast number of *canchus, carcas, umus, uscatus, huisas,* that there was not room for them all in Cuzco. The Ynca did not like to confide his secrets to so many, lest the people should lose their veneration for him, so he reprehended them publicly, saying that there were many wise men but little wisdom, and he dismissed them; but these enchanters, necromancers, wizards, and witches returned with more liberty than they had had before, and their idolatrous practices increased.

The Ynca Ruca died, and left the sovereignty to his eldest son Yahuar-huaccac Ynca Yupanqui, who began by being very free and liberal, but was finally so impoverished that he was obliged to draw tribute from the provinces, for the expenses of his house. At last the people rose in rebellion,

[1] See *G. de la Vega,* i, pp. 327, 317; ii, 62.

and, seeing this, the Ynca dissimulated, so that the people became quiet and brought him all kinds of presents. They say that this Ynca ordered the prisons to be made outside the town, that he might not see the punishment of criminals. As he grew old he began to undertake conquests, and ordered dresses to be made with plumes, and *purapuras* of gold and silver, and of copper for the soldiers, to put on the breast and shoulders as a protection against arrows and spears; and he distributed these among his captains and soldiers.

This Ynca's eldest son was named Uira-ccocha Ynca Yupanqui, whose mother was *Mama Chuqui - checya*, a native of Ayamarca, and great-great-grand-daughter of To- cay Ccapac. In the festival of his birth they represented plays called *añay saoca, hayachuco, llama-llama hañamsi.* The Ynca marched round Cuzco with his army, without making war upon any enemy. On his death he left the Ynca Uira-ccocha to succeed him.

The Ynca Uira-ccocha was married to Mama Runtucay, a native of Anta, and at the marriage and coronation all the people assembled, and among them Chuchi-ccapac of the Hatun-Collas, who came in a litter with his guards and servants, and with his idol or *huaca* richly adorned; and he often disputed with the Ynca, saying :—

Cam Cuzco-Ccapac ñuca Colla-Ccapac hupyasumicusu rimasu amapirima ñuca collque tiya cam chuqui tiya. Cam Uiracochanpa- chayachi mucha. Nuca Ynti-mucha.[2]

At last the Ynca, being affable and friendly, assented; for he is said to have been too gentle. His chief employ- ment was the building of houses, and of the fortress on the Sacsahuaman, and to cultivate and plant quiscuar and molli trees; but he neglected all warlike pursuits. He had a na-

---

[2] Thou art Lord of Cuzco. I am Lord of the Collas. I have a silver throne. Thy throne is of gold. Thou art a worshipper of Uira-ccocha- Pachayachachi. I worship the Sun.

tural son named Ynca Urcu, to whom he renounced the kingdom during his life time. This Ynca Urcu undertook the conquest of Colla-suyu with a great army. Before setting out
he sent a haughty demand for tribute, but all the tribes,
which had not acknowledged him as their lord, refused
compliance. Ynca Urcu then set out with a powerful army,
and undertook the conquest without securing the loyalty of
the intervening tribes. He passed through the country of
the Caviñas, taking with him the statue of Manco-Ccapac,
to secure good fortune for himself. But he was defeated
and killed at Huana-calla, by the hand of Yamqui Pachacuti,
the chief of Huayra-Cancha. Then the Hanco-allos and
Chancas besieged the city of Cuzco, which roused the Ynca
Uira-ccocha Yupanqui from his careless ease. He knew
not what course to pursue, and applied to the Hanco-allos
and Chancas. Eventually he came out to arrange a peace,
to Yuncay-pampa. Then his legitimate son, named Ynca
Yupanqui, whom his father detested, was afflicted at the
sight of his capital encompassed by an enemy. His heart
was emboldened and he took the road to Cuzco, but before
he arrived at Callachaca, as he travelled along the road
alone, he saw a very fair and beautiful youth on the top of a
rock, who said : "O son, I promise, in the name of the
Creator, on whom you have called in your troubles, that he
has heard you, and will give you the victory over your enemies. Fight then without fear." He then disappeared,
and the prince felt at once emboldened and capable of command. On reaching his palace, he cried out, saying :—
"*Cuzco Ccapac pac churacllay yana pahuay may pimcanqui.*"
Then he entered the house of arms, and took out all the
offensive and defensive weapons. At that juncture twenty
Orejones arrived, his relations, sent by his father. He armed
all the men and women and, entering the temple, he took
the *tupac-yauri*[3] and *ccapac unancha,*[4] and unfurled the

_____
[3] Sceptre.   [4] Standard.

standard of the Yncas. The city became a fortress, and the
enemy commenced the attack, but the prince had forgotten
the *tupac-yauri*. At the first encounter, the prince Ynca
Yupanqui was knocked down by a stone from a sling, and
remained half insensible. Then he heard a voice from
heaven saying that he had not got the sceptre of *tupac-yauri*.
So he went back to the temple and took the sceptre, and
returned to the battle, encouraging the captains and soldiers
to fight. Meanwhile an old Ynca, a near relation of the
prince's father, named Tupac Ranchiri, who was a priest of
the Ccuricancha, set some stones in a row, and fastened shields
and clubs to them, so that they might look at a distance,
like rows of soldiers sitting down. The prince, looking out
for succour from his father Uira-ccocha Yupanqui Ynca, saw
these rows from a distance, and cried out to the supposed
soldiers to rise, as his men were on the point of yielding.
The Chancas continued the attack with increased fury, and
then the prince saw that the stones had become men,
and they rose up and fought with desperate courage and
skill, assaulting the Anco-allos and Chancas; so the prince
gained a victory, and followed the enemy to *Quizachilla*,
where he beheaded the chiefs of the hostile army, named
Tomay-huaraca, *Asto-huaraca*, and *Huasco-Tornay Rimac*.
He thus gained a great victory;[5] and they say that a widow
named *Chanan Coricoca* fought valiantly in the battle like a
soldier. The prince sent presents of the heads of the Chancas
and Anco-Allos to his father. But the Ynca Uira-ccocha
Ynca Yupanqui was ashamed to return to Cuzco, and lived
at Puna-marca until his death. The young prince Ynca
Yupanqui assembled more troops, and followed the Anco-
Allos and Chancas, overtaking them at the river Apurimac,
where the flying enemy killed one of the bravest of the Ynca
captains, named Vilcaquiri, by hurling a stone upon him.

[5] This is the same battle described by *Garcilasso de la Vega*, ii, p.
53.

He exclaimed to the prince, "Is it possible that I must die without having fought or gained any glory?" They hollowed out the trunk of a tree, and buried the body in the tree, and the fruit of that tree yields a medicine called *villca*, which is good for all heated and feverish humours.[6]

The Ynca Yupanqui followed the enemy as far as Andahuayllas; and, on his return to Cuzco, he undertook the conquest of Colla-suyu; and other provinces submitted peaceably. Among them was that of the famous chief Yamqui-Pachacuti, whom the prince thanked for the death of Ynca Urcu, his brother. And the prince took his name and added it to his own, which became Pachacuti Ynca Yupanqui. He conquered all the land of the Colla-suyu, and invaded the provinces of the Chayas and Caravayas, where he destroyed a famous idol. He subdued the Chayas and Ollacheas, and, leaving a garrison in Ayapata,[7] he returned to Cuzco. He next marched to the country of the Chancas with fifty thousand men; and at Vilcas-huaman he found seven *huacas* in the form of very great Curacas, black, and very ugly. They were called *Ayssa-vilca, Pariacaca, Chinchacocha, Huallallu Chuquiracra;* and two others of the Cañaris. The prince took them and sent them to Cuzco, to work at the Sacsahuaman fortress, and also afterwards to labour at the look-out towers on the sea-shore, at Chincha and Pachacamac. Then Pachacuti Ynca Yupanqui conquered the provinces of the Angaraes, Chilqui-urpus, Rucanas, and Soras. He received news that the Huancas were preparing for war at Taya-cassa; so he encamped at Paucaray and Rumi-huasi, where he formed three armies, which were to invade the valley of Hatun-Huanca-Sausa simultaneously. They advanced from Paucaray, but the enemy

[6] *Huillca*, a tree, the fruit of which, like the lupin, is a purgative.—*Mossi*, p. 127.

[7] Ollachea and Ayapata are villages to the eastward of the Andes, in Caravaya.

submitted, and brought in provisions, and presents of maidens. The Ynca was pleased at the peaceful submission of these people, and he promised to confirm their three Curacas in their lordships, conferring upon them the additional title of *Apu ;* and he ordered one of them to be given shoes of gold. He then entered the valley of Sausa in pursuit of his enemy Anco-allo, passing by Tarma, Colla-pampa, Huanucu, and Huamalies, and Cassamarca, until he reached a province where the people feasted on their dead. He continued to advance until he came to the province of the Cañaris, which was full of sorcerers and *huacas*. Thence he marched to Huancavillca ; but the Anco-allos entered the forests, leaving their idol behind them.[8]

The Ynca Pachacuti obtained great sums of gold, silver, and *umiña* (emeralds) ; and he came to an island of the Yuncas, where there were many pearls called *churup-mamam*, and many more *umiñas*. Thence he marched to the country of Chimu, where was Chimu Ccapac, the chief of the Yuncas, who submitted and did all that was required of him. The Curaca of Cassamarca, named *Pisar-Ocopac*, did the same. The Ynca then marched along the coast to Rimac-yuncas, where he found many small villages, each with its *huaca*. Here he found *Chuspi-huaca*, and *Puma-huaca*, and a great devil called *Aissa-villca*. He then advanced, by Pachacamac, to Chincha, where he found another *huaca* and devil. Returning to Pachacamac, he rested there for some days. At that time there was hail and thunder, which terrified the Yuncas. The Ynca did not demand tribute here, as he had done in the other provinces.

He then pursued his way without stopping, by Mama and Chaclla to Xauxa, and went thence to Huancavilca, where he found two natural springs flowing with chicha, at a time when all his soldiers were suffering from thirst. The

---

[8] See the account of the flight of Hanco-hualla (Anco-allo) in *G. de la Vega*, ii, pp. 82 and 329.

natives presented him with *ychma* (colour), and the Yauyus brought him gold and silver. He next came to Huamañin, near Villcas, where he had first seen the seven evil *huacas*. In Puma-cancha,[9] a very hot place before coming to Villcas, his eldest legitimate son was born, named Amaru Yupanqui, and he rested there for some days. Here the news arrived of a miracle at Cuzco. A *yauirca* or *amaru*, a ferocious creature, half a league long and two *brazas* and a half wide, with ears, eye-teeth, and a beard, had come forth from the mountain of Pachatusan, and entered the lake of Quichui-pay. Then two *sacacas* (comets) of fire came out of Ausan-cata, and went towards Arequipa; and another went towards some snowy mountains near Huamanca. They were described as animals with wings, ears, a tail, and four legs, with many spikes on their backs; and from a distance they appeared to be made of fire. So Pachacuti Ynca Yupanqui set out for Cuzco, where he found that his father, Uira-ccocha Ynca Yupanqui, was now very old and infirm.

Then were celebrated the festivals of his return, and of the Ccapac Raymi of Pachayachachi, with great rejoicing. The Curacas and Mitmays of Caravaya brought a *chuqui-chinchay*, which is an animal of many colours, said to have been chief of the *uturuncus*.[1] This Ynca caused all the deformed and idiotic persons to be employed in making clothes. He was very fortunate in arms. When his father died, the mourning was vicuña wool of a white colour; and the soldiers were ordered to carry the body of the old man, with his arms and insignia, through the city, singing a war-song and bearing their shields and clubs, their *llaca-chuquis*,[2] *chasca-chuquis, suruc-chuquis*. The women came forth in another procession, with their hair shorn, and dressed in black, and their faces blackened, flogging themselves with

---

[9] The deep hot valley of the river Pampas.

[1] Jaguars.

[2] *Llaca*, a plumed lance (*Mossi*).

quichuas and *coyas, secsec, sihuicas.*[3] They say that these women mourned for a whole week, and sought for the body of the dead Ynca.

Afterwards Pachacuti undertook the conquest of the Cunti-suyus, and in the Collao he fell in with the Collas and Camanchacas, who are great sorcerers. Thence he marched to Arequipa, Chancha, and to the Chumpivillcas, and thence to Parina-cocha, returning to the city by the country of the Aymaraes, Chollques, and Papris. At that time they say that the Capacuyos sent a poor man with *hultis* (clay pots in which they keep *llipta*), who gave Pachacuti Ynca a blow on the head with the intention of killing him. The man was tortured, and confessed that he was a Caviña of the Quiquijanas, and that he had come to kill the Ynca at the request of the Capacuyos. So the Ynca ordered the province of the Caviñas to be laid waste; but they said that the fault was not theirs, but the Capacuyos, whose Curaca was Apu Calama Yanqui, and who numbered near 20,000 men, besides women and children. They were all put to death. They say that they tried to murder the Ynca, by advice of their *huaca*, Canacuay.[4] Then the Yuca's second son was born, named Tupac Ynca Yupanqui ; and the Ynca undertook the conquest of the Antisuyus with 100,000 men. But the *huaca* of Canacuay sent forth fire, and stopped the passage with a fierce serpent which destroyed many people. The Ynca raised his eyes to heaven and prayed for help with great sorrow, and a furious eagle descended, and, seizing the head of the serpent, raised it on high and then hurled it to the ground. In memory of this miracle the Ynca ordered a snake to be carved in stone on the wall of a terrace in this province, which was called *Anca-pirca*.

[3] Xhichca of *Mossi* (148); secsec of *Mossi* (278) ; sihui of *Mossi* (235). Different kinds of thorn bushes.

[4] Name of the mountain between Paucartampu and the eastern forests.—See *G. de la Vega*, i, p. 330.

The Ynca returned to Cuzco, and he was very old. News came that a ship had been seen on the sea; and after another year a youth entered the city with a great book which he gave to the old Ynca and then disappeared. The Ynca fasted for six months in Tococachi without ceasing. Afterwards the Ynca Pachacuti resigned the kingdom to his son Amaru Tupac Ynca, who would not accept it, but devoted his time to farming and building. Seeing this, Pachacuti transferred the succession to his second son, Tupac Ynca Yupanqui, whom all the tribes joyfully acknowledged. So he was crowned, and the sceptre called *Tupac-yauri* was delivered to him. He ordered that the soldiers of all the tribes should assemble in Cuzco, for he had heard that there was a rebellion in Quito. He marched to conquer the rebels with twenty thousand men; and another twelve thousand with their wives as garrisons and *mitimaes*.[5] He ordered the troops to join him from all parts, he punished the rebels, removed them from their native land to other parts, and divided the spoils among his soldiers. He distributed rich dresses of *cumpis* and *puracahuas* of plumes, shields, *pura-puras* of gold and silver; and to the officers shirts of gold and silver, and diadems called *huacra-chucu*.[6] Thus he arrived at Quito, always gaining the victory, and afterwards he returned to Tumipampa, after leaving *mitimaes* in Cayambis; but he did not punish the natives because they made very humble excuses and were pardoned.

In those days there was a great famine which lasted for seven years, and during that time the seed produced no fruit. Many died of hunger, and it is even said that some ate their own children. The Ynca was then living at Tumipampa. They say that Amaru Tupac Ynca, during those seven years of famine, obtained large harvests from

---

[5] Colonists.

[6] *Huacra*, a horn; and *chucu*, a head-dress. This was the name of a large tribe near Cassamarca.—See *G. de la Vega*, ii, p. 322.

H

his farms at *Calla-chaca* and *Lucrioc-chullo*, that the dews
always descended upon them at night, and that frost never
visited them, insomuch that the people would have worshipped him by reason of the miracle; but Amaru Tupac
would not consent to this insult to the Creator. He rather
humbled himself, feeding the poor during the seven years
of famine. For his disposition was to be humble and meek
to all. He had filled the *collcas* or granaries with food
many months before. His descendants were the *Ccapac-
Ayllu*. At that time Huayna Ccapac Ynca was born in
Tumipampa, a town of the Cañaris, his father being Tupac
Ynca Yupanqui, and his mother Coya Mama Anahuarqui.
The Ynca built the great palace of Tumipampa-Pachacamac;
and all the sorcerers were pardoned in honour of the prince's
birth, at the intercession of his mother, they having been
condemned to death. For the Ynca Tupac Yupanqui had
always been a great executor of justice upon *llaycas* and
umus, and a destroyer of *huacas*, but not for this did they
cease to increase in number.

Eventually the Ynca returned to Cuzco, sending a captain in advance, named Arequi Ruca, with twelve thousand
men, by the coast road, that he might visit the provinces
and punish all rebels. The Ynca went direct to Cuzco,
taking with him Cayambis, Cañaris, and Chachapuyas as
labourers. He also took many girls of the Quitus, Quilacus,
Quillasencas, Chachapuyas, Yuncas, Huayllas, and Huancas,
as chosen maidens for *Ticci Ccapac Uiracochan Pachacya-
chachi*, called *Yurac-aclla*, *Huayra-aclla*, *Paco-aclla*, and
Yana-aclla;[7] and much wealth of gold and silver and precious stones, and plumes of feathers. He then ordered
that all the provinces from Quitu to Cuzco should make
farms and *collcas* or granaries, roads and bridges and *tampus*;[8] that there should be *acllas*,[9] in all the provinces,

---

[7] See p. 82.   [8] Inns.

[9] Chosen virgins.

officers of *cumpis*,[1] smiths, *Paucar-camayoc*, *Pillcu-camayoc*,[2] and garrisons of soldiers for the security of the land, and *hampi-camayoc*.[3] The Ynca also gave orders that every village should supply food for the poor.

When the Ynca approached Cuzco, where Pachacuti Ynca Yupanqui had remained with thirty thousand men of war, the old man came out to meet him as far as Villca-cunca, with his chiefs or Apu Curacas, in litters ; and the two armies made a most brilliant appearance with their gold and silver and rich plumes. The two forces imitated skirmishes, and the good old man, from joy at seeing his son and grandson, made his son a general, and his grandson master of the camp. He then sent half his army with Uturuncu achachi[4] and *caçir ccapac* (this *caçir ccapac* means a vice-general or viceroy), and with all the Apu Curacas, that they might all be in order of battle on the Sacsahuaman fortress, to defend the city; that his grandson, Huayna Ccapac, might have a battle with fifty thousand men all armed with gold and silver. This was done by way of a representation or comedy, and those in the fortress were conquered, who were Cayambis and Pastus, and their heads were cut off (which was done by anointing them with the blood of llamas) and put upon lances. Then there was a triumphal march, with the *haylli*,[5] to the Ccuricancha, where they offered up their prayers to the simple image of the Creator. Then the captains came forth by the other door to the square of Huacay-pata-Cusi-pata, with the song of the *quichu*, and the Curacas sat on their *tiyanas*[6] in their order. Here also sat Pachacuti Ynca Yupanqui, with his sons Tupac Ynca Yupanqui, and Amaru Tupac Ynca, all on

---

[1] Fine cloth. [2] Keepers of plumes and garlands.
[3] Doctors. *Hampi*, medicine.
[4] Name of a general. The words mean "Grandfather of a jaguar". But *Achachi* is a grandfather in the Colla language. In Quichua a grandfather is *Machu*. He was probably a Colla general.
[5] Song of triumph. [6] Thrones.

equal *tiyanas* made of gold, all richly dressed with their *ccapac-llautus*,[7] and the old man held the golden sceptre of *tupac yauri*, while his sons only had *champis*[8] of gold.

But the administration of the empire was left to Tupac Ynca Yupanqui, and his child Huayna Ccapac remained in the Ccuri-cancha without coming forth during that year. The festival of Ccapac Raymi was kept with great solemnity by the three ministers of the temple of Ccuricancha, Apu-Rimac, and Auqui-Challcu-Yupanqui, and Apu-cama; who called the Ynca their son, and his house was on the site of the present convent of San Agustin.

At this time the old Pachacuti Yupanqui died, seeming to fall asleep, without feeling any pain, at whose death there was much mourning, and food, wool, and clothing were distributed among the poor, throughout the kingdom, and many old captains were buried with him, together with all his pages, whom, it was said, he would require for his service in the other life. They made them drunk before they were put to death. They say that this Pachacuti Ynca Yupanqui had great store of gold and silver, which was kept in a vault, divided into three chambers, in the valley of Pisac. The body of Pachacuti was placed in the house of the dead bodies of the other Yncas and their wives, where they are embalmed and arranged in their order, each in its recess.

On his death the provinces of the *Puquinas* and *Collas* rebelled, from Villcañota to Chacamarca, with all the *Urcosuyus* of Achacache, Huancane, Asillu, and Asancaru, and they made their fortress in *Llallahua Pucara* with two hundred thousand men; but as this fortress could not contain them all, those who had least courage went into two other strongholds in the province. So Tupac Ynca Yupanqui assembled an army to attack them; and the Hanan-Quichuas and Hurin-Quichuas, confident in their prowess,

---

[7] Royal fringe.   [8] Battle-axes.

petitioned to be allowed to march against the enemy. At last the Ynca yielded to their importunity, and a very powerful army of twelve thousand Quichuas marched from Cuzco, full of confidence, well armed, taking with them a *huaca,* or idol.

They began to fight in Huarmi-Pucara[9] with the women of the Quillacas, and the Quichuas were defeated. They retired to the principal fortress of Llahua-pucara, where they were besieged by the Collas and entirely cut to pieces. One man escaped, and brought the news to Tupac Ynca Yupanqui, who mourned for the flower of his army. Then he set out himself from Cuzco with one hundred and twenty thousand men, and marched against the Collas, laying siege to the said fortress of Llallahua-pucara. This siege lasted for three years. Then the Collas offered up sacrifices to the sun, of children and *cuis,*[1] and from the air there was an encouraging answer to their *Tayta*[2] (*Tayta* means a minister of the *huacas*). Then they waged war upon the Ynca without any fear ; but it fell out very differently from what they expected, for the Ynca attacked these Collas with renewed fury, and there was much bloodshed. Next day the Collas, to strike terror among the troops of the Ynca, began to sing and beat drums, after which there was another battle without any decisive result. On the third day the Ynca and his captains renewed the assault at sunrise and drove back the Collas. Then Chuchi-Ccapac and his chiefs escaped to the province of the Lupacas dressed as women. They were brought before the Ynca in the town of Cac-yaviri, with the *huaca* of *Ynti* and other *huacas.* Tupac Ynca Yupanqui ordered the chiefs and the *huacas* to be placed in the centre of their army of one hundred thousand men, where they were insulted, and, to increase the affront, he sent for the *huyachucos, suyuntus,*[3] *llama-llamas,* and *chuñires*

---

[9] *Huarmi*, a woman. *Pucara*, a fortress. [1] Guinea pigs.
[2] *Tayta* means father, master. [3] Turkey buzzards.

to trample upon them, and eventually they were thrown into the lake of Urcos, while the Collas were brought in triumph to Cuzco. In memory of these cruel wars of the Collas, the Ynca ordered two darts of gold and siver to be placed in Villcañota, and he left *mitimaes* and garrisons of loyal men for the security of the conquered provinces.

The Ynca then assembled 200,000 men to undertake a new conquest in the Andes, naming Uturuncu Achachi as general of the army, and Ccapac Huari, Poqui-llacta, and others of the Chillquis, Papris, and Canas, as officers. These did good service in the conquest of the provinces of Mana-resu and Upatari, as far as the confines of Huancavillca on one side, and to Caravaya on the other, where they met with a province inhabited entirely by women, called *Huarmi-auca*.[4] They then crossed a river of great volume; but at first, as no man could pass over, some audacious monkeys, belonging to a chief of the Manares, went across, and secured ropes and cables after overcoming great difficulties. This province is called the Golden, and in it they found a great and rich land called *Escay-oya*,[5] with a very warlike race of people who were said to be cannibals; and they make such deadly poison, that it would seem they have a pact with the devil. They fought two desperate battles, and in the third they were defeated by the soldiers of the Ynca, not because they were less brave, but by superiority of arms and discipline. They say that while these new provinces were being num-bered, and while arrangements were being made for leaving garrisons, news came that Tupac Ynca Yupanqui had banished a captain to a province of the Chirihuanas.[6] The captain, Apu Quillacta, proclaimed this news to his people, and they returned to their own land, leaving the Ynca army with the general, Uturuncu Achachi. This was the reason that the Escay-oyas, and Upataxis, and Manares

---

[4] *Huarmi*, a woman. *Auca*, a soldier.   [5] Illegible in MS.
[6] This passage is obscure.

again took up arms, for the forces of Uturuncu Achachi
were reduced; and he returned to Cuzco, abandoning the
conquests made by the labours of three armies and at great
cost of lives. If this had not happened these provinces
would now be subject to the crown of Spain, and their
inhabitants would have been Christians; but our Lord
knows it, and has reserved this good work for another time.

In those days the Ynca sent Caçir Ccapac as visitor-
general to the land, giving his commission in lines on a
painted stick; and before his departure Colla-chahuay,
the Curaca of Tarma, in Chinchaysuyu, was sent to travel
through the country, and eat and drink with all the Curacas,
for this Collcachahuay was the greatest eater and drinker
that God had created in those parts.

The Ynca was in the fortress of Sacsahuaman with all his
officers when Apu-Quillacta and his twelve thousand men
of Colla-suyu returned, and complained of the ill-treatment
of the exiles. The Ynca excused himself, saying that he
knew nothing of it. Then news came that the Chillis were
assembling warriors to attack the Ynca, and he sent a captain against them with twenty thousand men, and twenty
thousand of the Huarmi-aucas. The two commanders
marched as far as the Coquimpus, Chillis, and Tucumans,
who were easily subdued, and a great quantity of very fine
gold was brought back to Cuzco. When the Ynca received
this large quantity of gold, he ordered plates of it to be
made to cover the walls of the Ccuricancha. In the feast of
Ccapac-Raymi it was the usual custom of the Ynca to
invite all the people of Ttahuantin-suyu to drink in their
order. The Curacas and common people murmured that
there was stint in the liquor; and when this came to the
ear of the Ynca, he ordered enormous *querus*[7] for the ensuing
year, when portentously large *querus* were given three times
in the day.

[7] Bowls.

At this time there came from the Andes of Upatari three huudred Antis laden with gold in dust and tubes, and at the moment of their arrival it began to freeze, and all the crops were frozen to the roots. So, by advice of the old councillors, the Yncar ordered the three hundred men to carry their loads of gold to *Pachatusun*, a very high hill, and there to have them buried. So the unfortunates were killed and buried as a welcome.

The Ynca died, being very old, as well as his brother Amaru Tupac Ynca, who had attained a great age. Both the brothers died in the same year, leaving Huayna Ccapac Ynca as their heir, and Apu Hualpaya as governor, for the heir was of tender age. They mourned for the Ynca as they had done for Pachacuti, forming two armies, one of men and the other of women, and they buried many *yanas*,[8] *pachacas*,[9] women, and servants, who were beloved by the Ynca. The barbarous captains thought that their Ynca would require to be served in the next world by these people. They say that this governor and coadjutor intended to raise himself to be ruler of Ttahuantin-suyu, and that he ordered troops to be secretly assembled from all parts for a given day. They say that this governor began to worship the sun and moon and thunder; and Huayna Ccapac, being a young child, also adored them, and all things that were put into the Ccuricancha by his ancestors, supposing that they were put there to be worshipped. And they say that the governor assigned estates for these false gods, and that some evil disposed Curacas executed his orders with alacrity.

This Hualpaya was now ready to rebel without the knowledge of the provinces; and one night a bastard uncle of Huayna Ccapac was lying half awake and half asleep, very early in the morning, when he saw troops headed by Hualpaya surrounding the city, and pointing their arrows at the

---

[8] Servants.　　　[9] Officers in command of a hundred men.

child Huayna Ccapac. This was a dream; but the uncle
jumped up as if it had been true, went to the house of Cuys
Manco, and assembled all the councillors. The governor
entered the chamber where twelve grave councillors were
assembled, and asked the cause. The uncle had told them
his dream, and they made him repeat it three times. Then
one ordered the friends of the governor to be seized,
another that fifty men should watch the roads and see if
anything unusual was on foot; and finally, the most trusted
favourite of Apu Hualpaya confessed that many Indians
laden with coca were on the roads, with their arms concealed,
ready to rebel. Then the governor, with his numerous
followers, could not be seized by the councillors; so they
assembled five hundred of the most loyal and faithful
of the councillors of Ttahuantin-suyu, who were sworn to
defend the royal house, and he took the *ccapac-uancha*, or
standard of the Yncas, out of the temple, and went to
the governor, taking the infant Huayna Ccapac with
them. Hualpaya was well armed, and on the point of
coming forth with many captains, but he was seized with
his followers and his head was cut off, and those who came
from the provinces to help him were flogged. Then the
councillors continued to rule the whole realm without a
governor.

After three years they began to prepare for the feast of
the coronation; and they assigned as the wife of Huayna
Ccapac his own sister Ccoya Mama Cusirimay, according
to the custom of his ancestors. They were married on the
day of the coronation, when all the walls and roofs in the
city were covered with rich plumes of feathers, and the
streets were paved with golden pebbles. The people were
gorgeously dressed in *cumpis* and plumes. The Ynca came
forth from the house of his grandfather Pachacuti Ynca
Yupanqui, followed by all the Apu Curacas of Colla-suyu
and councillors; while Mama Cusirimay came out of the

palace of Tupac Ynca Yupanqui, attended upon by the
Apu Curacas of Chinchay-suyu, Cunti-suyu, and Anti-suyu,
with all their Auqui-cuna[1] according to their rank. They
were in litters, and Huayna Ccapac did not hold the *tupac-
yauri*, but only the *champi*. Many attendants of less note
surrounded him, all dressed in shining *churus*[2] and mother-
of-pearl, and well armed with their *purupuras*[3] and *chipanas*[4]
of silver. They say that fifty thousand men guarded the
city and the fortress of Sacsahuaman, and that the festival
was a wonderful sight.

The Ynca and his spouse then entered the temple, each
by a separate door, the temple being that of the Creator
Pachayachachi.[5] This is the name given by these heathens,
and the High Priest was called *Apu Challcu Yupanqui*.
The sovereign and his wife were shod in *llanques* of gold;
and afterwards they gave him the *chipana* of gold and raised
him to the platform whence he performed these ceremonies,
where he said a prayer in a loud voice, which concluded
the proceedings of that day, and they were considered to be
married. Afterwards they delivered to him the *tupac-yauri*[6]
and the *suntur-paucar*,[7] after three days, and the *ccapac-
llautu*[8] and the *unincha*[9] in the same place where they were
married, and in continuation of the same ceremony. They
also delivered to him the *ccapac-unancha*[1] or royal standard
to be carried before him, and the *huaman-champi*[2] of two
edges, with the shields or *huallcancas*,[3] *uracahuas*, and
uma-chucus.[4] The Ynca took an oath and touched the
ground, promising to emulate the deeds of his forefathers,
and to attend to the things of Pachayachachi and his Ccuri-

---

[1] *Auqui*, an unmarried prince. *Cuna*, the plural particle.

[2] A shell.

[3] I am uncertain of the exact meaning. *Puru* is a calabash; also
false. *Puru-ccayan*, mourning.   [4] A bracelet.   [5] See p. 11.

[6] Royal sceptre.   [7] Royal head-dress.   [8] Fringe.

[9] Fillet.   [1] Royal standard.   [2] Club.

[3] Shield.   [4] *Uma*, "head." *Chucu*, "head-dress."

cancha, and to do no evil to the kingdom of Ttahuantin-
suyu, keeping the laws of former Yncas, and favouring all
loyal servants. Then the *Apu Challca Yupanqui* said a
prayer to the Creator, beseeching him to guard and protect
the Ynca with his powerful hand, and to defend him from
his enemies. Those present then shouted out their acclama-
tions. Then they all praised the Creator called Pachayachachi Uiracochan. Then the Ynca went to the Huacay-
pata, where was his *ccapac-usnu*,[5] as in Villcas, and there
each chief and captain, in his order, promised obedience to
the new sovereign.

They say that the disposition of Huayna Ccapac was very
affable and knightly, and that Ccoya Mama Cusirimay was
beautiful. But before he married, Huayna Ccapac had a
son named Ynti Tupac Cusi Hualpa, whose mother was
Rahua Ocllo; and he was also the father, by a princess
named Tocto Ocllo Cuca, of another son named Tupac
Atahualpa. Then the Ynca had a son by his wife named
Ninancuyochi, whose mother, the Ccoya, died soon afterwards. Then Huayna Ccapac Ynca wished to marry his
second sister, named Mama Cuca, who refused her consent,
and he then ill-treated her and began to use force, but her
prayers and menaces made him desist. Then he went with
presents and offerings to the body of his father, praying
him to give her for his wife, but the dead body gave no
answer, while fearful signs appeared in the heavens, portend-
ing blood. This was called *Ccalla-sana*.[6] This made Huayna
Ccapac give up his intention in regard to his sister, so he
gave her to a very old and ugly Curaca who was a great
chewer of coca; and he did this, not for her good, but in
order to bring shame upon her. She wept; and leaving
the old man, whose name was *Hacaroca*, she entered the

---

[5] *Ccapac*, royal. *Usnu*, a station, land-mark, heap of stones; tribunal
or judgment seat.

[6] *Ccallani*, I break. *Sanampa*, a sign.

house of the *Acllas* as a princess, and became abbess, never
having submitted to the old man. The Ynca Huayna Ccapac
was then married a second time, but not with such ceremonies as on his union with his first wife, to *Ccoya Chimpu
Runtucay*.

Then he set out for the provinces of Colla-suyu, to order
the assembly of an army to march to Quito. On the road
his second wife bore a son, named Manco Ynca Yupanqui,
and they went through all the land, and the chiefs and
army assembled at Puma-cancha to march against Quito
and the Cayambis, for every day news came that these
provinces had rebelled. Then the Ynca distributed clothes
and arms and provisions to the soldiers, and the chiefs took
oaths, and the army prepared for the war. The Ynca
named Mihicnaca Mayta as general of the army, and as
generals of the four provinces he nominated four of the
oldest and most experienced chiefs.

The festival of Ccapac Raymi was celebrated in Villcas,
where there was another plate of gold. Here the chiefs
remembered that they had forgotten the statute of *Huayna
Ccapac*, and the Ynca, consenting to their wishes, sent for
it. In those days messengers came from Rimac, bringing
word that, within the Ccuricancha of Pachacamac (the Ccuricancha was a temple, and there were many in different
parts, the largest being in Cuzco), the *huaca* had said that
it desired to see the Ynca. So he went to visit Pachamac,
and the *huaca* spoke to him alone, saying that he must take
riches to Chimu, and honour him more than Uiracochan
Pachayachachi. The Ynca consented, and the wizards rejoiced. The army reached the town of Tumipampa, where
the Ynca ordered water to be brought from a river by
boring through a mountain, and making the channel enter
the city by curves in this way.[7]

Half the army was employed in building the edifices for a

---

[7] See opposite page.

Ccuricancha, a wonderful work. Then the Ynca departed with his army, numbering a million and a half of men, and came to Picchuya Sicchupuruhuay. All the inhabitants, with the Cayambis, Quillisencas, and Quillacus, fled to fortresses to defend themselves against the Ynca. The two

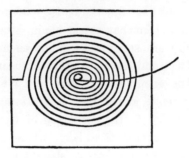

armies then began to fight, and much blood was shed. The Colla-suyu troops had been ordered to take the enemy in the rear, but meanwhile the Cayambis did great injury to the royal camp, and discovered that the Colla-suyus were marching very leisurely. So they fell upon them furiously, and caused great slaughter, so that few escaped in the fine and powerful army of Colla-suyu. The Ynca felt this misfortune deeply, for the general of Colla-suyu was one of his wisest councillors. But the Ynca was to blame for having confided in the promises of the *huaca* at Pachacamac and other idols. His men were now left starved and in rags, while the war became more fierce than ever. At last the Ynca sent to Cuzco for reinforcements; but news came that the Chirihuanus had invaded his territory, which caused him fresh anxiety. He despatched his most experienced captains for the conquest of the Chirihuanus, with 20,000 men of the Chinchay-suyus. Thus his army was reduced to 100,000 men, and with this he continued the war. He sent the Colla-suyu troops over the mountains to attack the fortress of the Cayambis, while he Chinchay-suyus marched by the plains. The Ynca himself advanced by the direct

road. They fought more furiously than ever, and the
Colla-suyus climbed to the fortresses of the Cayambis and
attacked them fiercely, sparing neither age nor sex. The
Ynca also fought in person, attended by the Mayus,
Sancus, and Quillis-cachis. The enemies were worn out
with fatigue; but next day the battle was renewed, and the
Colla-suyus and Chinchay-suyus again attacked the fortresses, which were steep rocks. The enemy began to fly
to another place, and the Ynca ordered his army to rest for
that day. The enemy took refuge in a stronger fortress,
and reinforcements joined the Ynca's army from Cuzco.
The Cayambis fled to the *montañas* of Otabala,[8] and assembled on the shores of a lake, where they were surrounded, and there was great slaughter. The warriors
washed their arms in the lake, and there was a mass of
blood in the centre, so the lake was called *Yahuar-ccocha*.[9]

Then the Ynca went to Quito to rest, and to establish his
government and laws. He then advanced beyond Pasto,
·but returned to Quito, where he solemnized the Ccapac-
Raymi. At the hour for eating a messenger arrived in a
black mantle, who reverently kissed the Ynca, and gave
him a *pputi*[1] covered up. The Ynca told the messenger to
open it, but he excused himself, saying, that the command
of the Creator was that the Ynca alone should do so. So
the Ynca opened it, and there came flying out a quantity of
things like butterflies or bits of paper, which spread abroad
until they disappeared. This was the pestilence of *Sarampion* (?), and in a few days the general Mihcnaca Mayta died,
with many other captains, their faces being covered with
scabs. When the Ynca saw this, he ordered a house to be
built of stone, in which he hid himself, and there died.
After eight days they took out the body quite dried up, and

---

[8] Otavalla. See *G. de la Vega*, ii, p. 350; and *Cieza de Leon*, p. 138.
[9] See *Cieza de Leon*, p. 133; and *G. de la Vega*, ii, p. 449.
[1] *Puti*, a trunk, parcel.

embalmed it, and took it to Cuzco on a litter, richly dressed and armed as if it had been alive.

A son, named Tupac Atahualpa, was left in Quito, and many chiefs and captains, called Quis-quis, Challcuchima, Unacchuyllu, Rumi-ñaui, Ucumari, and many more.

The body of Huayna Ccapac was conveyed to Cuzco with much ceremony, and the people made obeisances to it. After it was deposited with the other bodies of the Yncas, there was general mourning for his death. Then Yuti Tupac Cusi Huallpa Huascar Ynca made his mother, Rava Ocllo, marry the dead body, in order that he might become legitimate, and the ministers of the temple performed the ceremony out of fear. Thus Tupac Cusi Huallpa took the title of legitimate son of Huayna Ccapac, and called upon all the chiefs of Ttahuantin-sayu to swear obedience to him, which was done. He then prepared for his coronation, and induced the great Curacas to ask the ministers of Ccuricancha to deliver to him the *ccapac llautu, suntur-paucar, tupac-yauri,* and *ccapac-uncu*. Great preparations were made for the coronation, and there was a distribution of rich dresses, plumes, and arms, which was merely done to gain over the chiefs. At the end of a year he received the *ccapac-llautu*, with the name of Yuti Cusi Huallpa Huascar Ynca.[2] He married his sisters, named *Chuqui-huy-pachu-quipa*, and *Ccoya Mama Chuqui huypa chuquipa*.

Afterwards Tupac Cusi Huallpa took 1200 Chachapuyas and Cañaris for the servants of the palace, and dismissed

---

[2] This Ynca Cusi Huallpa caused a garden to be made at Sappi, near Cuzco, with many animals of gold and silver, amongst the trees. Then he caused a very long chain to be made, of gold, and each link was in the form of a serpent twined with the tail in the mouth, and adorned with colours like a serpent's skin. This Ynca was not called Huascar, as some say, on account of this chain; but because he was born at Huascar-pata, near Molina. It is a tradition that the chain was thrown into this lake of Molina (Muyna) when the Spaniards came, and not into that of Urcos-ccocha.

those of his father. He also began to punish his father's captains with death because they had left Tupac Atahuallpa and the other captains in Quito. Then he marched into the provinces of Colla-suyu, and came to Titicaca, where he ordered a golden image of the sun to be set up. He worshipped it as Uiracocha Ynti, thus adding the name of Ynti. On his return to Cuzco he came to Pocana-cancha, where he found all the Apu Curacas coming in their litters according to the privilege granted by former Yncas, and Huascar Ynca laughed at this, although he did not take away the privilege. In this place he ordered the Acllas, of all four classes, to be brought into the open square, in the middle of all the Apu Curacas and the whole army. Then he told a hundred Indians of the Llamallamas and Hayacuchos, while they were performing their dances, to seize the damsels and ravish them in public. The damsels, when they were thus treated, cried out and raised their eyes to heaven ; and all the great men of the kingdom resented such conduct, and looked upon this Huascar Ynca as half a fool, and only treated him with reverence from fear.

At that time Tupac Atahuallpa sent to Huascar Ynca, beseeching him to give him the title and nomination of Governor of the Provinces of Quito, and the Ynca Huascar granted the request, and gave him the name of Ynca-ranti.[3] Then the chief of the Cañaris, named Urco-calla, brought false news to Huascar Ynca, asking him why he consented that Tupac Atahuallpa should have the title of Ynca. This enraged the Ynca, and when Tupac Atahuallpa sent him rich presents he caused them to be burnt, and drums to be made of the skins of the messengers who brought them, except a few, whom he sent back to Quito dressed as women, and with very shameful messages to Auqui Atahuallpa. They were followed by a chief named Huaminca-atoc, whom

---

[3] *Ranti*, a deputy. *Ynca-ranti*, viceroy.

the Ynca sent against Atahuallpa with 1200 men, and orders to take him and the other captains prisoners. This captain rested at Tumipampa. Meanwhile the surviving messengers arrived at Quito, and reported what had happened to Auqui Tupac Atahuallpa, who received the news in great sorrow, but in silence. Then he sent to the captain Huaminca-atoc, asking him to declare for what purpose he had come with an army; and the captain replied that he would answer by his deeds. Then Auqui Atahuallpa, with the consent of all his captains, determined to take up arms, and the people of Quito swore to obey him. He assumed the title of Ynca, and began to use a litter, and assembled 13,000 warriors. After a few days the captain Atoc reached Mullu Hampatu,[4] near Quito, and Atahuallpa came out against him. There was a battle, in which Atahuallpa was defeated, and all the Mitimaes[5] were terrified. But he resolved to attempt further resistance. So he appointed Challcuchima to be general, and Quis-quis to be master of ·the camp, who defeated and captured the captain Atoc and put out his eyes. When Huascar Ynca heard the news of the disaster he was transported with greater rage, and sent his brother Huanca Auqui, with 12,000 men, to attack Atahuallpa. He was ordered to increase his army on the road; and he advanced to Tumipampa, and thence to Quito. Atahuallpa came out with 16,000 men. In the first battle Huanca Auqui ordered a retreat to Yana-yacu, where both sides fought valiantly, and again at Tumipampa; but Huanca Auqui was defeated between the country of the Cañaris and Chachapuyas. Atahuallpa returned to Quito, punishing the Cañaris with great cruelty. Thus the army of Huanca Auqui was defeated in four battles. Challcuchima remained at Tumipampa, Atahuallpa returned to Quito, and Huanca Auqui conquered the province of the Pacllas of Chachapuya, in the name of Huascar Ynca. He fought the

---

[4] See *Cieza de Leon*, p. 153.   [5] Colonists.

enemy between Chachapuya and Caxamarca, and was again
defeated, retreating to Huanuco. After many challenges,
the two armies met once more at Bombon, each with
100,000 men. After having been arrayed for the encounter,
the soldiers on both sides ate and drank. The battle lasted
for three days, and on the last day Quis-quis and Challcuchima, the captains of Atahuallpa, were victorious, 20,000
having fallen. Huanca Auqui, now almost despairing,
retreated to Xanxa, where he met another fine army which
had been sent from Cuzco to reinforce him; and the captain who commanded angrily reprehended Huanca Auqui.
The defeated general had drinking bouts with his uncles in
the valley of Xauxa, and sent thence to the *huaca* at Pachacamac for help, and received a hopeful reply.

So Huanca Auqui ordered all the Huancas, Yauyus, and
Aymaras to come to the defence of Huascar Ynca, and
thus he assembled 200,000 men. The army of Quis-quis
entered the valley of Xauxa, where he rested for some days
and sent to Quito for reinforcements. He also sent to the
huaca at Pachacamac, which replied that he would gain the
victory. At the same time Huascar sent for a true answer,
and the *huaca* promised him the victory. He must take
heart and assemble all his power, and that then he would
conquer. Then Huascar Ynca sent to all the huacas and
idols in the land, and they all promised that he should gain
a victory in Villcas. He likewise ordered all the *layccus,*
umus, canchus, vallavicas, contivicas, canavicas, auzcovicas,
to come and offer up sacrifices and to divine; and they
foretold that the enemy would not advance beyond Ancoyacu,
and that Huascar would gain the victory.

At that time a captain from Cuzco, with 12,000 men,
offered battle to the enemy on the river of Ancoyacu, and
Huanca Auqui refused to send him any help; yet he
detained them for a month; but at last he was defeated,
and all his men were destroyed. This news reached Huascar

when he was engaged in the *mucha*[6] of the *huacas*. There were forty *huacas* assembled, and the Ynca began to abuse them with many insulting words, saying :—

Llulla vatica hauchha auca supay, chiquiy manta pallcaymantam chirmayñaymantam camcam Cuzco capacpa aucan-cunacta muchar-cayque callpaays ayran callpari cuyhuan aspacay niyhuan runa arpay ñiy huan camcam hillusu huaccunacatacay chapas camcam acoycunacataca runa huallpaquiypa hahocha aucana catamuscam-pas canquichic, chicallatac hinallatac mitaysanay villcaycunapas camcuna huaca rimachun camca cunactam, ari tonapa tarapaca Uiracochan Pachayachip yanan ñiscaca chienisus canqui.

Saying this he took an oath, shaking his mantle and kissing a little earth; and from that time he became an enemy of the huacas, idols, and sorcerers. Then he sent messengers throughout the realm of Ttahuantin-suyu to summon his vassals, as far as Chile, Coquimbo, Chirihuana, the Andes of Caravaya, the country of the Hatun-runas, who were giants; and in a few days a countless multitude assembled. The news soon arrived that Quis-quis and Challcuchima were encamped in Villcas-huaman, and the Ynca sent orders to Huanca Auqui to attack them; but he sustained another defeat, and the enemy advanced to Andahuaylas. Then Huascar Ynca Ynti Cusi Huallpa sent his three millions of men of war to try what Quis-quis and Challcuchima were made of. The enemy had at least a million and a half of men, and the captains alone numbered fifteen hundred; but the army of Huascar contained double the number.

Huanca Auqui, on coming to Curampa, left a million of men at Huancarama and Cocha-cassa to keep the enemy in check, while he went to Cuzco to report to the Ynca the reasons of his reverses; and the two princes made a brotherly reconciliation. Then the Ynca set out from Cuzco, taking all the Apu-Curacas and Auquis, and the

———
[6] Worship.

I 2

chiefs called Mancop-churin-cuzco, who are knights, and
the Ayllun-cuzcos as body-guards; and as a vanguard he
had the Quehuars and those of Colla-suyu, the Tambos,
Mascas, Chillquis, Papris, Quichuas, Mayus, Sancus, Quillis-
cachis; and as supports came the Chachapuyas and Cañaris.
All were in good order, and so the Ynca Huascar reached
Utcu-pampa surrounded by an imperial pomp and majesty
never before seen. Each tribe, with its general, was in
battle array from Ollanta-tambo to beyond Huaca-chaca.
The enemy extended from Chuntay-cassa to the river of
Pollcaro; and thus the plains were covered with the men
of both armies.

On that day the two armies were formed ready for battle,
and the Ynca Huascar ascended a high hill near the Apurimac, and beheld, with feelings of pleasure, the people covering the land like flour; and all the hills, *huayccus*,[7] and
plains glistening with the gold and silver and bright-coloured
plumes of the warriors, so that there was no spot unoccupied
for twelve leagues by six or seven. Each nation and province had its war songs and musical instruments. On the
next day Huascar Ynca sent messengers to order each company to make the assault with all possible fury, and the
battle then began. They continued to fight from dawn
until dark, and they say that twenty thousand men were
killed. Next day they began again after breakfast, and a
most fierce battle raged until sunset. On the third day it
was again renewed, and at the hour for eating both armies
were nearly worn out, and they rested, and all the plains
were covered with dead bodies, and well irrigated with
blood. On the fourth day they began again with still greater
fury; and Quisquis and Chalcuchima, the captains of Atahuallpa Ynca, retreated to three high hills with only half a
million of men. Here they entrenched themselves, and at
dawn next day the men of Colla-suyu attacked them fiercely,

[7] Ravines.

while the Ynca ordered the hills to be surrounded and assaulted on all sides. Then Quisquis and Chalcuchima, having lost many men, collected the survivors and retreated to the highest of the three hills, which was covered with grass, with groves of trees at the base. An Indian of the Canas suggested that the trees and grass should be set on fire, and the Ynca gave the necessary orders. A high wind arose and burnt the men of Chincha-suyu, while the troops of the Ynca killed them like flies in honey. Chalcuchima and Quisquis escaped with only two thousand three hundred men. They say that rivers of blood flowed from the battle field, which was covered with dead bodies.

The two captains, with their surviving followers, fled under cover of the night, and Huascar Ynca ordered his troops not to continue the pursuit until the following day; but, by that time, Quisquis and Challcuchima had reached the hill of Cochacassa, ten leagues from the battle field, with only seven hundred men.

At midnight Challcuchima and Quisquis lighted a fire on their left hands with a piece of grease; putting one lump of grease to represent the camp of Huascar Ynca, and the other for the camp of Atahuallpa. And the one in the place of Huascar Ynca burnt much more than that in the place of Atahuallpa, so that the grease of Huascar, burning up so high, went out very quickly, while that of Atahuallpa went on burning. Then Challcuchima and Quisquis sang the *haylli*, and told their men that all would go well. They set out for Utcu-pampa in search of Huascar Ynca, and got there at sunset with six hundred and forty men, when the Ynca was asleep, and took him prisoner, routing the Rucanas[8] who were his bearers, and so they carried him to Sallcantay. When the army found that Huascar Ynca was taken they were terrified, and each tribe went off to its own land. As soon as Quisquis and Challcu-

----

[8] See *G. de la Vega*, i, p. 267; ii, p. 147, 358.

chima had got possession of the body of Ynca Huascar, they desired nothing more. They did not enter the city, but posted their men at Quepay-pampa, whence they sent orders to all the Apu-curacas and Auquis to come to them, with the mother of Huascar, the general Huanca Auqui, and his captains.

They insulted the Ynca by tying a rope round his neck, and Quisquis called him *Cocahacho* and *Sulluya*, which means bastard, eater of coca, and offered him many other affronts. Then Quisquis and Challcuchima abused the mother of the Ynca, saying : " Come here, Mama Ocllo, you who were the concubine of Huayna Ccapac." When Huascar heard this, he asked them who they were that they should pass judgment on his descent; upon which Quisquis struck him, and gave him *chillca* leaves instead of coca. When he was thus outraged, Huascar raised his eyes, and cried out : " O Lord and Creator, how is it possible ? Why hast thou sent me these burdens and troubles." In those days Quisquis ordered all the children of Huascar Ynca to be slain, and all his servants, up to fifteen hundred persons, who were within the palace of Puca-marca.[9]

Huascar Ynca, his wife and mother, and two children, with Huanca Auqui and the chief officers and councillors of the Ynca, were sent with a guard of a hundred men to Atahuallpa. But in a few days the news arrived that the Spaniards had landed, and there was great dismay. By the advice of Quisquis great riches were buried in the earth; and it is also said that Huascar had previously ordered a chain of gold and three thousand loads of gold, with as many of silver, to be concealed in Cunti-suyu. They also hid all the *cumpis* and rich dresses of gold. One named Barco and Candia arrived at Cuzco without meeting Huascar Ynca, and Challcuchima was seized on the way to Caxamarca. Francisco Pizarro captured Atahuallpa in the

[9] See *G. de la Vega*, ii, p. 246.

midst of a vast concourse of Indians, after he had spoken with the friar Vicente de Valverde, when twelve thousand men were killed. For the people thought that they were the messengers of Pachayachachic Uiracocha; and when they fired off their guns, it was supposed to be Uiracocha.

When Atahuallpa was in prison the cock crowed, and he said that even the birds knew his name. From that time they called the Spaniards *Uiracocha*, because they declared to Atahuallpa that they brought the law of God. Hence they called the Spaniards *Uiracocha*, and the cock *Atahuallpa*. This Atahuallpa sent messages to Antamarca with orders that Huascar should be killed; and after he had sent them he began to pretend to be sad, trying to deceive the captain, Francisco Pizarro. So, by orders of Atahuallpa, they killed Huascar Ynca in Antamarca, with his son, wife, and mother, with great cruelty, and the Marquis knew all this through the complaints of the Curacas. Atahuallpa was baptized and called Don Francisco, and afterwards he was put to death as a traitor. Then the captain, Francisco Pizarro, accompanied by the friar Vicente, set out for Cuzco, taking with him a bastard son of Huayna Ccapac as Ynca, who died in the valley of Xauxa. The captain Francisco Pizarro reached the bridge of the Apurimac with sixty or seventy men, where he was met by Manco Ynca Yupanqui, with all the Curacas, who had come to offer obedience and become Christians. On reaching Villca-cunca, these Curacas, out of pure joy and satisfaction, began to make skirmishes. At Sacsahuana, on the following day, the friar Vicente, with the captain Francisco Pizarro, said to Manco Ynca Yupanqui that they wished to see the dresses of Huayna Ccapac Ynca, his father. He showed them, and they said they must see richer dresses, and the same Pizarro put them on him in the name of the Emperor. Then they all set out for Cuzco, with Manco Ynca Yupanqui borne in a litter.

In passing the village of Anta they came upon Quisquis, the tyrant captain of Atahuallpa. Then they all entered Cuzco with great pomp and majesty, and the marquis, with his grey hairs and long beard, represented the Emperor Charles V, while the friar Vicente, in his robes, personified his holiness the Pope. The Ynca, in his litter lined with rich plumes of feathers, his sumptuous clothes, the *suntur-pauçar* in his hand, and the royal insignia of the *ccapac unancha*, was greeted with great joy by the people. The friar Vicente went straight to the Ccuricancha, the house erected by the ancient Yncas in honour of the Creator; and at length the holy evangel entered upon possession of a new vineyard, which had been so long usurped by the ancient enemies of the faith. There the friar preached like another Apostle St. Thomas, the patron of these kingdoms, without ceasing, filled with zeal for the conversion of souls, baptizing Curacas; and if he had known the language his labours would have borne still more fruit; but he spoke through an interpreter. May God be praised for ever and ever.

A NARRATIVE

OF THE ERRORS, FALSE GODS, AND OTHER SUPERSTITIONS AND
DIABOLICAL RITES IN WHICH THE INDIANS OF THE PRO-
VINCES OF HUAROCHIRI, MAMA, AND CHACLLA LIVED
IN ANCIENT TIMES, AND IN WHICH THEY
EVEN NOW LIVE, TO THE GREAT
PERDITION OF THEIR SOULS.

COLLECTED

By the Doctor Francisco de Avila, Presbyter (Cura of the parish of
San Damian in the said province of Huarachiri, and vicar of the three
above mentioned), from trustworthy persons who, with special diligence,
ascertained the whole truth, and that, before God enlightened them,
they lived in the said errors, and performed these ceremonies. It is an
agreeable subject and well worthy to be understood, that the great
blindness in which those souls walk, who have not the light of faith,
nor desire to admit it to their understandings, may be known.

At present nothing more is given than the narrative, but our
Lord will thus be well served if the said illustrious
Doctor, God sparing his life, would adorn it with
reflections and interesting notes.

In the year 1608.

Chauca-chiipita was the name of the Indian we found with the new shirt; and the cloaks show whether they are of *Masnu-yauri* or *Carhuayalli*.

Conopa is the general name for all the small stone idols that we found.

Uncuraya is the name of the jar with the figure of the Devil. They used it in the feast of *Massuma*.

Chellcascayu is the idol that we went to search for.

THE PROVINCE OF HUAROCHIRI.

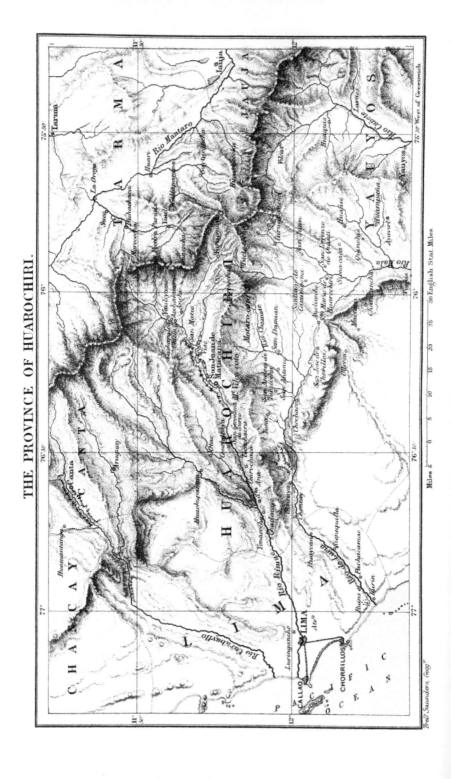

Fred. Saunders, Geog.r

Miles 5   0   5   10   15   20   25   30 English Stat. Miles

CHAPTER I.

Of the first and most ancient God of these people, and how the men of these provinces say that, in ancient times, it was a very hot country, and how afterwards some other idols were adopted, after the first.

It is a most ancient tradition that, before any other event of which there is any memory, there were certain huacas or idols, which, together with the others of which I shall treat, must be supposed to have walked in the form of men. These huacas were called *Yananamca Intanamca*; and in a certain encounter they had with another huaca called *Huallallo Caruincho*, they were conquered and destroyed by the said *Huallallo*, who remained as Lord and God of the land. He ordered that no woman should bring forth more than two children, of which one was to be sacrificed for him to eat, and the other,—whichever of the two the parents chose,—might be brought up. It was also a tradition that, in those days, all who died were brought to life again on the fifth day, and that what was sown in that land also sprouted, grew, and ripened on the fifth day; and that all these three provinces were then a very hot country, which the Indians call *Yunca* or *Ande*; and they say that these crops were made visible in the deserts and uninhabited places, such as that of Pariacaca and others; and that in these Andes there was a great variety of most beautiful and brilliant birds, such as macaws, parrots, and others. All this, with the people who then inhabited the land (and who, according to their account, led very evil lives), and the said idol, came to be driven away to other Andes by the idol *Pariacaca*, of whom I shall speak presently, and of the battle he had with this *Huallallo Carrincho*.

It is also said that there was another idol called *Coniraya*, of which it is not known certainly whether it existed before or after the rise of *Pariacaca*. It is, however, certain that it was invoked and reverenced almost down to the time when the Spaniards arrived in this land. For when the Indians worshipped it they said, " *Coniraya Uiracocha* (this name is that which they gave, and still give, to the Spaniards), thou art Lord of all: thine are the crops, and thine are all the people." In commencing any arduous or difficult undertaking, they threw a piece of coca (a well-known leaf) on the ground, as an oblation, and said, " Tell me, O Lord *Coniraya Uiracocha*, how I am to do this?" The same custom prevailed among the weavers of cloths, when their work was toilsome and difficult. This invocation and custom of calling the idol by the name of Uiracocha certainly prevailed long before there were any tidings of Spaniards in the country. It is not certain whether *Coniraya* or *Pariacaca* were first; but as it is more probable that *Coniraya* was the more ancient, we will first relate his origin and history, and afterwards that of *Pariacaca*.

CHAPTER II.

In which the account of *Coniraya* is continued, and how he became enamoured of the goddess *Cavillaca*, and of other things which are worthy to be known.

They say that in most ancient times the Coniraya Uiracocha appeared in the form and dress of a very poor Indian clothed in rags, insomuch that those who knew not who he was reviled him and called him a lousy wretch. They say that this was the Creator of all things; and that, by his word of command, he caused the terraces and fields to be formed on the steep sides of ravines, and the sustaining walls to rise up and support them. He also made the

irrigating channels to flow, by merely hurling a hollow cane,
such as we call a cane of Spain; and he went in various
directions, arranging many things. His great knowledge
enabled him to invent tricks and deceits touching the
huacas and idols in the villages which he visited. At that
time they also say that there was a woman who was a
huaca. Her name was Cavillaca, and she was a most
beautiful virgin, who was much sought after by the *huacas,*
or principal idols, but she would never show favour to any
of them. Once she sat down to weave a mantle at the foot
of a *lucma* tree, when the wise Coniraya succeeded in
approaching her in the following manner : He turned
himself into a very beautiful bird, and went up into
the lucma tree, where he took some of his generative
seed and made it into the likeness of a ripe and luxurious
lucma, which he allowed to fall near the beautiful Cavillaca.
She took it and ate it with much delight, and by it she was
made pregnant without other contact with man. When the
nine months were completed she conceived and bore a son,
herself remaining a virgin ; and she suckled the child at
her own breast for a whole year without knowing whose it
was nor how it had been engendered. At the end of the
year, when the child began to crawl, Cavillaca demanded
that the *huacas* and principal idols of the land should
assemble, and that it should be declared whose son was
the child. This news gave them all much satisfaction, and
each one adorned himself in the best manner possible,
combing, washing, and dressing in the richest clothes, each
desiring to appear brighter and better than the rest in the
eyes of the beautiful Cavillaca, that so she might select him
for her spouse and husband. Thus there was an assembly
of false gods at Anchicocha, a very cold inhospitable spot
between the villages of Chorrillo and Huarochiri, about half
way. When they were all seated in their order, Cavillaca
addressed them as follows : " I have invited you to assemble

here, O worthies and principal persons, that you may know
my great sorrow and trouble at having brought forth this
child that I hold in my arms. It is now aged one year: but I
know not, nor can I learn, who was its father. It is notorious
that I have never known man nor lost my virginity. Now
that you are all assembled, it must be revealed who made me
pregnant, that I may know who did this harm to me, and
whose son is this child." They were all silent, looking at
each other, and waiting to see who would claim the child,
but no one came forward. They say that, in this assembly,
in the lowest place of all, sat the god Coniraya Uiracocha
in his beggar's rags ; and the beautiful Cavillaca scarcely
looked at him, when she addressed the gods ; for it never
entered into her head that he was the father. When she
found that all were silent, she said :—" As none of you will
speak, I shall let the child go, and doubtless his father will
be the one to whom he crawls, and at whose feet he rests."
So saying, she loosed the child, who crawled away, and,
passing by all the others, he went to where was his father
Coniraya in his rags and dirt, and when the child reached
him, it rejoiced and laughed, and rested at his feet.

This conduct caused Cavillaca great shame and annoyance,
and she snatched up the child, exclaiming :—" What dis-
grace is this that has come upon me, that a lady such as I
am should be made pregnant by a poor and filthy creature."
Then she turned her back and fled away towards the sea-
shore. But Coniraya Uiracocha desired the friendship and
favour of the goddess, so, when he saw her take her flight,
he put on magnificent golden robes, and, leaving the astonished assembly of gods, he ran after her, crying out :—
" O my lady Cavillaca, turn your eyes and see how handsome and gallant am I," with other loving and courteous
words ; and they say that his splendour illuminated the
whole country. Yet the disdainful Cavillaca would not turn
her head, but rather increased her speed, saying :—" I have

no wish to see any one, seeing that I have been made pregnant by a creature so vile and filthy."[1] She disappeared, and came to the sea coast of Pachacamac, where she entered the sea with her child, and was turned into a rock. They say that the two rocks may still be seen, which are mother and child. Coniraya continued the pursuit, crying out, and saying, " Stop ! stop ! lady. Turn round and look ! where are you, that I cannot see you?" As he ran, he met a condor, to whom he said :—" Brother, tell me whether you encountered a woman with such and such marks ?" The condor answered :—" I saw her very near this place, and if you go a little faster, you will certainly overtake her." To whom Coniraya, rejoicing at the good news, thus made reply, blessing the condor, and saying :—" You shall live for ever, and I give you power to go whithersoever you please, to traverse the wildernesses and valleys, to search the ravines, to build where you shall never be disturbed ; and I grant you the faculty of eating all things that you find dead, such as huanacu, llamas, lambs, and even when they are not dead but merely neglected by their owners, you shall have power to kill and eat them. I further declare that he who kills you shall himself be killed."

Coniraya then continued his journey, and met a small fox of the kind that emits a strong odour, and asked him the same question touching Cavillaca. The fox answered that it was in vain for him to run fast, to seek, or to follow, because the goddess was now far off, and he could not overtake her. Then Coniraya cursed the fox, saying :—" As a punishment for the bad news you have given me, I command that you shall never go abroad but at night, that a bad smell shall always come from you, and that men shall persecute and hate you."

The god went on and met a lion which, in reply to his

[1] They say that the word she used was *cachca-sapa*, which means " itchy".

question, told him that he was very near the goddess Cavillaca, and that if he made a little more haste he would overtake her. This good news pleased the sage, and he blessed the lion, saying :—" You shall be respected and feared by all, and I assign to you the office of punisher and executioner of evil doers, you may eat the llamas of sinners, and after your death you shall still be honoured ; for when they kill you and take your skin they shall do so without cutting off the head, which they shall preserve, with the teeth, and eyes shall be put in the sockets so as to appear to be still alive. Your feet shall remain hanging from the skin with the tail, and, above all, those who kill you shall wear your head over their own, and your skin shall cover them. This shall they do at their principal festivals, so that you shall receive honour from them. I further decree that he who would adorn himself with your skin, must kill a llama on the occasion, and then dance and sing with you on his back."

After having given the lion this blessing, he continued his journey and met a fox, which said that his running was useless, for that the lady was far off, and it was impossible to overtake her. In payment for such news, the wise Coniraya pronounced the following curse :—" I command that you shall be hunted from afar, and then when the people see you, even at a great distance, they shall come out and hunt you ; and when you die you shall be of no account, and no one shall take the trouble to use your skin, or to raise you from the ground."

He then met a falcon, which said that the lady Cavillaca was very near ; so Coniraya declared that the falcon should be highly esteemed, that in the morning it should breakfast on the *alquenti*,[2] which is a very delicate and beautiful little bird living on the honey within the flowers (I do not know its name in Spanish),[3] and during the day that it should

---

[2] *Ccenti*, the humming bird.   [3] *Tominejo*.

eat any other bird it choose; and that he who killed it should also kill a llama in its honour; and that when he came out to sing and dance at the festivals, he should have the falcon's skin on his head.

Next he met some parrots that gave him bad news; so he declared that they should always give out cries and shrieks, and that, as they said the lady was far off, they should be heard from afar; that when they wished to feed they should not be safe, for their own cries should betray them, and that they should be hated by all people.

Thus he rewarded and granted privileges to all the animals that gave him news that accorded with his wishes, and cursed all those whose tidings were not agreeable to him.

When he reached the sea-shore he found that Cavillaca and her child were turned into stone; and as he walked along the beach he met two beautiful young daughters of Pacha-camac, who guarded a great serpent, because their mother was absent, visiting the recently arrived Cavillaca in the sea. The name of this wife of Pachacamac was *Urxayhua-chac*.[4] When Coniraya found these girls alone without their mother, he did not care for the serpent, which he could keep quiet by his wisdom; so he had intercourse with the elder sister, and desired to do the same with the younger, but she flew away in the shape of a wild pigeon (called by the Indians *urpi*); hence the mother of these girls was called *Urpi-huachac*, or mother of the doves.

In those days it is said that there were no fishes in the sea, but that this *Urpi-huachac* reared a few in a small pond. Coniraya was enraged that Urpi-huachac should be absent in the sea, visiting Cavillaca; so he emptied the fishes out of her pond into the sea, and thence all the fishes now in the sea have been propagated. Having done this, Coniraya continued his flight along the coast. When the mother of

[4] *Urpi-huachac.*

the girls returned they told her what had happened, and
she pursued Coniraya in a great fury, calling out, until at
last he determined to stop and wait for her. Then she addressed him with loving and tender words, saying,—"Coniraya, do you wish that I should comb your head and pick
out the lice?" So he consented, and reclined his head on
her lap; but while she was pretending to do this, she was
forming a rock over which she might hurl him when he was
off his guard. He knew this through his great wisdom, and
told her he must retire for a few minutes. She agreed to
this; and he went back to the land of Huarochiri, where he
wandered about for a long time, playing tricks both to whole
villages and to single men or women. The end of this
huaca will be related presently.

The above traditions are so rooted in the hearts of the
people of this province at the present time that they preserve them most inviolably; and thus they hold the condors
to be sacred, and never kill one, believing that he who kills
one will die himself. I know that there was a condor in
the ravine of San Damian, near the bridge, which was
unable to fly from extreme old age; but there was not an
Indian who would touch it, and it lived there for thirteen
or fourteen years. When I had killed some of these condors, the people asked me how it was that I dared to do so,
but I did not understand why they should ask the question
until I had heard this fable. They also have a great horror
of the small fox; and they do to the lion all that was
ordained in the blessing of Coniraya, bringing out the skin
on great occasions, while he who owns it kills a llama. I
have often seen this done in my own parish in Huarochiri,
on occasion of the drinking bouts called *Huantachinaca*.[5]

Also as regards the fox, I have seen, in the village of San
Juan, near that of Santa Ana, because one man cried out

---

[5] Or *Ayrihua*. A harvest dance. The *huantay-sara* was the fertile
stalk of maize round which the dance was performed.

that he saw a fox, the whole village turned out, and ran in chase of it without knowing where it was, but all following the first, and I after them to see what was the matter. I have seen this happen twice in that village, and the same custom prevails in the others.

As to the falcon, there is scarcely a festival in which one does not appear on the heads of the dancers and singers; and we all know that they detest the parrots, which is not wonderful considering the mischief they do, though their chief reason is to comply with the tradition.

Who will not grieve at the blindness of these poor people, and at the small fruit which the preaching of the Catholic truth has borne during so many years. Yet they can neither plead ignorance, nor can they complain that they have not been taught. It is true that in some parishes the priests have been negligent in teaching, but in others it is not so; and we have seen that the people are as much and more attached to their errors in those parishes where the preaching has been attended to, as in those where it has been neglected.

CHAPTER III.

Of an eclipse of the Sun which is said to have taken place in ancient times.

In all the stories and fables of these people I have never been able to make out which came first, or in what order they should be placed, for they are all very ancient traditions. They relate that, a long time ago, the sun disappeared and the world was dark for a space of five days; that the stones knocked one against the other; and that the mortars, which they call *mutca*, and the pestles called *marop*, rose against their masters, who were also attacked by their sheep, both those fastened in the houses and those in the fields. This

may have been the eclipse which occurred when our Re-
deemer died ; but I cannot clearly make this out, for when
it was day in that hemisphere it was night here, so that
here the eclipse would have taken place at night. The rest
of the story consists of lies, for, as these people had no
watches, how could they tell that the sun was absent for
five days, seeing that we count days by the absence and
presence of the sun ?

CHAPTER IV.

Of a deluge which is said to have taken place ; with a refutation of all
the preceding fables.

It is necessary to go back a step in this chapter, for this
should be the third, and the preceding chapter the fourth.
For what I have to mention here is a saying of the Indians
which is more ancient than the eclipse. They relate that
there was nearly an end to the world, which happened in
the following way : An Indian was tethering his llama in a
place where there was good pasture, and the animal resisted,
showing sorrow and moaning after its manner, which it does
by crying *yu' yu'*. The master, who happened to be eating
a *choclo*, observing this, threw the core (which they call
coronta) at the llama, saying, "Fool, why do you moan and
refrain from eating ? Have I not put you where there is
good pasture ?" The llama thus replied : "Madman ! what
do you know, and what can you suppose ? Learn that I am
not sad without good cause ; for within five days the sea
will rise and cover the whole earth, destroying all there is
upon it." The man, wondering that his llama should speak,
answered it by asking whether there was any way by which
they could save themselves. The llama then said that the
man must follow it quickly to the summit of a high moun-

tain called Villca-coto, which is between this parish[6] and San Geronimo de Surco, taking with him food for five days, and that he might thus be saved. The man did as he was told, carrying his load on his back and leading the llama, and he arrived on the summit of the mountain, where he found many different kinds of birds and animals assembled. Just as he and his llama reached the top the sea began to rise, and the water filled the valleys and covered the tops of the hills, except that of Villca-coto; but the animals were crowded together, for the water rose so high that some of them could hardly find foothold. Among these was a fox, whose tail was washed by the waves, which they say is the reason that the tips of foxes' tails are black. At the end of five days the waters began to abate, and the sea returned to its former bounds; but the whole earth was without inhabitants except that solitary man, from whom, they say, descend all the people who now exist. This is a notable absurdity, for they do not say that any woman was saved; and they make out that the man had intercourse with some devil; and, as the commentator of the books of the city of God (Lib. xv. cap. 23) says, they glory and rejoice, like some others of those times, at being the sons of a demon. The Egyptians denied that a man could have connection with a demon, though they affirmed that it was possible with a female demon; but the Greeks related stories of many men having been, with this object, beloved by the Devil, such as Hyacynto, Phæbus, Hypolito, all of whom the Devil loved.

According to the most certain and true opinion there could not have been inhabitants in this land before the universal deluge; for as it is certain that all men sprang from our father Adam, and that in the period between Adam and Noah so wide a dispersion could not have taken place, how is it possible that these Indians can have had

[6] San Damian.

any knowledge of the deluge? They declare that, in the days of Coniraya Uiracocha, their country was *yunca*, and that the crops ripened in five days. This is also impossible, for the situation of this province is the same as that of all the country which slopes from the snowy chain of mountains to the sea, from Pasto to Chile, a distance of more than twelve hundred leagues. If this small portion was ever *yunca*, the whole of the rest of that region which slopes towards the sea must also have been *yunca*, which the people deny; therefore this district cannot have been so. For there cannot have been a change of climate affecting this small district without breaking the chain of mountains, and then continuing it again, which is absurd. How, too, could they know this if, as they say, it was before the deluge, when there can then have been no inhabitants; and if the deluge, as is certain, destroyed all, including even the llama on Villca-coto?[7]

It is certain that there were no inhabitants in this land until many days and years after the deluge; for it was necessary that the descendants of those who were saved in the ark should spread themselves to the new world, and it is certain that they cannot have handed down these fables to their sons. It follows that the Devil, who has been so great a lord over these people, made them believe in lies, and in the matter of the deluge told them about the llama that spoke, the fox that wetted its tail, and the other stories. If any Indian would object that, if there was no *yunca* in Parracaca, how is it that there are remains and ruins of farms and cultivation? I reply that, God permitting, the Devil could easily make those terraces to deceive those who, leaving the natural light of God, served him.

[7] The origin of the tradition is clear enough. The people of Huarochiri originally came from the coast, and hence they said that the land of their ancestors was hot.

CHAPTER V.

Relates who was Huathiacuri, and how a certain man made himself a God, and perished; also of the origin of Pariacaca and his brothers.

We have related the most ancient traditions of these people, and how they assert that, after the deluge, they were all descended from that one man. It must now be understood that in the time after the deluge, in every district, the Indians chose the richest and most valiant man among them for their leader, and this period they call *Purunpacha*,[8] which means the time when there was no king. They say that in those days there appeared five large eggs on a mountain between Huarochiri and Chorrillo, towards the south, (and this is the origin of *Pariacaca*) called Condorcoto. At that time there lived a poor and ill-clad Indian named *Huathiacuri*, who, they say, was a son of Pariacaca, and who learnt many arts from his father. They say that he was called Huathiacuri because his food was all *huatyasca*, which means parboiled, not properly cooked, or, as we say here, roasted " *en barbacoa*." Being poor, he could afford nothing better. At the same time they say that a very rich and great lord had his house on Anchicocha, about a league and a half from the place where the five eggs appeared. His house was very richly and curiously adorned, for the roof was made of the yellow and red feathers of certain birds, and the walls were covered with similar and even more curious materials. This lord had a great number of llamas—some red, others blue and yellow and of other bright colours, so that, to make mantles, it was unnecessary to dye the wool, and he had many other kinds of riches. For these reasons people came to him from all directions to pay their respects; and he made himself to be very wise, even saying that he was the God and Creator. But at last

[8] See page 70.

a great misfortune befell him, which was that he fell sick of
a tedious and disgusting disease, and everybody wondered
that a man who was so wise and rich, and was a God and
Creator, should be so ill and be unable to cure himself. So
they began to murmur against him. During all this time
the pretended God did not fail to seek for remedies, trying
various cures, procuring extraordinary medicines, and sending for all who had any knowledge of the healing art. But
all was of no avail, and there was no man who understood
either the disease or the cure. At this time they say that
Huathiacuri journeyed towards the sea, and slept on that
height, called Latallaco, where the ascent commences in
going from Lima to Cienequilla. While he was there he
saw a fox going towards the sea, and another coming from
the coast towards Anchicocha. The one coming from the
sea asked the other whether there was any news, and the
other answered that "all was well except that the rich man
was very sick, and was taking extraordinary pains to get
cured, and to assemble learned men who could tell him the
cause of his illness, and that no one understood it. But,"
added the fox, "the real cause is that, when his wife was
toasting a little maize, one grain fell on her skirt, as happens every day. She gave it to a man who ate it, and
afterwards she committed adultery with him. This is the
reason that the rich man is sick, and a serpent is now
hovering over his beautiful house to eat it, while a toad
with two heads is waiting under his grinding-stone with
the same object. But no one knows this," concluded the
fox ; and it then asked the other fox whether it had any
news. The other fox replied that a very beautiful daughter
of a great chief was dying for having had connection with a
man. But this is a long story, which I shall tell presently;
and now we will return to the proceedings of Huathiacuri.

Having heard what the foxes said, he went to the place
where the rich man was lying sick, and, with much dissimu-

lation, he asked a young and beautiful girl (who, with another elder sister already married, was daughter to the sick God) if any one was ill. She said, " Yes, my father is sick." He replied : " If you will consent to show me favour and to love me, I will cure your father." The name of this girl is not known, although some say that she is the same who was called *Chaupiñaca*. But she did not wish to consent, so she went to her father and told him that a dirty ragged man said he could cure him. Then all the wise men who were assembled laughed heartily, saying that none of them could effect a cure, and how much less could this poor wretch succeed. But the sick man, by reason of his earnest desire to be cured, did not refuse to place himself in the hands of the stranger, and ordered that he should be called in, whoever he might be. He entered, and said that he could certainly effect a cure if the sick man would give his young daughter to him for a wife. The sick man replied that he would willingly do so ; which the husband of his elder daughter took very ill, holding it to be a shame that his sister-in-law should be the wife of so poor a man, who would thus appear to be the equal of himself, being rich and powerful. The contention between these two will be related presently.

The wise Huathiacuri commenced the cure by saying— " Do you know that your wife has committed adultery, and that this is the reason of your sickness ? Do you know that there are two great serpents above your house waiting to eat you ? and that there is a toad with two heads underneath that grind-stone ? Before everything else we must kill those animals, and then you will begin to recover your health. But, when you are well, you must worship and reverence my father, who will appear before many days, for it is quite clear that you are neither God nor Creator. If you were God you would not be ill, nor would you be in need of a cure." The sick man and those who stood round were astonished.

The wife said that the accusation against her was a wicked
lie, and she began to shout with rage and fury. But the
sick man was so desirous to be cured that he ordered search
to be made, and they found the two serpents on the top of
the house and killed them. Then the sage reminded the
wife that when she was toasting maize one grain had fallen
on her skirt; that she had given it to a man; and that
afterwards she had committed adultery with him. So she
confessed. The sage then caused the grindstone to be
raised, and there hopped from underneath a toad with two
heads, which went to a spring that now flows by Anchicocha,
where they say that it still lives, making those who go to
it lose their way, and become mad, and die. Having done
all this, the sick man became well, and the wise Huathiacuri
enjoyed the girl. They say that he generally went once a
day to that mountian of Condor-coto where were the five
eggs, round which a wind blew, and they say that before
this there was no wind. When the sage wanted to go to
Condorcoto, the sick man, now recovered, gave him his
daughter to take with him, and there the pair enjoyed
themselves much to their own satisfaction.

To return to the brother-in-law of the girl, that rich man
who, as we have said, was displeased that she should be
given to Huathiacuri,—he was very angry when he was told
that Huathiacuri had enjoyed her, and declared that he was
a poor wretch and not a sage. He resolved to make others
think this. So one day he said to Huathiacuri, "Brother, I
am concerned that you, as my brother-in-law, should be
ragged and poor, when I am so rich and powerful and so
honoured by the people. Let us choose something at which
we may compete, that one may overcome the other." Hua-
thicuri accepted the challenge. Then he took the road to
Condorcoto, and went to the place where his father Parracaca was in one of the eggs, and told him what had taken
place. Pariacaca said that it was well to accept any chal-

lenge, and that he should come back and tell him what it was. So with this advice Huathiacuri returned to the village.

One day his brother-in-law said—" Now let us see which can vanquish the other in drinking and dancing on such a day." So Huathiacuri accepted the challenge, and posted off to his father Pariacaca, who told him to go to a neighbouring mountain, where he would turn into a dead huanacu. Next morning a fox with its vixen would come to the place, bringing a jar of chicha on her back, while the fox would have a flute of many pipes called *astara*. These would have to approach Pariacaca, because the object of their coming was to give him drink, and to play and dance a little; but when they should see the dead huanacu on the road, they would not wish to lose the opportunity of filling their stomachs; and that they would put down the chicha, the drum, and the flute, and would begin to eat; that then he would come to himself and return to his own shape, and begin to cry aloud, at which the foxes would take to flight, and that he would then take the things they had left behind, and might be sure of victory in the challenge with his brother-in-law.

All this happened as Pariacaca had said; and Huathiacuri went to the place where his brother-in-law was drinking to those who stood round with great quantities of chicha, and was dancing with many of his friends. His drums were beaten by more than two hundred women. While this was going on Huathiacuri entered with his wife, dancing with her, and she charging his cup and playing on a drum. At the first sound of her drum the whole earth began to shake, as if it was keeping time to the music, so that they had the advantage of the rich man, for not only the people but the earth itself danced. Presently they went to the place where they kept the drinking bouts, and the brother-in-law and all his friends came to beat Huathiacuri in drinking, thinking

that it was impossible for him to drink alone as much as the
rich man and all his friends. But they were deceived, for
he drank all they gave him without showing a sign of having had enough. Then he rose and began to drink to those
who were seated, his wife filling the cups with chicha from
the fox's jug. They laughed, because they thought that
before he had given cups to two of them the jug would be
empty; but the chicha never failed, and each man that
drank fell down in a state of intoxication. So in this also
he came out as a conqueror.

When the brother-in-law saw how badly he came out of
this encounter he determined to try another, which was that
each should come dressed in festive attire, with splendid
plumes of various colours. Huathiacuri accepted this challenge also, and went for help to his father Pariacaca, who
dressed him in a shirt of snow, and so he vanquished his
brother-in-law once more.

Then the brother-in-law challenged him once more, saying that people should now see who could enter the public
square, with the best lion-skin on his shoulders, for dancing.
Huathiacuri went again to his father Pariacaca, who sent
him to a fountain, where he said he would find a red lion-
skin with which to meet the challenge; and when he entered the square, men saw that there was a rainbow round
the lion's head; so Huathiacuri again obtained a victory.

Still the conquered brother-in-law was determined to
have a final trial. This was a challenge for each to build a
house in the shortest time and in the best manner. Huathiacuri accepted it; and the rich man at once began to
collect his numerous vassals, and in one day he had nearly
finished the walls, while Huathiacuri, with only his wife to
help him, had scarcely begun the foundations. During the
night the work of the rich man was stopped, but not that
of Huathiacuri. For, in perfect silence, an infinite number
of birds, snakes, and lizards completed the work, so that in

the morning the house was finished, and the rich man was vanquished, to the great wonder of all beholders. Then a great multitude of huanacus and vicuñas came next day laden with straw for the roof; while llamas came with similar loads for the rich man's roof. But Huathiacuri ordered an animal that shrieks loudly, called *oscollo*,[9] to station itself at a certain point ; and it suddenly began to scream in such a way as to terrify the llamas, which shook off their loads, and all the straw was lost.

At the end of this competition Huathiacuri, by advice of his father Pariacaca, determined to put an end to the affair; so he said to the rich man, " Brother, now you have seen that I have agreed to everything that you have proposed. It is reasonable, therefore, that you should now do the same; and I propose that we should both see who dances best, in a blue shirt with a white cotton *huara* round the loins. The rich man accepted the challenge, and, as usual, was the first to appear in the public square, in the proposed dress. Presently Huathiacuri also appeared, and, with a sudden shout, he ran into the place where the other was dancing; and he, alarmed at the cry and the sudden rush, began to run, insomuch as, to give him more speed, he turned, or was turned by Huathiacuri, into a deer. In this form he came to Anchicocha, where, when his wife saw it, she also rose up saying, " Why do I remain here ? I must go after my husband and die with him." So she began to run after him, and Huathiacuri after both. At last Huathiacuri overtook the wife in Anchicocha, and said to her, " Traitress ! it is by your advice that your husband has challenged me to so many proofs, and has tried my patience in so many ways. Now I will pay you for this by turning you into a stone, with your head on the ground and your feet in the air." This happened as he said, and the stone is there to this day ; and the Indians go there to

[9] A wild cat.

worship and to offer coca, and practise other diabolical superstitions. Thus the woman was stopped; but the deer ran on and disappeared, and it maintained itself by eating people; but after some time the deer began to be eaten by men, and not men by deer.

They say that those five eggs in Condorcoto, one of which contained Pariacaca, opened, and five falcons issued from them, who were presently turned into five men, who went about performing wonderful miracles; and one was that the rich Indian, whom we have mentioned in this chapter as having pretended to be God, perished, because Pariacaca and the others raised a great storm and a flood which carried him and his house and wife and family away into the sea. The site of this man's house is between two very lofty mountains, the one called *Vicocha*, near the parish of *Chorrillo*, and the other *Llantapa*, in the parish of *San Damian*, and between them flows the river of Pachacamac. There was a sort of bridge, consisting of a great tree called *pullao*, forming a most beautiful arch from one hill to the other, where a great variety of parrots and other birds passed to and fro. All this was swept away by the flood.

CHAPTER VI.

Having come forth from the five eggs with his four brothers, and having caused the above tempest, Pariacaca aspired to perform great and mighty deeds throughout the world, though the region he traversed did not exceed twenty leagues in circuit. Especially he conceived the idea of encountering the valiant Caruyuchu Huayallo, to whom they sacrificed children, as we have related in the first chapter. So Pariacaca went in search of Caruyuchu, of whose end and defeat I shall speak presently; but first I must relate what happened to Pariacaca on the road.

On his way from Condorcoto to the residence of Caruyu-chu, he came to the place where now stands the village of Santa Maria de Jesus de Huarochiri, at the bottom of the ravine in which the river flows, and by which one goes to the parish of Quinti.[1] Here there was a village called Huagaihusa, where they were celebrating a great festival. It is to be noted that all this country was then *yunca*, with a hot climate, according to the false opinion of the Indians. Pariacaca entered the place, where all the people were drinking, in the dress of a poor man, and he sat down with the others, but at the end of all, as is the custom with those who are not invited. But no man drank to him nor gave him to drink during the whole day. Seeing this, a girl was moved with pity and compassion, and she said, "How is it that no one gives a drink to this poor man or takes any notice of him?" and she put a good draught of chicha into one of those large white calabashes called by the Indians *putu*, and took it to Pariacaca, who received it with thanks, and told her she had done a very good deed, and had gained his friendship. "This," he added, "is worth to you the same as your life, for at the end of five days wonderful things will happen in this place, and none of the inhabitants shall remain alive, for their neglect has enraged me. You must put yourself in safety on that day, with your children, that you may not share their fate; but if you reveal this secret to any other inhabitant of the village, your death is also inevitable."

The woman was thankful at receiving this warning, and on the fifth day she took good care to go far away from the village with her children, brothers, and relations; leaving the rest of the inhabitants off their guard, and still engaged in drinking and feasting. But the enraged Pariacaca had ascended a high mountain called Matro-coto, which over-hangs the village of Huarochiri, and below which there is

[6] San Lorenzo de Quinti.

another mountain peak called Puipu-Huana, which is on the road from San Damian to Huarochiri. Then an enormous quantity of rain began to fall, with hail and yellow and white stones, which carried the village away into the sea, so that no man escaped. This flood is still a tradition among the people of Huarochiri, and some high banks were left, which may be seen before arriving at the village. Having completed this work, Pariacaca, without speaking to any-one in the other villages, or communicating with them, crossed over to the other side of the river, where he did what I shall describe in the following chapter.

CHAPTER VII.

How Pariacaca gave water in abundance to the Indians of the Ayllu Copara, for their fields; how he became enamoured of Choque Suso, an idol which is still very famous.

Having crossed the river, Pariacaca travelled over the fields which now belong to the Ayllu Copara, and which then were in great want of water for irrigation. They did not then procure it from the river, but from a spring on the mountain called Sienacaca, which overhangs the village now called San Lorenzo.[2] A large dam was built across this spring, and other smaller dams were thrown across it lower down, by which means the fields were irrigated. In those days there was a very beautiful girl belonging to the Ayllu Copara, who, seeing one day that the maize crop was drying up for want of water, began to weep at the small supply that came from one of the smaller dams she had opened. Pariacaca happened to be passing by, and, seeing her he was captivated by her charms. He went to the dam, and taking off his *yacolla* or cloak, he used it to stop

---

[2] San Lorenzo de Quinti.

up the drain that the girl had made. He then went down
to where she was trying to irrigate the fields, and she, if
she was afflicted before, was much more so now, when she
found that there was no water flowing at all. Pariacaca
asked her, in very loving and tender words, why she was
weeping, and she, without knowing who he was, thus
answered :—" My father, I weep because this crop of maize
will be lost and is drying up for lack of water." He replied
that she might console herself and take no further thought,
for that she had gained what he had lost, namely, his love ;
and that he would make the dam yield more than enough
water to irrigate her crop. Choque-suso told him first to
produce the water in abundance, and that afterwards she
promised willingly to yield to his wishes. Then he went up
to the dam, and, on opening the channel, such a quantity of
water flowed out, that it sufficed to irrigate the thirsty
fields, and to satisfy the damsel. But when Pariacaca asked
her to comply with her promise, she said that there was
plenty of time to think about that.   He was eager and
ardent in his love, and he promised her many things, among
others to conduct a channel from the river which should
suffice to irrigate all the farms. She accepted this promise,
saying that she must first see the water flowing, and that
afterwards she would let him do what he liked.

He then examined the country, to see whence he could
draw the water ; and he observed that above the site of the
present village of San Lorenzo (in which that Ayllu Copara
now resides) a very small rill came from the ravine of *Coca-
challa*, the waters of which did not flow beyond a dam which
had been thrown across it. By opening this dam and leading the water onwards, it appeared to Pariacaca that it
would reach the farms of the Ayllu Copara, where were the
fields of his lady-love. So he ordered all the birds in those
hills and trees to assemble, together with all the snakes,
lizards, bears, lions, and other animals ; and to remove the

L

obstruction. This they did; and he then caused them to widen the channel and to make new channels until the water reached the farms. There was a discussion as to who should make the line for the channel, and there were many pretenders to this duty, who wished to show their skill as well as to gain the favour of their employer. But the fox managed, by his cunning, to get the post of engineer; and he carried the line of the canal to the spot just above the present site of the church of San Lorenzo. Then a partridge came flying and making a noise like *Pich-pich*, and the unconscious fox let the water flow off down the hill. So the other labourers were enraged, and ordered the snake to take the fox's place, and to proceed with what he had begun. But he did not perform the work so well as the fox; and the people to this day deplore that the fox should have been superseded, saying that the channel would have been higher up and better, if this had not taken place : and because the course of the channel is broken, just above the church, they say that is the place where the fox let the water flow off, and which has never since been repaired.

Having brought the water to irrigate the farms in the way that is still working, Pariacaca besought the damsel to keep her promise, and she consented with a good grace, but proposed that they should go to the summit of some rocks called *Yanacaca*.[3] This they did, and there Pariacaca obtained his desires, and she was well repaid for her love when she knew who he was. She would never let him go anywhere alone, but always desired to accompany him; and he took her to the head-works of the irrigating channel, which he had constructed for her love. There she felt a strong wish to remain, and he again consented, so she was converted into a stone, while Pariacaca went up the mountains. Thus Choque Suso was turned into a stone at the head of the channel, which is called Cocochalla.

[3] *Yana*, black. *Caca*, a rock.

Above this channel there is another called *Vim-lompa*,[4] where there is another stone, into which they say *Coniraya* was turned.

CHAPTER VIII.

How the Indians of the Ayllu of Copara still worship Choque Suso and this channel, a fact which I know not only from their stories, but also from judicial depositions which I have taken on the subject.

(Here was to be added that which I saw, and the story of the hair of *Choque Suso*, and the rest of the depositions that were taken, concerning this irrigating channel.)

HERE THE MANUSCRIPT ENDS ABRUPTLY.

[4] Corrupt.

REPORT

POLO DE ONDEGARDO.

Written in a memorandum book, apparently as a rough Draft, among
the papers of the Licenciate Polo de Ondegardo.

(Manuscript in the National Library at Madrid. 4to, on parchment, B. 135.)

REPORT

POLO DE ONDEGARDO.

Of the Lineage of the Yncas, and how they Extended their Conquests.

It must be understood, in the first place, that the lineage of these Yncas was divided into two branches, the one called Hanan Cuzco, and the other Hurin Cuzco. From this it may be concluded (and there is no memory of anything to the contrary) that they were natives of the valley of Cuzco, although some pretend that they came from other parts to settle there. But no credit should be given to them, for they also say that this happened before the flood. From what can be gathered and conjectured in considering the traditions of the present time, it is not more than three hundred and fifty to four hundred years since the Yncas only possessed and ruled over the valley of Cuzco as far as Urcos, a distance of six leagues, and to the valley of Yucay, which is not more than five leagues.

Touching the Lords that the people can remember, their recollection does not carry them back beyond the time already stated. They preserve the memory of these Lords by their *quipus*, but if we judge by the time that each is said to have lived, the historical period cannot be placed further back than four hundred years at the earliest.

It must have been at about that period that they began to dominate and conquer in the districts round Cuzco,

and, as would appear from their records, they were sometimes defeated. For, although Andahuaylas, in the province
of the Chancas, is only thirty leagues from Cuzco, they did
not bring it under their sway until the time of Pachacutec
Yupanqui Ynca, who defeated those Chancas. The history
of this event is given in the record of the *Pururunas*, or
huacas, which originated and resulted from this battle with
the Chancas, the commencement of all the Ynca victories.[1]
On the other side of Cuzco is the road of Colla-suyu ; and
they also retain a recollection of the time when the Canas
and Canches, whose country is even nearer, were paid to
go with the Yncas to the wars, and not as vassals following
their lords ; and this was in the same battle in which Pachacutec Ynca fought against *Usco-vilca*,[2] Lord of the Chancas. They also recollect the time when they extended their
dominion along this road to the lake of Villca-ñota, the
point where the Collao begins. Two powerful rivers flow
out of this lake, one going to the north sea, and the other
to the south. The lake was worshipped by the natives, and
looked upon as a noted *huaca*. A long interval of time
elapsed before the Yncas advanced beyond this point. It
was the successor of that lord who conquered the Chancas
who began to advance beyond this point, and those provinces had no peace until the time of Tupac Ynca, father of
Huayna Ccapac. We found these wars recorded in the
registers of the Yncas, but each province also had its registers of wars, so that, if it were necessary, we might very
easily fix the time when each province was subjugated by
the Yncas.

But it is enough to understand that these Yncas at first
extended their conquests by violence and war. There was
no general opposition to their advance, for each province

[1] See *G. de la Vega*, ii, p. 57 ; and the present volume, p. 92.
[2] Should be Ancohualla, or Hanco-hualla. See *G. de la Vega*, ii, 58,
82, 329.

merely defended its land without aid from any other ; so
that the only difficulty encountered by the Yncas was in the
annexation of the districts round Cuzco. Afterwards all the
conquered people joined them, so that they always had a
vastly superior force as well as more cunning in the art of
war. Thus it was seldom that they were completely defeated,
although sometimes they were obliged to retreat, and desist
from a war during a year.

No province ever attempted to disturb them in their own
land, only seeking to be left in quiet possession of their
territories, and this seems to me to have been a great advantage to the Yncas. There is no memory of such an
attempt in their registers ; but, after the districts were reduced to obedience, the great natural strength of this region
conduced to its security. The four roads which diverge
from Cuzco are all crossed by rivers that cannot be forded
at any time in the year, while the land is very rugged and
strong. There cannot, therefore, be a doubt that in this,
and in possessing better discipline and more knowledge,
lay the advantage they had over all the other nations of this
region. This superiority is shown in their edifices, bridges,
farms, systems of irrigation, and in their higher moral lives.
If other nations have anything good, it has all been taught
them by the Yncas. The Yncas also had a different system
of warfare, and were better led, so that they could not fail
to become lords over the rest. Thus they continued to extend
their dominions and to subjugate their neighbours.

The second thing that may be taken for granted is that
having resolved to conquer and subjugate other nations, the
Yncas sought some colour and pretext for prosecuting their
objects. The first story that these Yncas put forward,
though it was not the title which they finally asserted, was
an idea that, after the deluge, seven men and women had
come out of a cave which they call *Paccari-tampu*, five leagues
from Cuzco, where a window was carved in masonry in most

ancient times; that these persons multiplied and spread
over the world. Hence every province had a like place of
worship where people came forth after the universal destruction; and these places were pointed out by their old men and
wizards, who taught them why and how the Yncas venerated
the cave of *Paccari-tampu*. Thus in every province these
places of worship are to be found, each one with a different
tale attached to it.

With this title the Yncas were for a long time unable to
conquer more than the provinces bordering on Cuzco until
the time of Pachacuti Ynca Yupanqui. His father had been
defeated by the Chancas, and retreated to Cuzco, leaving
his troops in a *Pucara* or fortress. Then the son formed an
army out of the fugitives, and out of the garrison of Cuzco,
and out of the men of Canes and Canches, and turned back
to attack the Chancas. Before he set out his mother had a
dream that the reason of the victory of the Chancas was
that more veneration was shown for the Sun than *Pachayachachic*, who was the universal Creator. Henceforward a
promise was made that more sacrifices and prayers should
be offered to that statue. Then the son was promised a
victory over the Chancas, and that men should be sent from
Heaven to reinforce him. With this title he went forth
and conquered, and thence arose that idea of the *Pururaucas*,
which was one which was most important for the Yncas as a
title in extending their conquests . . . . . sacrifices of many
kinds were continually invented, and all who were subjugated
were taught that Cuzco was the abode and home of the
gods. Throughout that city there was not a fountain, nor
a well, nor a wall, which they did not say contained some
mystery, as appears in the report on the places of worship
in that city, where more than four hundred such places are
enumerated. All this continued until the arrival of the
Spaniards; and even now all the people venerate the
huacas given them by the Yncas.

The third thing to be understood is that as soon as the Yncas had made themselves lords of a province, they caused the natives, who had previously been widely scattered, to live in communities, with an officer over every ten, another over every hundred, another over every thousand, another over every ten thousand, and an Ynca governor over all, who reported upon the administration every year, recording the births and the deaths that had occurred among men and flocks, the yield of the crops, and all other details, with great minuteness. They left Cuzco every year, and returned in February to make their report, before the festival of Raymi began, bringing with them the tribute of the whole empire. This system was advantageous and good, and it was most important in maintaining the authority of the Yncas. Every governor, how great lord soever he might be, entered Cuzco with a burden on his back. This was a ceremony that was never dispensed with, and it gave great authority to the Yncas.

The fourth thing is that in every place where a settlement or village community was formed, the land was divided in the following manner : one portion was set apart for the support of religion, being divided between the Sun and the *Pachayachachic*, and the thunder, which they called *Chuquilla*, and the *Pacha-mama* and their ministers, and other *huacas* and places of worship, both general and such as were peculiar to each village. It would take long to enumerate them, for they were so numerous that, if they had had nothing else to do, the sacrifices alone would have given them occupation. For each town was divided in the same way as Cuzco, and every notable thing was made an object of worship, such as springs, fountains, streams, stones, valleys, and hill summits, which they called *apachetas*. Each of these things had its people whose duty it was to perform the sacrifices, and who were taught when to sacrifice and what kind of things to offer up. Although in no part were there so many objects

of worship as in Cuzco, yet the order and manner of worshipping was the same.

A knowledge of the *huacas* and places of worship is very
important for the work of conversion. I have a knowledge
of them in more than a hundred villages ; and when the
Lord Bishop of Charcas doubted whether the custom was
so universal, at a time when we were in a joint commission by order of his Majesty, I showed him the truth of
it in Cuzco. And although the discovery of these things
has taken time, yet it has been necessary as regards the
question of tribute and contributions. For a very large
portion of the harvests was set apart for this service, and
stored in places prepared for the purpose. Part was ex-
pended on the sacrifices of the villages, and a larger share
was taken to Cuzco from all parts. The portions thus set
apart were from a third to a fourth, varying in different districts. In many villages all belonged to the Sun, such as
in *Arapa* and others. In these the greater part was devoted to sacrifices, in others (belonging to the Ynca) not
so much.

Another share of the produce was reserved for the Ynca.
This was stored in the granaries or sent to Cuzco, according to the necessities of the Government. For it was not
always disposed of in the same way. The Ynca supplied
with food all his garrisons, his servants, his relations, and
the chiefs who attended upon him, out of this share of the
tribute, which was brought to Cuzco from all parts of the
country. In time of war the provisions from some parts
were sent to others, in addition to the ordinary consump-
tion, and there was such order in these arrangements that
no mistake ever occurred. Sometimes the stores were sent
from the magazines in the mountains to the coast, at others
from the coast to the interior, according to the exigencies
of each case, and this was done with never-failing speed and
exactness. When there was no demand the stores remained

in the magazines, and occasionally there was an accumulation sufficient for ten years.

There can be no doubt that this share of the Ynca was well managed. I visited many of the store-houses in different parts, and they were, without comparison, larger and better than those set apart for the service of religion.

The lands set apart for the tribute of the Ynca and of religion were sown and reaped in the same order; but it must be understood that when the people worked upon them, they ate and drank at the cost of the Ynca and of the Sun. This work was not performed by gangs, nor were the men told off for it, but all the inhabitants went forth except the aged and infirm, dressed in their best clothes, and singing songs appropriate for the occasion. In these two kinds of tribute there were two things that seem worthy of note. One is that the aged, infirm, and widows did not join in it. The other is, that although the crops and other produce of these lands were devoted to the tribute, the land itself belonged to the people themselves. Hence a thing will be apparent which has not hitherto been properly understood. When any one[3] wants land, it is considered sufficient if it can be shown that it belonged to the Ynca or to the Sun. But in this the Indians are treated with great injustice. For in those days they paid the tribute, and the land was theirs; but now, if it is found convenient to tax them in some other way, it is clear that they will pay double tribute—in one way by being deprived of their land, and in another by having to pay the tax in the form that may be now fixed. If any one, as is often done, sets up a claim by saying the Ynca had power to appropriate the land, the injustice and wrong is all the greater; because if such was the right, his Majesty succeeds to it; and, as regards *encomiendas* for a life or lives, it is clear that it is not the intention to grant them, nor is it just as regards the estate

[3] That is, any Spanish settler.

of the Ynca. .Such tribute or tax was levied by the Ynca as King and Lord, and not as a private person. Hence arose a notable mistake. It was declared that all the farms of *coca* belonged to the Ynca, which was true, and therefore they appertain to his Majesty. He could grant them in *encomienda,* and resume them at the end of the term, if he so pleased, as is the case with the *alcabalas* of Valladolid. The Fiscal exerted himself to prove that the farms belonged to the Ynca, and that the *encomienda* only extended to the Indians, and this was through not comprehending the nature of the tribute that was given to the Ynca. In effect the Ynca took the produce of all the *coca* farms throughout the Andes for his own use, except a few small patches granted to chiefs and *camayus*.[4] All the rest was taken to Cuzco, but there was not then so much as there is now, nor one fiftieth part; for in this too the reports were deceptive, as I have more particularly shown in my report on the *coca*.

The Ynca did the same with all the males in the flocks, which were appropriated for the service of himself and of religion, being left, however, in the same district where they were bred, and merely counted. No female was included in the tribute. The pastures and hunting-grounds were demarcated, that the flocks might not be passed from one province to another; but that each might have its assigned limits. This rule has also given rise to pretensions on the part of some, to the flocks, on the ground that they belonged to the Sun or the Ynca; and, before order was established, a great quantity was seized on this pretext. It is very certain that if his Majesty took the tribute of the flocks, he would not wish that it should be given out of what the Indians held as their own, and enjoyed as such; but only from that which belonged to him, from having been given by them to the Ynca and to religion.

After I had become thoroughly acquainted with the sub-

---

[4] Officials.

ject, I severely censured some who took a quantity of flocks from the *Aymaraes* and other parts, on this pretext. But, on an appeal to the Audiencia, it was permitted on the ground that his Majesty succeeded to the right.

It was not all the flocks that were treated in this way; for a portion, though a small one, was left to the district, and another to the chief, who afterwards granted some to his servants. Those belonging to religion and to the Ynca were called *Ccapac-llama*, and the others *Huachay-llama;* which means rich and poor beasts. A division was prohibited, and to this day they are all enjoyed in common.

In the matter of the flocks they made many rules, some of which were so conducive to their preservation that it would be well if they were still observed. It may be said that, in a great part of the kingdom, the people are maintained by the flocks. They flourish in the coldest regions, and there also the Indians are settled, as in all parts of the Collao, and on the sides towards Arequipa and the coast, as well as throughout *Carancas, Aullagas, Quilluas,* and *Collahuas.* All those districts, if it were not for the flocks, might be looked upon as uninhabitable; for though they yield *papas, quinuas,* and *ocas,* it is an usual thing for three out of five years to be without harvests, and there is no other kind of produce. But, by reason of the flocks, they are richer and can dress better than those who live in fertile districts. They are very healthy, and their villages are more populous than those in the warm lands, and the latter are even more frequently without their own products, than those who possess flocks. For the flocks are sent down with wool, and return laden with maize, *aji,* and pulses. This is the reason that, in the rules, a hundred Indians of the barren land, though they be far from the mines, give more than two hundred from the fertile land. Then Indians who take their flocks to Potosi gain more in a month than any other ten in a year, and they return with their flocks improved.

There was a rule that females should never be killed, and thus the flocks multiplied exceedingly, for neither were those of the Ynca or of religion killed except for sacrifices. If any beast was attacked with *carache*,[5] which is the disease by which so many have been lost in our times, the rule was that they should not be fed or cured, but buried at once, deep in the ground, as the disease was infectious.

The flock of the community was shorn at the proper season, and the wool was divided amongst the people, each getting the quantity he required for himself, his wife, and children ;. so that all were clothed. A portion of the flocks of the Ynca and of religion were also shorn, and cloth was made out of the wool and taken to Cuzço, for the use of the Ynca, and for the sacrifices. It was also used for clothing the attendants of the Ynca, or was stored in the magazines. Thus in each village they had workmen, called *cumpicos,* to weave the rich cloth which they made in great quantities. The store-houses were quite full of cloth when the Spaniards came, as well as with all other things necessary to sustain life and for war.

One thing should here be noted, which is that when they distributed the cloth to each man according to the quantity required for clothing his family, no account was taken of what such a person might have of his own, because he was supposed to enjoy this without prejudice to his enjoying his share with the rest, even if a family possessed a large quantity. It is important to decide how this tribute may now be taken, with due regard to justice, from the estates of religion, of the Ynca, and of the community. For in the event of there being sufficient for the payment of this class of contribution, and of that which results from it and is made from the wool, but a deficiency under some other class, it would not be reasonable to make up such deficiency by an exaction from every head, which is the way that it is

[5] See *G. de la Vega,* ii, p. 378.

now made up. For if one Indian only has a single head of
flock it will be taken for the tribute, while if another possesses a hundred head no more than one will be taken.
This consideration gave rise to their own custom that no
man should pay tribute from his own personal property, but
only from the work of his hands, all working as a community.
It is clear that the tribute of religion and the Ynca was
levied from the whole community for the public service,
while the private property of each man was held by favour
from the Ynca, and, according to their laws, they had no
other title to it. From this private property no tribute of
any kind was exacted, even when it was considerable in
amount. But all were obliged to do their part in producing
the tribute demanded from the community. It is not
right, therefore, that they should now be taxed by the head,
but rather according to their estates. If there are a thousand
Indians in a *Repartimiento*, among whom there are five
hundred *mitimaes*[6] who never possess any sheep, and if the
tribute amounts to five hundred head, it is impossible to
raise it. Consequently when, by reason of the flocks, the
tribute is to be paid in sheep, it is necessary to ascertain to
whom the sheep belong, and to assess the *mitimaes* and the
natives separately. Thus the difficulty will be overcome,
and the injustice will be avoided. The community is composed of rich and poor, and the tribute of sheep should
be distributed among those who breed them, without including any poor man who happens to have acquired a single
sheep. For this immunity should be granted, and the matter
is of sufficient importance to justify this digression.

The same remark applies to the tax which is exacted
throughout the Collao and the province of Charcas where
they have flocks. This consists in having to convey to
Potosi a quantity of provisions in proportion to the number
of sheep in the flock. This class of tribute was well known

[6] Colonists.

M

in the time of the Yncas, because they carried tribute to
Cuzco on the sheep of the Sun and of the Ynca in great
quantities. But in assessing this burden the *mitimaes* were
treated with great injustice; for, as they were all taxed
together, the natives received their share, and the *mitimaes*
theirs, so that the natives conveyed their provisions on their
beasts, while the *mitimaes* had to carry them on their own
backs, for a distance of forty leagues and more. It is a serious
matter for an Indian to have to carry three *arrobas* on his
back, which is the weight of a *fanega* of flour, besides his
own food, and the loss of time.

The ancient tribute was to sow the crops for the Ynca and
for religion, and to reap them and carry the harvests to the
store-houses, where there was always a superfluity.

Another mistake that has been made in levying taxes,
especially in the Collao, through which the Indians have
been much oppressed, is through their being ordered to pay
a quantity of provisions according to the extent of the land
they possess for sowing with *papas*, from which they make
chuñus. For out of five years, there is but a small yield in
three, so that the Indians have to pay all they possess.
Thus the men and their families suffer throughout the year
by reason of the tribute.

On the death of an owner of land, the heirs and descendants possessed it in common, without the power of dividing
it; but the person who represented the *Ayllu* had the
charge, and all the rest enjoyed the fruits in common, which
were divided among them in the following manner: If a son
of the first possessor had six sons, and another son had two,
each one had equal shares, and there were as many shares
as persons. At the time of sowing they all had to be present to divide the crop; and at the harvest if any one, even
though a descendant, had not been at the sowing, he could
neither take his share nor give it to another. Yet even if
he was absent ten years, he did not lose his right, if he

chose to be at the sowing; and even when there were so many descendants as that there was scarcely a mazorca of maize for each, the rule was still observed; and it is still kept up in the district of Cuzco, where the lands are held in this manner.

This custom of each descendant having a right to a share, should be known when any business connected with the levying of taxes is to be arranged. Thus the lands belonged to the whole village, and he who did not work at the sowing had no share in the harvest.

The reason may now be understood why, in so many lawsuits that are submitted to the Corregidores and Audiencias, scarcely any are between an Indian and another of the same village, but between one village and another.

After the Spaniards came, the Indians continued for a long time to till the lands of the Ynca and of religion, and to store up the harvests according to the old custom, and to burn a portion in sacrifice, believing that a time would come when they would have to give an account to the Ynca. When the President Gasca marched through the valley of Xauxa against Gonzalo Pizarro, I remember that he rested there for seven weeks, and they found stores of maize there for several years, upwards of fifteen thousand *fanegas* near the road. When they understood that these reserved lands might be sown for their own profit, the people of different villages began to sow them, and hence arose many lawsuits.

When people went to work on land out of their own district, it was also for the Ynca and religion, and the land set apart for this was called *suyus*. But there were also some Indians left to irrigate and guard these *suyus*, who, though in a land beyond their own district, were always subject to their chiefs, and not to the chiefs in the land where they resided. These are a different class of men from the *mitimaes*, who were removed from the jurisdiction of the chiefs under whom they were born.

It should be understood how those lands which were tilled belonged to the sowers. In the Collao, where no maize can be raised, the people had lands on the coast, and sent men down to till them, near Arequipa for instance. In the time of the Marquis of Cañete, who was Viceroy of these kingdoms,[7] owing to information which I supplied, these *suyus* were returned as belonging to the province of Chucuito, but all the others suffer by reason of this custom not being understood.

The order which, up to this time, has been adopted for the conversion of the Indians, is for the priests to visit each village, with a book showing who are baptized, who are married, who have more than one wife. Thus the shepherd knows his sheep and is known by them. The ancient custom by which no man moved from his district, was a marvellous aid.

The rules of New Spain, where the country is very populous, are not applicable to this land. This was well understood by that prudent and illustrious worthy Don Antonio de Mendoza,[8] whose memory will long be cherished, and whose loss will be felt more every day by his Majesty and by the people of the Indies. At the end of a year, during which he had studied the affairs of this land, though he was suffering from illness, he said that before issuing any orders it was necessary to do three things—first, to see the country ; second, to know the capacity of the Indians ; and third, to understand their customs, rules, manner of living, and ancient system of taxation. For all this it was necessary that he should have had better health and fewer years.

The order established by the Ynca in matters relating to the chase, was that none should hunt beyond the limits of his own province ; and the object of this was that the game, while proper use was made of it, should be preserved. After

---

[7] From 1555 to 1561.

[8] Viceroy of Peru from 1551 to 1555.

the tribute of the Ynca and of religion had been paid, leave
was given to supply the requirements of the people. Yet
the game multiplied by reason of the regulations for its con-
servation, far more rapidly than it was taken, as is shown
by the registers they kept, although the quantity required
for the service of the Ynca and of religion was enormous.
A regular account was kept of all the hunts, a thing which
it would be difficult for me to believe if I had not seen it.

The Ynca made similar regulations with regard to the
forests, in the districts where they were of any importance.
They were assigned for the use of the regions where there
was a want of fuel, and these forests were called *moyas* of
the Ynca, though they were also for the use of the districts
in the neighbourhood of which they grew. It was ordained
that they should be cut in due order and licence, according
to the requirements. It should therefore be understood
that the pastures, the hunts, and the forests were used in
common under fixed regulations; and the greatest benefit
that his Majesty could confer on these Indians, next to their
conversion, would be to confirm the same order established
by the Yncas, for to frame new rules would be an infinite
labour.

There was another kind of contribution in the time of the
Yncas, which was as heavy and onerous as all the others.
In every province they had a house called *Aclla-huasi*, which
means " the house of the chosen ones," where the following
order was kept : There was a governor in each province
whose sole duty was to attend to the business of these houses,
whose title was *Apu-panaca*. His jurisdiction extended over
one *hunu*, which means ten thousand Indians, and he had
power to select all the girls who appeared to him to be of
promising dispositions, at the ages of eight or nine years,
without any limit as to the number chosen. They were
put into this house in company with a hundred *Mama-cunas*,
who resided there, where they were taught all the accom-

plishments proper for women, such as to sew, to weave, to make the drinks used by the Indians; and their work, in the month of February, at the feast of Raymi, was taken to the city of Cuzco. They were strictly watched until they reached the age of thirteen or fourteen years and upwards, so that they might be virgins when they should arrive at Cuzco, where they assembled in great numbers from all the provinces in the middle of March. The order of distribution was as follows :—

Women were taken for the service of the Sun, and placed in the temples, where they were kept as virgins. In the same order women were given to the service of Pacha-mama, and of other things in their religion. Then others were selected for the sacrifices that were offered in the course of the year, which were numerous. On these occasions they killed the girls, and it was necessary that they should be virgins; besides offering them up at special seasons, such as for the health of the Ynca, for his success in war, for a total eclipse of the sun, on earthquakes, and on many other occasions suggested by the Devil. Others were set apart for the service of the Ynca, and for other persons to whom he showed favour. When any man had received a woman as his legitimate wife or *mamanchu*, he could not take another except through the favour of the Ynca, which was shown for various reasons, either to one who had special skill in any art, or to one who had shown valour in war, or had pleased the Ynca in any other way. The number of women who were set apart for these uses was very great, and they were selected without any regard to whom they belonged, but merely because they were so chosen by the *Apu-panaca*, and the parents could not excuse or redeem them under any circumstances. Estates were set apart for the support of the houses of the chosen ones, and this tribute would have been felt more than any other if it had not been for the belief that the souls of the girls that were sacrificed went to enjoy infinite rest, which was the reason that sometimes they voluntarily offered themselves for sacrifice.

One of the chief articles of tribute was the cloth that was given for the service of the Ynca and of religion. Great quantities of this cloth were distributed by the Ynca among the soldiers, and were given to his relations and attendants. The rest was deposited in the store-houses, and was found there in enormous quantities when the Spaniards arrived in these kingdoms. This cloth was of many textures, according to the uses to be made of it. Large quantities were made of the very rich *cumpi*, woven with two fronts. A more common kind was made for the sacrifices, for in all the festivals much cloth was offered up. For these supplies the beasts of the Ynca were shorn at the proper time, worked up, and sent to Cuzco, with the other tribute, in the month of February, besides what was stored in the magazines, in accordance with the instructions issued in each year.

The beasts required for Cuzco were sent in the same month, in the quantity that had been ordered, all being males, for females were never wasted either for sacrifices or for food. The *Pachayachachic*, whom they held to be the universal Creator, the Sun, the thunder called *Chuquilla*, the *Pachamama*, and an infinite number of other objects of worship, all had their flocks set apart, and the wool from them was distributed in the city of Cuzco for the sacrifices, and to clothe the people who served the *huacas*. A quantity of cloth was also used for the service of the houses where the embalmed bodies of the Lords Yncas were kept. Here also were taken all kinds of food, such as maize, *chuñu*, aji, and every other kind of provision that was raised in the farms. All these things were arranged with such order, that it is difficult to understand how the accounts and registers can have been so well kept.

An immense quantity of personal service from all the provinces was also required in the city of Cuzco, for the Ynca and his court. Every province that was conquered had to send its principal idol to the city of Cuzco, and the same province continued to provide for its service and sacrifices in the same order as when it was in the province.

Another very heavy burden consisted in the supply of men for war, as there were frequent rebellions in various parts of the empire, and it was necessary to guard all the frontiers, especially along the river of Maule in Chile, and on the Bracamoras in the province of Quito, and towards that of Marcas, and in the province of the Chirihuanas, bordering on Charcas, and towards the forests of the Chunchus and Mosus. On all these frontiers we still meet with *pucaras* or fortresses where the garrisons were assembled, with roads leading to them. *Mitimaes* also were sent, from different provinces, to live on these frontiers.

Those who performed special services were exempted from other classes of tribute. There is an example of this in the province of Lucanas, where the people were trained to carry the litter of the Ynca, and had the art of going with a very even and equal pace. In Chumpivilcas the people excelled in dancing, and many were exempted on that account. In the province of Chilcas there is a red wood of excellent quality for carving, and the Chilcas brought it thence to Cuzco, a distance of two hundred leagues, in very great quantities, with many representations carved and painted on it. The wood was burnt for sacrifices in fires kindled in the great square, in presence of the Ynca and of the embalmed bodies of the dead lords. Thus the best product of each province was brought to Cuzco.

In the arrangement of tribute, men were also set apart for the construction of public works, such as bridges and roads. In all the royal roads from Quito to Chile, and still further on to the borders of the government of Benalcazar,[9] and the branch road to Bracamoras, there were *chasquis* stationed at the end of every *tupu*, both on the road of the coast and of the mountains. A *tupu* measures the same as a league and a half. At these points there were small houses adapted to hold two Indians, who served as postmen, and were relieved once a month, and they were there night and day. Their duty was to pass on the messages of the Ynca from Cuzco to any other point, and to bring back those of the governors, so that all the transactions and events of the empire were known. When the Ynca wished to send anything to a governor, he said it to the first *chasqui*, who ran at full speed for a league and a half without stopping, and passed the message to the next as soon as he was within hearing, so that when he reached the post the other man had already started. They say that from Cuzco to Quito, a distance of five hundred leagues, a message was sent and another returned in twenty days. I can believe this, for in our wars we have sometimes used these *chasquis*, and as it was an ancient custom, they readily made the arrangement. In this way letters have been brought from Cuzco to Lima in three days, a distance of a hundred and thirty leagues, over a very bad road. The Yncas also used these *chasquis* to bring up fresh fish from the sea ; and they were brought up, in two days, a distance of a hundred leagues. They have records in their *quipus* of the fish having sometimes been brought from Tumbez, a distance of more than three hundred leagues. The food of the *chasquis* was provided from the store-houses of the Ynca; for those who worked for the Ynca's service, or for religion, never ate at their own expense.

[9] Sebastian de Benalcazar, one of the first conquerors of Peru, and Governor of Popayan.

N

EDIFICES AND FORTRESSES.

One other contribution and tribute in the time of the Yncas imposed heavy labour, and this was the demand for Indians to work at the edifices of Cuzco. This work was very toilsome, for all their buildings were of masonry, and they had no tools of iron or steel, either to hew the stones out of the quarries or to shape them afterwards. All this was done with other stones, which was a labour of extreme difficulty. They did not use lime and sand, but adjusted one stone to another with such precision that the point of junction is scarcely visible. If we consider the number of times they must have fitted and taken off one stone before this accuracy was attained, an idea may be formed of the toil and of the number of workmen that was required. To this labour was added the conveyance of stones from great distances by force of men's arms. Any one who has seen their edifices, will not doubt their statements that thirty thousand men were employed. For not only are these works above the ground, such as those in the city and for-tress, but there is also much well-cut masonry underground, as well hewn as any that can be found in Spain. As they had nothing but stone tools, it seems to me that a hundred Indians could not work and shape a single stone in a month, and any one who likes to look at them will certainly think the same. These edifices are not only in Cuzco, but in many other parts where the work must have been much more heavy and difficult, by reason of the stones being more distant. For at Cuzco, from Santa Ana, which is in Carmenca, where the city commences, to Angostura, there is a distance of three leagues, a little more or less; and within this space all kinds of stone for building are to be found, black and white, hard and soft; and all the stones of the neighbouring hills are excellent for lime and plaster. I have examined the quar-ries, and have seen their ingenious contrivances, in company with dexterous artificers from Spain, and they assured me they had never seen so many kinds of excellent stone within so small a space. He who has seen the work which the Yncas commenced in Tiahuanacu, near Chuqui-apu,[1] and considers that the stone is not met with within a hundred leagues of the spot, will understand the advantage enjoyed by Cuzco.

This service was exacted throughout the kingdom; it being arranged in Cuzco in each year, as regards the number of men to be employed and the work to be done.

NOTE.—This report is incomplete at the end, and the copy at Madrid has been made by a very ignorant clerk who left blank spaces when he did not understand a word or passage.

[1] The modern city of La Paz.

THE END.

INDEX.

I.—SUBJECTS.

Administration (*Civil*), 155, 156 (see *Laws*)

Agriculture. Irrigation, 19; sowing, 19; ploughing, 48; harvest, 52; patronage of, 78; method of labour, 157

Antiquity of Ynca civilization, 151

April. Harvest time, 52

August. Ceremonies in, 20; rains commence, 21

Bathing. At installation of knights, 45

Breeches. Ceremony of conferring knighthood, by giving, 35, 36, 43

Building. Tribute, 170; materials, 171

Cable. Ceremony of, 48, 111 (*note*)

Celibacy of youths, 82 (see *Virgins*)

Ceremonies at festival of the Sun, 17; at the driving forth of evils (*situa*), 21, 24, 26, 33; at the installation of knights, 35-46: of the cable, 48; of the water sacrifice, 50; when a woman conceived, 53; when a child was named, 53; when a girl reached the age of puberty, 53, 80; of worshipping heaps of stones on mountain passes, 78; of coronation, 105

Cloth. Distribution, 160; tribute, 167

Comets, 95 ·

Confession. Custom of, 15

Conquests. Of first Ynca, 76; of Pachacutec, 93-96; progress of by the Yncas, 152 (see *War*)

Coronation. Ceremony, 105

Costumes (see *Dresses*)

Creation. Tradition of, 4, 5, 6, 7

Creator. Attributes, 6, 7; argument for existence of, 11; prayer to, 20, 28, 33, 89; precedence given to, 26; representation of, 76; honour paid to, 84, 167; temple to, 11

Cultivation (see *Agriculture*)

Dancing (see *Music*)

December. Sham-fight in, 47

Deluge. Traditions of, 4, 5, 9, 132, 153

Devils. In early times, their power, 70, 71, 78; exposure of, 86 (see *Huacas* in list of Quichua words)

Dramas, 90

Dresses. Of young knights, 36, 40, 44; of maidens, 37; of parents and relations, 37, 49; of villagers, 77

Drinking (see *Libations*)

Ears. Ceremony of boring, 35, 46

Emeralds, 94

Famine, 97

Farm, 98 (see *Agriculture*)

Fasting, 82, 85, 97

February, 52

Festival of the Sun, 16; for driving forth evils, 21; of knighthood, 35-46; for multiplication of flocks, 46 (see *Ceremonies*)

Fish. Sent fresh from the coast to Cuzco, 169

Flocks. Feast for, 46; management of, 158, 160, 161

Forest conservancy, 165

Fortress of Cuzco. Commenced, 88; building, 90

Future state. Belief as to, 48; speculations as to, 85

Hair. Ceremony of shearing, 37, 53; combing of girls', 80; men ordered to shave, 82

Harvest, 52

Heads. Practice of compressing, 78, 82

Human sacrifices, 54, 79, 85, 100

Hunting. Rules as to, 164

Insignia (see *Royal*)
Irrigation, 19

January, 51
July. Occupations in month of, 19
June. Festival in sowing-time, 19

Knighthood. Festival of admission to, 35, 36 ; Races, 41 ;
    installation, 43, 44 ; ceremony of bathing, 45 ; piercing
    the ears, 46 ; breeches, 43 ; discipline, 39, 40, 42, 46 ;
    cultivate maize, 52 (see *Youths, candidates for*)

Land tenures, 155
Landmarks, 83
Laws enacted by Yncas, 76, 83, 158-61, 164
Legends (see *Traditions*)
Libations, 26, 49, 103
Lineages. Enumeration of, 23 ; of each tribe, 77
Love. Excessive, between youths and maidens, 81
——— Charms, 81, 88

Maidens. At installation ceremony, 37 ; their duties, 41 ;
    encourage youths at the races, 42
Maize. Cultivated by young knights, 52 ; used as a charm, 63
March. Month of, 52
Marriage ceremony, 54, 76, 80, 107
May. Festivals in months of, 16
Moon. Idol of, 37
Mourning for the Ynca, 95, 100
Mummies. Honours paid to, 26, 27, 48, 50
Music, songs, and dancing, 18, 26, 32, 39, 42, 44, 48, 50,
    51, 52, 59, 89, 99, 167

November, 36

October. Festival of boring ears of youths, 35
Origin of tribes, 4 : of Cañaris, 8 ; of Yncas, 74, 153

Paintings, representing lives of Yncas, on boards, 4
Pearls, 94
Plays (see *Dramas*)
Ploughing. Time of, 48

Prayers. To the Creator, 20, 23, 28, 89; for fruitful flocks, 29; for the Huacas, 29, 32; for the Sun, 30, 56; for the Yncas, 31; to Huanacauri, 38; of the first Ynca, 79

Priest, 17, 18, 38, 41, 52, 83, 89, 98, 114 (see *Sorcerers, Wizards*)

Races. Run by candidates for knighthood, 41, 80

Rainbow. Appearance of, 75

Rope (see *Cable*)

Royal Insignia, 6, 19, 39, 41, 44, 91, 100, 105, 106, 111, 120

Sacrifices, 17, 20, 27, 32, 38, 43, 46, 49; by water, 50, 52; human, 54, 58, 79, 85, 100, 166; various kinds, 81

Sheep. Images of, 19, 41 (see *Flocks*)

Shearing (see *Hair*)

Shepherds, 46, 81

Songs, 59, 84, 89, 99; war, 95 (see *Music*)

Sorcerers, 89; cursed by Huascar Ynca, 115 (see *Wizards*)

Sun. Festival of, 16; not looked upon as God, 17; legend of, 18; prayers for, 30, 56; worship of, contemned, 83; worship of by Colla chief, 90

Staff of Tonapa, 74

Superstitions respecting Spaniards, 60 (see *Devils, Traditions*)

Tenure (see *Land*)

Traditions of earliest age, 70; of Tonapa, 71, 87; of Huanacauri, 75; in Huarochiri, 123; of Coniraya and Cavillaca, 124; of Huathiacuri, 135; of Pariacaca, 144 (see *Creation, Deluge, Origin*)

Tribute. Of crops, 162; virgins, 165; cloth, 167; soldiers, 168; labour, 168

Virgins. Houses of. Different classes, 82, 98, 108, 112; ravished by order of Huascar Ynca, 112; rules as to, 165; sacrifice of, 166

War. Of the Chancas, 91, 154; with the Collas, 101; with Quito, 108; of Huascar and Atahualpa, 113 (see *Conquests*)

Weaving, 78 (see *Cloth*)

Wives, 54, 80, 166 (see *Marriage*)

Witches, 63

Wizards, 13, 63 (see *Sorcerers*) ; persecuted, 83

Worship (see *Ceremonies*, *Festivals*)

Youths. Candidates for knighthood, 36 ; discipline they
were subjected to, 39, 40, 42, 46 ; races run by, 41 ;
breeches given to, 35, 36, 43 ; dress and ornaments of,
44, 45, 80 ; bathe, 45 ; sham-fights, 47 ; ears bored,
46 ; celibacy of, 82 (see *Knighthood*) ; cultivate maize, 52

II.—NAMES OF PLACES.

Words with a † also occur in Garcilasso de la Vega, and with a ‡ in
Cieza de Leon.

Acahuara. A plain in the valley of the Vilca-mayu, south
of Cuzco, near the modern village of Andahuaylillas, 18

†‡*Acari.* A valley on the Pacific coast, 62. See *Cieza de
Leon*, pp. 28, 265 ; and *G. de la Vega*, i, 244, 267

Achacache. On the shores of lake Titicaca. Inhabitants
called *Urcos-suyus*, 100

Achpiran. A hill visible from the temple at Cuzco, behind
which the sun sets, 17

Acoya-puncu, Angostura de. The first stage from Cuzco, in
the direction of Colla-suyu, 22, 170

Allcayriesas. Aborigines of Cuzco (see *Cullinchinas* and
Cayaucachis), 76

Amaybamba. A place beyond Ollantay-tampa, 29

Anahuarqui. Hill, two leagues from Cuzco, 41, 42

Ancasmarca. A province five leagues from Cuzco, in Anti-
suyu, 9

Anchi-cocha. In the province of Huarochiri, 125, 136

Anco-yacu river, 114

†‡*Andahuaylas (Antahuaylla)*, 18, 22, 152

†*Angaraes (Ancara)*, 78, 93. See *G. de la Vega*, ii, p. 132

Anta. Near Cuzco, 9, 59, 120

Antamarca. Huascar Ynca slain at, 119

†*Anti-suyu* province, 22, 27, 54, 96
Apu-tampu (see *Paccari-tampu*)
†‡*Apurimac* river, 23, 92, 116, 119
Arapa. A village north of lake Titicaca, 156
†‡*Arequipa*, 95, 96, 159
†‡*Asancaru* (*Azangaro*), 100. See *G. de la Vega*, i, p. 76;
    Cieza de Leon, p. 369
†‡*Asancata* peak, 87, 95. See *G. de la Vega*, i, p. 159
Aullagas. A province in Upper Peru (modern Bolivia), 159
†*Ayamarca*, 35, 90. See *G. de la Vega*, i, p. 80
Ayapata. A district in the province of Caravaya, 93
†*Aymara*, 96, 114, 159. See *G. de la Vega*, i, pp. 235, 237;
    ii, p. 50

†‡*Bombon* (*Pumpu*), 114. See *G. de la Vega*, ii, p. 130

†‡*Cacha*, 18. See *G. de la Vega*, i, p. 159; ii, p. 69
Cacha-pucara. Fortress at Cacha, 72
Cachona village. Probably *Cachora*, a small village near
    Abancay, 41
†*Cac-yaviri.* On the south side of lake Titicaca, 101
Cajamarca (see *Cassamarca*)
Callachaca, 91, 98
Capi-mayu. River flowing through Cuzco; now called
    Huatanay, 50
Carapucu mount, 72
†*Carancas.* In the south of Bolivia, 159
†‡*Caravaya* province, 72, 93, 95, 102, 115
†‡*Cassamarca* (Caxamarca), 7, 67, 94
†*Cayambi.* In the kingdom of Quito, 97, 98, 108, 109
Ccapac-uilca. Sacrifice on hill of, near Cuzco, 17
Chacamarca. There is a place in the district of Vilcas-
    huaman with this name (*Alcedo*, i, p. 353), 73, 78, 100
†‡*Chachapuyas* province, 98, 111, 113, 116
Chaclla. A district of Huarochiri, 94, 121
Chayas province, 93
†*Chilli*, 103, 115
Chillqui (*Chollqui*). A district south of Cuzco; now called
    Paruro (*Alcedo*, i, p. 443), 96

Chillqui-urpu, 93

†*Chimu*, 94, 108. See *G. de la Vega*, ii, pp. 195, 424

†*Chincha-suyu*. Northern division of the Ynca empire, 22, 27, 54, 103

†*Chincha-yunca*. On the coast, 88, 93, 94

†*Chirihuana*, 102, 109, 115, 168. See *G. de la Vega*, i, pp. 50, 54; ii, pp. 274, 277

†*Chita*. Heights a league and a half from Cuzco, 23. See *G. de la Vega*, i, p. 341; and ii, p. 71

†*Chollques*. (Probably *Chillqui* of *G. de la Vega*, i, p. 80). Near Paruro, 96

Choco village, 41

Chorrillo. A village in Huarochiri, 125, 142

†‡*Chumpivillcas*, 96, 168. See *G. de la Vega*, i, p. 229

†*Chunchus*, 168. See *G. de la Vega*, ii, p. 263

Chuntay-cassa, 116

†*Chuqui-apu*, 171. See *G. de la Vega*, i, p. 225

Chuqui-chaca, 29

Chuqui-cancha, 56, 57

Chuqui-chinchay, 95

Churicalla. Two leagues south west of Cuzco, 23

Cienequilla. On the road from Lima to Huarochiri, 136

Coca-challa. A ravine in Huarochiri, 145

Cocha-cassa. Near Huancarama, a lake somewhat off the road from Cuzco to Andahuaylas, 115, 117. See *G. de la Vega*, i, p. 266

†*Colcapata*, 19. See *G. de la Vega*, i, p. 179; ii, pp. 7, 109, 168, 237

†*Colla-suyu*. South division of the empire of the Yncas, 22, 27, 54, 67, 93, 105, 108

†‡*Collas*. A tribe in the northern part of the basin of lake Titicaca, 96, 100, 109

†‡*Collao*. A general name for the region round lake Titicaca, 164

†*Collahua*, or Caylloma. A lofty region between Cuzco and Arequipa (*Alcedo*, i, p. 492), 159

Collo-chahuay, 103

Colla-pampa, 94

Collca-pampa, 74, 75

Condorcoto. A mountain in Huarochiri, 138

†‡*Coquimpu.* In Chile, 103, 115

Cullinchinas. An aboriginal tribe of Cuzco, 76

†*Cunti-suyu.* Western division of the empire of the Yncas, 23, 27, 54, 96

†*Curampa*, 115. See *G. de la Vega*, i, p. 323 ; and *Alcedo*, i, p. 565

Cusipampa. A tributary of the Apurimac, 23

†*Cusi-pata.* Great square in Cuzco, 87. See *G. de la Vega*, ii, pp. 159, 252, 254

Cuti. A hill in the puna of Pumacancha, 18

†*Cuzco-ccapac* (see *Hurin, Hanan*), 79

Cuzco-cara-urumi. A rock so called, which gave the name to the city, 76

†*Hanan-Cuzco.* Upper Cuzco, 26, 33, 43, 44, 47, 48, 76, 79, 151

Hatun-Huanca Sausa. Valley of Xauxa, 93. See *G. de la Vega*, ii, pp. 128, 517. (See *Sausa*)

Hayacuchos (or *Hayachuco*). Indians who performed dances at Cuzco. The latter form is probably correct, 90, 112

†*Huaca-chaca.* A bridge over the Apurimac, 116. See *G. de la Vega*, i, pp. 234, 241

†*Huaca-puncu-mayu.* River also called *Capi-mayu* and Huatanay, flowing through Cuzco, 50

†*Huacay-pata.* Great square at Cuzco, 17, 39, 43, 53, 87, 99

†*Huacra-chucu*, 97. See *G. de la Vega*, ii, p. 322

Huamalies province, 94

†*Huamanca* (Guamanga), 95

Huaman-cancha, near Cuzco, 43

Huamañin,, near Vilcas, 95

Huanacu (see *Tia-huanacu*), 16

Huana-calla, 91

†‡*Huancas.* Great tribe of, 87, 93, 98, 114

Huancarama. Between the Apurimac and Andahuaylas, 115

†*Huancane.* On the north side of lake Titicaca, 100

†*Huancavillca.* The modern Huancavelica, 94, 102

†‡*Huanucu* province, 94, 114

Huaray-pacha, 22

Huarmi-pucara, 101

Huari, 15

Huarochiri province, 125, 135, 143

†*Huaruc,* 88. See *G. de la Vega,* i, p. 80

Huascar-pata, 111

†‡*Huayllas,* 98. See *G. de la Vega,* ii, p. 132

Huayparya. South of Cuzco, 22

Hucuru, 87

†*Hurin Cuzco,* or Lower Cuzco, 22, 33, 43, 44, 47, 48, 76, 151

†*Jaquijahuana* (see *Sacsahuana*), 23. See *G. de la Vega,* i, p. 80; ii, p. 53. Also *Cieza de Leon,* pp. 9, 32, 150, 320, 321

Lanqui-supa, Yayanacota de. The lake of Lanqui in the lofty region west of the vale of Vilcamayu, 88

Latallaco hill, near Lima, 136

Llallahua-pucara, 100, 101

Llantapa, in Huarochiri, 142

Lucrioc-chullo farm, 98

Lupaca province, in Colla-suyu, on the western shore of lake Titicaca, 101

Mama province, a district of Huarochiri (*Alcedo,* ii, p. 433), 94, 121

Manares province, 102

Mantucalla. Ynca remained at, during sacrifices, 18

Maras. A village north of Cuzco, 43

†*Marca-huasi.* About ten leagues from Cuzco, in the province of Abancay (*Alcedo,* ii, p. 457), 23

†*Mascas.* Vanguard in Ynca's army, 116. See *G. de la Vega,* i, p. 80

Matahua. A place near Cuzco, 38

Matra-coto. Mountain in Huarochiri, 143

Mauli, river, 168

Mulli-pumpa. In Urcos, 18

‡*Mulla-hampatu.* In the kingdom of Quito, 113

Musus (Moxos), 168

†*Muyna,* 111. See *G. de la Vega,* i, pp. 80, 86, 190, 306, 349 ; ii, pp. 306, 485

Ollachea. In the province of Caravaya, 93

Ollanta-tampu. In the vale of Vilcamayu, near Cuzco, 51, 116

Omoto-yanacauri. Sacrifice at, 17

†‡*Otabala.* In the kingdom of Quito, 110

†‡*Paccari-tampu,* 6, 38, 71, 173. See *G. de la Vega,* i, p. 65

†‡*Pachacamac.* On the coast of Peru, south of Lima, 29, 31, 33, 60

Pachatusam. A high hill near Cuzco, 95, 104

†*Papris,* 96, 102, 116. See *G. de la Vega,* i, p. 80

†*Parinacochas,* 59, 96. See *G. de la Vega,* i, p. 231

†‡*Pastus,* 99, 110. See *G. de la Vega,* i, p. 40 ; ii, p. 241, 350

Pati. A plain near Andahuaylillas, 18

Paucaray, 93

Pisac. In the vale of Vilcamayu, near Cuzco, 23, 100

Pocama-cancha, 112

Pollcaro river, 116

Poquen-cancha. Temple where historical records were kept, near Cuzco, 4

†*Poqui-llacta,* 102. See *G. de la Vega,* i, pp. 79, 86

†*Potosi.* In Upper Peru, 161

†*Puca-marca,* at Cuzco, 21, 118. See *G. de la Vega,* ii, p. 246

†‡*Pucara.* In the Collao, 6, 7, 100, 101

Puipu-huana. A mountain peak in Huarochiri, 144

Puma-cancha, 18, 95, 108

†*Puma-chupa.* A suburb of Cuzco, 50. See *G. de la Vega,* ii, pp. 239, 242, 247

Puma-huaca, 94

Puna-marca, 92

Puquina. Near Moquegua, 100 (*Alcedo,* iv, p. 236)

Puquinque, 47

Putina. In the province of Azangaro, near lake Titicaca, 83

†*Quehuar*. Vanguard in the Ynca's army, 116. See *G. de la Vega*, i, p. 80. *Quehue* became a village near Checacupe, in the vale of Vilcamayu (*Alcedo*, iv, p. 284)

Quepay-pampa, 118

Queros-Huanacauri. Sacrifice at, 17

Quihuar-cancha. In Cuzco, 21

†*Quichuas*, 100, 116

Quichuipay lake, 95

†*Quilacu*. In Upper Peru, 98

†‡*Quillasenca*, 98, 109 (*Alcedo*, iv, p. 290). A tribe between Quito and Pasto

Quilli-yacolca. Ravine near Cuzco, 41

Quillis-cachis. Aborigines of Cuzco, 110, 116

Quilluas, 159

†*Quiquisuna*. A village in Quispicanchi, in the vale of Vilcamayu, south of Cuzco (*Alcedo*, iv, p. 293), 18, 22, 96

Quinti. In Huarochiri, 143

Quiras-manta ravine, 39

†‡*Quito*, 97, 98, 108, 110

Quiza-chilla. Final victory over the Chancas at, 92

†*Quispi-cancha*. A province south of Cuzco (*Alcedo*, iv, p. 295), 18

Quisuar-cancha. Temple at Cuzco, 11

Quiyancatay mountain, 87

†*Rimac-pampa*, at Cuzco, 20. See *G. de la Vega*, ii, p. 239

Rimac-yuncas, 94, 108

Rontoca. In the Quehuars, 18

†*Rucanas* (*Lucanas*), 93, 117. See *G. de la Vega*, i, p. 267; ii, pp. 147, 358

Rumi-huasi, 93

Rurama, near Quiquijana, 18

†*Rurucachi*, 18, 88. See *G. de la Vega*, i, p. 159

Sacalpiña. A league from Cuzco, 54

†*Sacsahuaman*. Fortress at Cuzco, 88, 90, 93, 99, 103, 106

†‡*Sacsahuana*, 12, 119
Sallcatay mountains, 87, 117
Sancus, 110, 116
Santa Ana. A village in Huarochiri, 130
——————— A church in Cuzco, 170
San Agustin. Site of the palace of Tupac Ynca Yupanqui at Cuzco, 100
San Damian. A village in Huarochiri, 130, 142, 144
Santo Domingo. On the site of the temple at Cuzco, 17, 37
San Geronimo de Surco. A village in Huarochiri, 133
San Juan. A village in Huarochiri, 130
San Lorenzo de Quinti. A village in Huarochiri, 144
Santa Maria de Jesus de Huarochiri, 143
Santiago de Hanalucayhua y Hurinhuayhuacanchi, 67
Sañuc, 74
Satpina, 22
Sausa, 6, 87, 88, 93
Sausiru farm, 52
Sienacaca, 144
Sihuana. In Cacha, 18
Soras. In the province of Lucanas (*Alcedo*, iv, p. 445), 93
Succanca hill, 17
Sulcanca, 18
Suntu hill, 18
Surco. In Huarochiri, 133
Susur-puquio, 12
Sutic-toco. In Paccari-tampu, 77

†*Tampu*, 29, 77, 98, 116
Tancar village, 82
†‡*Tarma*, 94, 103
Tautar, 23
Taya-cassa. An island near Huanta, formed by the river Anco-yacu, which divides the province of Huanta from that of Angaraes (*Alcedo*, iv, p. 515), 93
†‡*Tiahuanacu*, 4, 5, 6, 7, 73, 171
Tilca, 23
Tiquina. South part of lake Titicaca, 73

†*Titicaca*, 5, 60, 112

†*Tococachi*. Suburb of Cuzco, 85, 97. See *G. de la Vega*, ii, p. 249

†*Ttahuantin-suyu*. Empire of the Yncas, 68, 76, 87, 103, 107, 111

†‡*Tumi-pampa*, 97, 108, 113
———————— *Pachacamac*, 98

†*Tucuman*, 103

† *Uacay-pata* (see *Huacay-pata*)
†*Uiscaca-bamba*. Wizards kept at, 60
†‡*Urcos*, 18, 29, 102, 151
†*Urco-suyu*, 67, 100. See *G. de la Vega*, i, p. 159
Utcu-pampa. Huascar taken prisoner at, 117

Vallollo mountain, 87
Varivilca (see *Huarivilca*)
Villca-coto, 133
†*Vilcañota*, 18, 83, 88, 152. See *G. de la Vega*, ii, pp. 179, 255
†*Vilca-cunca*, 99, 119. See *G. de la Vega*, ii, pp. 51, 511
† *Vilca-pampa*, 63. See *G. de la Vega*, ii, pp. 270, 301
†‡*Vilcas-huaman*, 93, 95, 108, 114, 115. See *G. de la Vega*, i, pp. 324, 326 ; ii, p. 58

†*Xauxa* (see *Sausa*)

Yacachacota. Huaca at, 88
Yacolla hill, 18
†‡*Yahuar-ccocha*, 110
Yamquesupa village
Yana-cocha, 88
Yana-yacu, 113
Yana-yana. Sacrifice at, 18
Yaurisquis. Near Paruro, south of Cuzco (*Alcedo*, i, p. 443), 23
†*Yauyus*, 114. See *G. de la Vega*, ii, p. 143
†*Yunca*, 31, 94, 123, 134. See *G. de la Vega*, ii, p. 224
†*Yuncaypampa*, 91
†*Yucay*, 151

III.—QUICHUA WORDS.

Some are *corrupt,* and cannot be made out, owing to errors in transcription.
Words with a † also occur in Garcilasso de la Vega, and with a ‡ in Cieza de Leon.

Accari. This word occurs in a prayer for the Ynca. *Acca* is the fermented liquor called chicha. *Ri* is a particle meaning ' but,' ' but however' (*Holquin,* pp. 264, 267), 31

Achacuc, 29 ⎰ Sorcerers who told fortunes by maize or llama's
Achicoc, 14 ⎱ dung, according as they came out odd or even. *Mossi* No. 3 ; *Von Tschudi,* p. 17

Achus. *Achu* or *Achuch.* An interjection of reprehension at one who exaggerates (*Mossi,* No. 4 ; *Von Tschudi,* p. 19), 79

†*Aclla.* Chosen women (see *Yurac, Huayra, Pacu, Yana*) 82, 98, 108, 112

†*Aclla-huasi.* House of chosen women, 165. See *G. de la Vega,* i, p. 292

Acnupu, 29, 33. *Acnapuy* (*Von Tschudi,* p. 9), or *Acnopuy* (*Mossi,* p. 5), richly dressed. *Acnani,* to prepare ceremonies. *Acnapuy,* pretty, handsome (*Markham,* p. 67)

Acoy-cunacataca. *Accoy,* innumerable (*Markham,* p. 65), *Cuna,* the plural particle. *Taca,* a particle of affirmation (*Holquin,* p. 265)

Acsa. The only word resembling this is *Acsu,* the skirt or petticoat, 29

Ahuapichu. *Ahua,* woven. *Pichu,* a hollow bone, or small pipe. *Ahua* is also a macaw. Then *pichu* is probably for *pichiu* or *piscu,* a bird, 28, 33

Alan-Situa-saqui. A song at the Situa festival. *Alan* should probably be *Alau,* an interjection, 26

Allastu. *Allani* is the verb " I dig". Possibly *stu* should be *stin,* when the word would mean ' the time for digging,' or it might be *huaca,* a proper name, 32

Allcachispa. *Allcachini,* to interpret, 31

Allcañañiy. From *Allcani,* to leave anything undone, 79, 89
—— *ñancyran*

Alquenti (see *Ccenti*)

Allpamantaca. Mortal (*Allpamantucac*), or that which becomes earth (*Allpayac*), 79

Allparnumachun. For *Allpamanac,* mortal, 79

Ama. Not, 31, 56

Amacaçachunchu, 30

Amacacharihuay. Amacha or *Amacacha,* a defender. *Ri,* a particle, denoting a beginning, as *Amachani,* 'I defend', *Amacharini,* "I prepare to defend", 32

Amachu-pichu-pichu-chunchu. Chu is an interrogative adverb. *Pi,* the preposition " in". *Pichu,* 30

Amamanachispa, 56

Amahunuchispa. Ama, not. *Hunu,* a million, or *Huñu,* all. *Mana,* none, 30

Amalla. Lla is a particle meaning "only", "no more than", 31

Amananu. An interjection, 30

Amapirima, 90

Amaquaquinta, 30

Amaru. A serpent, 95

Amatisca

Amaycay. Perhaps *Amancay,* a lily

Amusca. Amu, "dumb", 32

Anac-pacha (or *Hanac*), high. *Hanac-pacha,* heaven, 32

†*Anatuya. Añas,* a skunk, 79. See *G. de la Vega,* ii, p. 384

Añay saoca. A drama. *Añay,* an interjection of praise. *Sauca,* pleasure, 90

†*Anca.* An eagle, 96. See *G. de la Vega,* ii, p. 457

Ancalluasu. Dress of a girl. *Ancallu,* woman's attire in ancient times (*Mossi,* No. 15), 53

Ancha. Superlative, 89

Apa. Apani, I carry, 79

Apacha-mama-achi. A compound of Ynca and Colla words. *Apachi,* is grandmother in the Colla dialect. *Mama* is mother iu the Ynca language, 77

Apachinarcanqui. You shall have caused to be carried, 79

†*Apachita.* A heap on the road side, 78, 115. See *G. de la Vega,* ii, p. 356

Apacochan. (*Corrupt*)

Apoyunay. *Apuyupa,* " one in high authority", 79

†*Apu.* Chief, 25, 79. See *G. de la Vega,* i, p. 225 ; ii, pp. 39, 318

—— *Punchau,* sun idol, 25

—— *Quilla,* moon idol, 102, 103

—— *Panaca,* governor of the convents of women, 165

Armicachun. Probably *Armachachun.* *Arma,* bath. *Chachun,* third person singular imperative of *Cani,* "I am", 33

Arpay. Blood sacrifice, 79, 85, 115

Aspaca. *Aspacacuni,* to sacrifice by invitation, 115

Astara. A flute, 139

Atalli, 31

Atic. A conqueror, 79

Aticoclla. *Aticlla,* preparation, 31

Aticuc. *Aticani,* to keep or guard, 31

†*Atoc.* A fox, 112. See *G. de la Vega,* ii, p. 384

Attolihuay, 33

Atun (see *Hatun*)

†*Auca.* Enemy, soldier, 102, 115. See *G. de la Vega,* i, p. 185 ; ii, pp. 76, 528

†*Auqui.* Prince of the blood royal, unmarried, 106. See *G. de la Vega,* i, p. 97; ii, p. 352

Auscovicas. Soothsayers. The word is corrupt. Perhaps *Cusco-vica,* 114

Ayamarca Raymi. October, 35

Aycay. *Ayquiy* ? flight, 32

Ayma. A song, 89

Ayman, 79

Ayrihuay. April, 33, 52

Ayuscay-rutu-chica-quica-chica. Ceremonies. Garcillasso says that *Ayusca* is a baby that pines (i, iv, 2). *Ayuni* now, but not in ancient times, means to commit adultery. *Rutu,* to shear, and *Quicu,* to comb. *Chica,* as, as well as, so. The *Ayuscay* was when a woman conceived ; *Rutu,* when a child was named and shorn at the age of one ; *Quicu,* when a girl reached the age of puberty, 53

Cachra. A song, but the word is corrupt, 89

Cachun. The third person present imperative of the verb *Cani,* I am, 31, 56

†*Caçi-caçi.* Commandments, precepts, 71. Also a fast, according to *G. de la Vega,* ii, p. 229

Caçicta. Accusative form of the above, 30, 56

Cac-yoc. An old form of *ca,* "but"; *yoc,* a particle of possession, 32

Cahuariusinay. The word *Cahuari* is to look up; and *Cahuarina* a look-out place, 89

Cahuac. He who looks, 79

Callapallatichinay. Callpalla is sterile, barren, 89

Calli. Valorous, courageous, 37

Callpanchan. Callpa, force, vigour. *Callpanchani,* to strengthen, 77

Callpari. To regain strength, 115

Callparicu. A wizard, one who gives strength. 13

Callpay. Work, 115

Callurac. Clever, able

Calparica (see *Callparicu*)

†*Cam.* Thou, 90, 115. *G. de la Vega,* i, p. 197

Cam-cam, 115

Can-cuna. Ye, 115

Cama. The soul, 31. *G. de la Vega,* i, p. 106

Camac. Participle of *Camani,* I create, 33, 79. *G. de la Vega,* i, p. 101

Camac-churac. Churani, I put, 30

Camac-pacha. Pacha, the earth, 79

Camac-chiscan, 79

Camachun. Third person singular imperative, 30

Camachurac, 28

Camanchacas, 96

Camanmi. An optative form of the indicative, 79

Camantera-pichiu. Name of a bird, 46

Cama-quimpa, 86

Cumas. Perhaps for *Camac,* 28

Camascayqui. Imperative future second person, 29, 31, 32, 33

Camasca. A wizard, 14

Camay-quilla. December, 47

Camchomcanquiman. Probably for *Cachcanquiman.* Preterite of the optative second person singular of the verb *Cani*, I am. *"O that you were".* 79

Camtaca, 81

Canahuisa. Sorcerer, 89, 114

Canay. June, 19

Canca. They will be, or he will be. From *Cani*, I am, 28, 29

Cançachihuay. A thrush, 33

Cancha-ri. *Cancha*, a place, yard, court. *Ri*, a particle meaning but, but however, 30, 56

Canchu. A wizard, 83, 89, 114

†*Cancu* (see *Sancu*)

Cani. I am, 79

Canqui. Thou art, 33, 79, 115. *G. de la Vega*, Pt. ii, lib. i, cap. 23

Canquichic. We are, 115

Canipu. Medal of gold or silver worn by nobles on their foreheads, 16

Capaucha-cocuy. Human sacrifice. *Ccapachani* means to do a thing with pleasure, also to cut by the root. *Cocuy*, an offering. *Cocuni*, to offer oneself, 85

Canta, or *Camta.* Accusative of *Cam*, thou, 30

Cantoray. A way of making chicha, 35

†*Carachi.* The itch in llamas, 160. *G. de la Vega*, ii, p. 378

Carca. A sorcerer, from the dung of llamas ; diviner by odds and evens, 89

Carcan. Third person singular perfect indicative of *Cani*, "I am," 79

Carhua-yalli. A term unexplained by Dr. Avila, 122

Cari (*Ccari*). A man, 28, 86

Cari-cachun. *Ccari*, a man. *Cachun*, imperative third person of *Cani*, "I am"

Cari-cachuyu. Probably for *Cari-cachun*, 33

Cari-llacta. *Ccari* and *llacta*, a village, 56

Casilla. *Casi*, vain. Casilla, in vain, 28, 30, 56

Casillacta, 30, 31, 56

Catamuscampas. Catani, to cover, roof, 115

Catuiman, 32

Cauchay. Cauchani, to pick leaves, 30

Causachun. Third person imperative of *Causani*, to live, 30

Causamus, 33

†*Cay.* This. Also the infinitive of *Cani*, I am. Applied to nouns to denote the nature of a thing, as *Runa*, a man; *Runa-cay*, humanity, 30, 79. *G. de la Vega*, i, p. 198

Cay-lla. Lla, a particle of love, liking, preference, 28, 29, 33

Cay-cama. Cama, a preposition, with, as for as, according to, 81

Cay-cari-cachun, 79, 86

Cay-huarmi-cachun. Cay, this; *Ccari*, a man; *Huarmi*, a woman; *Cachun*, third person imperative of *Cani*, I am, 79, 86

Cay-colla. Proper name *Colla*, 38

Cay-coscay. Proper name, 86

Caycustaymi. (*The word is corrupt*), 29

Cayhuacyanquital. Cayhua, a certain plant; *quita*, wild. But the word is corrupt, 81

Cayqui. Cay-yqui, *thine*, 28, 33

Cayquita. Ta, accusative ending, 78

Cayquichu-ras. Chu, a particle of interrogation, 30

Cayquiquisicas-pilla. Quiqui, the same, 30

Cayu. A song, 89

Ccacca. A rock, 87

Ccalla-sana. A portent; *Ccallani*, I break; *Sanampa*, a sign, 107

Ccallac-pacha. "Beginning of time", 70

Ccamantira. Small bright feathers that birds have under their beaks, 80

†*Ccapac.* Rich, royal, 29, 78. *G. de la Vega*, i, p. 95; ii, pp. 27, 345

——— *acchama quispisutuc umu.* Water in the spring at Titicaca; *Chama*, joy; *Quispisutu*, crystal drops; *Umu*, water. "The royal joy bringing crystal water drops", 87

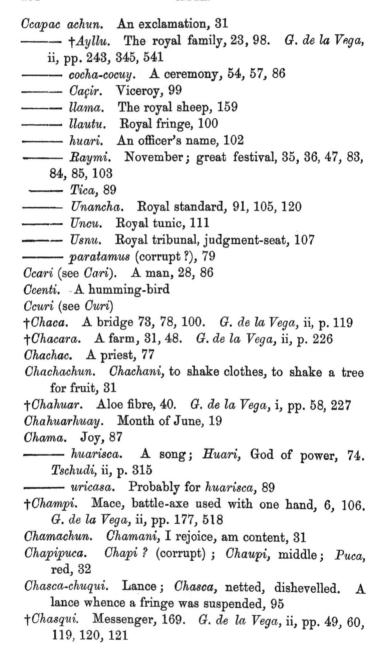

Ccapac achun. An exclamation, 31

——— †*Ayllu.* The royal family, 23, 98. *G. de la Vega,* ii, pp. 243, 345, 541

——— *cocha-cocuy.* A ceremony, 54, 57, 86

——— *Caçir.* Viceroy, 99

——— *llama.* The royal sheep, 159

——— *llautu.* Royal fringe, 100

——— *huari.* An officer's name, 102

——— *Raymi.* November; great festival, 35, 36, 47, 83, 84, 85, 103

——— *Tica,* 89

——— *Unancha.* Royal standard, 91, 105, 120

——— *Uncu.* Royal tunic, 111

——— *Usnu.* Royal tribunal, judgment-seat, 107

——— *paratamus* (corrupt ?), 79

Ccari (see *Cari*). A man, 28, 86

Ccenti. A humming-bird

Ccuri (see *Curi*)

†*Chaca.* A bridge 73, 78, 100. *G. de la Vega,* ii, p. 119

†*Chacara.* A farm, 31, 48. *G. de la Vega,* ii, p. 226

Chachac. A priest, 77

Chachachun. Chachani, to shake clothes, to shake a tree for fruit, 31

†*Chahuar.* Aloe fibre, 40. *G. de la Vega,* i, pp. 58, 227

Chahuarhuay. Month of June, 19

Chama. Joy, 87

——— *huarisca.* A song; *Huari,* God of power, 74. *Tschudi,* ii, p. 315

——— *uricasa.* Probably for *huarisca,* 89

†*Champi.* Mace, battle-axe used with one hand, 6, 106. *G. de la Vega,* ii, pp. 177, 518

Chamachun. Chamani, I rejoice, am content, 31

Chapipuca. Chapi ? (corrupt) ; *Chaupi,* middle ; *Puca,* red, 32

Chasca-chuqui. Lance ; *Chasca,* netted, dishevelled. A lance whence a fringe was suspended, 95

†*Chasqui.* Messenger, 169. *G. de la Vega,* ii, pp. 49, 60, 119, 120, 121

Chasquihuoy, 29

Chapa. Sentry, watch, 115

Chay. This, 31

Chayan. Chayman, here, 79

Chayariyuya. Chaya, return ; *Yuya*, mind, memory, 79

Chica. So, as, 75

Chica-llacta. Llacta, a village, 115

Chiccha. Chicchi, hail ; *Chicha*, a shoe, 75, 78

Chicpa (corrupt), 78

Chihuay. A bird, 29

†*Chilca.* A shrub (*Baccharis scandens*), 118. *G. de la Vega*, i, p. 187

†*Chipana.* A woman's breast; a lens of metal for concentrating the sun's rays; a bracelet worn by the High Priest, 45, 106. *G. de la Vega*, ii, pp. 30, 163

Chipicñispa. Chipicñini, I wink, 89

Chiqui. Misfortune, 75

Chiqui-manta. Manta, from 32

Chiquiy. My misfortune, 115

Chiraoca. Clear, genial season; *Ca*, an old form of genitive, 79

Chirmayñaymantan. Chirma, harmful, 115. *G. de la Vega*, ii, p. 326. To be unquiet or to do harm

Chispa. (Corrupt), 30

Chocanaco. A trial of strength. Should be *Choccanacuy*. A throwing of stones. (*Mossi*, No. 77), 47

Chucup-mama. Should be *Churup*, genitive of *Churu*, a shell ; *Mama*, mother ; mother of the shell. A pearl, 94

‡*Chumpi.* A belt (see *llama*) ; also a dark brown colour (*Cieza de Leon*, p. 146)

Chuñires. (Corrupt), 101

†*Chuñu.* Frozen potato, 162, 167. *G. de la Vega*, pp. 17, 359

Chupasitas. Worshipping the summit of a pass. *Chupa*, a tail, 59

Chuqui. A lance, 16, 20, 21, 25, 36, 115, 167, 95. *G. de la Vega*, i, p. 225 ; ii, p. 171

Chuqui-yllayllapa. Thunder and lightning

Chuqui. Gold, in the Colla dialect, 90

†*Churac.* Participle of *Churani,* to put, 31, 33. *G. de la Vega* i, p. 198

Churachay. Chay, that, 33

Churacllay. Llay, a particle, denoting pleasure or endearment, 91

Churaspac. Preposition, for, 31

Churasquayqui. Yqui, second possessive pronoun, 28, 32

†*Churi.* Son, 56. *G. de la, Vega,* i, pp. 91, 214

Churinta. Accusative, 31

Churu. A shell, 106

†*Chuspa.* A bag for coca, 20, 38. *G. de la Vega,* i, p. 296

Chutarpu. (Corrupt). Chutani, I tighten. *Chutasca,* a thing well fastened (see *Huanarpu*), 81

Cicapac. Dative case of *Çica,* a corrupt word ; perhaps *Sicya,* a measure, or *Sicra,* a small basket, 79

Citua (see *Situa*)

Coca-hacho. " Eater of coca ". *Hachu,* " chewer" (*Mossi*) 118

†*Cocha.* Lake, 117. *G. de la Vega,* i, p. 49 ; ii, p. 66

Cochaman. Man, against, or to, 79

Cochamanturayocpa. Tura, brother of a sister. *Yoc,* a particle of possession. *Pa,* genitive particle, 86

Cochispa. (Corrupt), 56

Coco. Missiles ; thistle heads ; a game, 47

Colla-chicha, 62

†*Collca.* A granary, 98. *Ramos,* cap. 18 ; *G. de la Vega,* ii, p. 237

Collca-uncu. A dress ; *Uncu,* a tunic ; *Collca,* a granary ; also the Pleiades (*Acosta* from *Balboa,* p. 58), 37

†*Collque.* Silver (see *Napa, Chachac*), 19, 47, 77, 90

Concaraca. Cunca, neck. *Rac,* before, 79

Conca-qui. Yqui, second possessive pronoun, 89

Conopa. Household god, not among the Yncas ; but among the coast tribes

Conti-vicas. Sorcerers (*Cunti-uica*), 114

Cori (see *Curi*)

†*Coya.* Queen (see *Mama*), 23, 96. *G. de la Veya,* i, pp. 68, 96, 293

—— *Raymi.* August, 20

Coya facssa. (*Corrupt.*) A woman dedicated to the sun, 25

Coyñiy-pashinatapac (*Corrupt.*) *Coñiy*, warmth, 79

Cozco (see *Cuzco*)

Cucunari (see *Coco*), 89

Cuchi. Rainbow, *Ccuychi*, 75

Cuchuy, 32

†*Cumpi.* Fine cloth, 88, 97, 99, 105, 118. *G. de la Vega,* ii, p. 324

Cumpicu. Weaver of fine cloth, 160

Cunacuy-camayoc. *Cunacuy*, a preacher; *Camayoc*, one who has charge of anything, 71

Cunti-huisa, Sorcerer, 89

†*Curaca.* A lord, 87, 99

Curayoc. *Ccoray*, the act of hoeing. *Yoc*, particle of possession

†*Curi.* Gold, 19, 47, 78, 89, 90

—— †*Cancha.* Temple, 16, 17, 76, 78, 89, 92, 99, 100, 103, 104, 108. *G. de la Vega,* i, p. 283

—— *ccacca.* A bowl to hold water from Titicaca, 87

—— †*napa.* Golden figure of a llama, 19, 47

—— *chachac.* A priest in some parts (*Arriaga*), 77

Cuscayqui. Equal; *Yqui*, thy, 89

†*Cusi.* Joy, 81. *G. de la Vega,* ii, pp. 159, 423

Cusi-cullasun. To feel joy, 89

Cusi-simirac. A happy smile; good news, 81

Cusi-llacta. A happy village, 31

Cusinchicpi. Giving rewards; *Pi*, from; *Cusinchini*, I console, 80

Cusi-ussa-pochoy. A good ripening, 30

Cuspalla, 89

†*Cuy Cuyhuan.* *Cuy*, a guinea pig; *Huan*, with, 85, 101

Cuyllu or *Cuyru.* A white llama; *Coyru*, white, applied to metals and animals, 27

Cuyru-mama. "White mother", applied to the earth, 56

†*Cuzco* (see *Hanan, Hurin*)

—— *asu ycochilliquilla*, 37

Gualanpapi (see *Hualanpapi*)

Hahocha. Perhaps *Hahua* (outside) ; *Hucha* (sin), a slight offence, 115

†*Hahuay.* Grandchild. Hence *Hahuanina*, a lineage, 29. G. de la Vega, ii, pp. 531, 533

Hampi-camayoc. A doctor, one who has charge of medicines or poisons, 99

Hamuttapty. Subjunctive of *Hamutani*, I understand, 79

†*Hanan-Cuzco.* Upper Cuzco, 26, 33, 43, 44, 47, 48, 76, 79, 151

Hanan-hamuyrac. *Hamuy*, to come ; *Rac*, even, 89

Hanan-pichun. *Hanan*, upper ; *Pichu*, a bird, 79

Hanantarac. *Hananta*, dative case ; *Rac*, even, first, 89

Hapa-cochan. To boast, 29

Hapi-ñunu. Devils; *Hapi*, to seize; *Nuñu*, breast, 68, 78, 87

Hatallihuay. To hold, to have charge of, 29, 31, 56

Hatallimuchun. To hold, 31

†*Hatun.* Great, 29

———— *pucuy.* January, 51

———— *runa.* A giant, 115

Hauca. May, rest, repose, 16

Hauchha. Cooked herbs, 115

Haycay. How much, how great, 29

———— *Pachacamac*, 28

Hayllayqui-pac. *Haylli*, song ; *Yqui*, thy, 39

Haymiquay. Help (*but corrupt*), 28

Hayñillalay (*corrupt*), 79

Hicrinpachap. Perhaps for *Hurin-pacha*, 86

Hillacunya-chuquicunya. Men dressed up as lions, so called, 45

Hillusu. Greedy, 115

†*Hinalla.* So, in this way, 89

Hinallatac. *Tac*, a final particle, 115

Hinatac, 81

Hinamatima (*corrupt*). Probably *Hinantin*, all together, 79, 89

†*Huaca.* Sacred, a sacred thing, 5, 27, 29, 32, 34, 55, 58, 76, 83, 93

———— *camayoc.* Priest in charge of a *huaca*, 43, 58

Huaca mucha. Worship of a *huaca*, 83, 86

Huacanqui. A love philtre, 81, 88

†*Huacay-pata.* Great square at Cuzco, 31

———— *chaspa.* Guard

———— *chamuy. Chamay,* joy

†*Huaccha* (see *Huachay*). Poor, 30. *G. de la Vega,* i, pp. 90, 97

Huaccunacatacay. Huaccani, to mourn, 115

Huachay-llama. The llama of the poor, 159

Huacra-chucu. Horn head-dress, 97. *G. de la Vega,* ii, p. 226

Huacus-chaspa (corrupt?), 30

†*Huahuay.* A child, 31, 56. *G. de la Vega,* i, p. 314

Hualanpapi or *Huallanpani.* A large tuft of feathers, 49

†*Hualcanca,* Shield, 106. *G. de la Vega,* ii, p. 171

Hualla-huisa. A sorcerer, 89, 114

Huallina (see *Taqui*). A song, 18. *Haylli* of *G. de la Vega,* ii, p. 8

Huallana-chamayariscca. A joyful song, 89

Huallpaquiypa. Hualpac, Creator, 115

Hualpay. Creation, formation, 29

Huallparillac. Two particles, *ri* and *lla,* 30

†*Huaman-cancha.* Place of a falcon, 43

———— *tiana.* Seat of a falcon, 76

———— *champi.* Club, 106

———— *ñin,* 95

Huan. With, 89

Huana. Correction, 29

†*Huanacu.* Wild species of llama. Guanaco, 16, 41

Huanarpu (see *Chutarpu*). The female form of *Chutarpu,* 81

Huanchurin. With, 30

Huanchin. With, 30

Huanta-chinaca. A drinking bout, 130

Huara. Breeches, 36, 141

†*Huaraca.* Sling, belt, 36, 38, 39, 40, 47, 53. *G. de la Vega,* ii, pp. 134, 167

Huarachicu. Ceremony of breeching, 34, 80

Huarayaru, 43

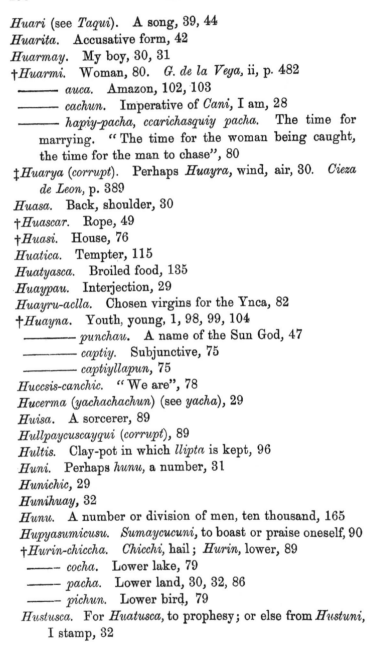

Huari (see *Taqui*). A song, 39, 44

Huarita. Accusative form, 42

Huarmay. My boy, 30, 31

†*Huarmi.* Woman, 80. *G. de la Vega,* ii, p. 482

————— *auca.* Amazon, 102, 103

————— *cachun.* Imperative of *Cani,* I am, 28

————— *hapiy-pacha, ccarichasquiy pacha.* The time for marrying. " The time for the woman being caught, the time for the man to chase", 80

‡*Huarya (corrupt).* Perhaps *Huayra,* wind, air, 30. *Cieza de Leon,* p. 389

Huasa. Back, shoulder, 30

†*Huascar.* Rope, 49

†*Huasi.* House, 76

Huatica. Tempter, 115

Huatyasca. Broiled food, 135

Huaypau. Interjection, 29

Huayru-aclla. Chosen virgins for the Ynca, 82

†*Huayna.* Youth, young, 1, 98, 99, 104

————— *punchau.* A name of the Sun God, 47

————— *captiy.* Subjunctive, 75

————— *captiyllapun,* 75

Huccsis-canchic. " We are", 78

Hucerma (yachachachun) (see *yacha*), 29

Huisa. A sorcerer, 89

Hullpaycuscayqui (corrupt), 89

Hultis. Clay-pot in which *llipta* is kept, 96

Huni. Perhaps *hunu,* a number, 31

Hunichic, 29

Hunihuay, 32

Hunu. A number or division of men, ten thousand, 165

Hupyasumicusu. Sumaycucuni, to boast or praise oneself, 90

†*Hurin-chiccha. Chicchi,* hail ; *Hurin,* lower, 89

————— *cocha.* Lower lake, 79

————— *pacha.* Lower land, 30, 32, 86

————— *pichun.* Lower bird, 79

Hustusca. For *Huatusca,* to prophesy; or else from *Hustuni,* I stamp, 32

Huya-chucu. Chucu, a head-dress, 101
Huyarihuay. Perhaps *Ayrihuay,* April, 28

Itari-panaca. Panaca, name applied to lineages or families, 23

Laycca. A priest, 83, 98, 114
Llaca-chuqui. A lance adorned with plumes, 95
†*Llacta.* A village, 76, 31, 115
———— *pachacasilla.* Head man of a village (see *Pachaca*)
Llanca (see *Llama*)
†*Llama huacar paña.* Right hand is *paña; Llama,* a
    sheep, 16
———— *huanacu.* A wild llama, 16
———— *pacos cuyllos.* White alpacas, 16
———— *paucar paco.* Beautiful alpacas, 16
———— *uqui paco,* 16
———— *chumpi.* Dark brown llama, 16
———— *llanca.* Working llama, 16
———— *ccapac.* Belonging to the crown, 159
———— *huachay.* Belonging to the people, 159
———— *cuyllu.* White llama, 27, 31, 32
———— *michec.* Shepherd, 81
———— *llama-hañamsi.* Drama, 90, 101
Llanay (corrupt), 70
Llanca-pata. Small plates of gold, 19
Llanquisi. Shoes, 80, 106
Llantu-pichu. Shade, 28, 33
Llapan. All, 89
Llasac. Heavy, 79
Llauraruna, 29
Llaychunca. A soothsayer by odds and evens, 89. The
    Llayca of *G. de la Vega,* i, ix, 14
Llayman, 79
Llautu. Royal fringe, 12, 16, 36, 58, 100, 106, 111
Lliclla. Mantle, 9, 24, 40. *Cieza de Leon,* p. 146
Llipta. Lime chewed with coca, 62, 96
Llusque. Month of May, 17
Llutacticci-capac. A name for the god, 89

Machiyqui. Thigh. *Yqui,* second possessive pronoun, 86

Mactamñiqui. A boy (*Macta*), 86

Mamanchu. Wife, 166

†*Mama-cuna.* Matrons in charge of the virgins of the Sun, 18, 165. *G. de la Vega,* i, pp. 293, 294, 300, 302

†*Mana.* No, not, 30, 32

Manayllay. From *Mañani,* I ask, pray for, 89

Manchuricayquiman. For *Mancharini,* I tremble, 79

Manamyancanchu. *Manam,* not. *Canchu,* 79

Manaracpas. Before that, 79

Manares. Before, 102

Manta. From, 32, 115

Mantapas. From, 81

Manchachic. *Manchani,* I fear. Imperative, 79

Manchay-simi-yocpa. *Manchay,* fear, 86

†*Maquiy-lluttaquey.* *Maqui,* hand; *Lluta,* to cover, 79

Maras-ttoco. Window at Paccari-tampu, 77

†*Marca-ri.* Village; *Marccani,* I carry, 31

Marca-rihuay, 29

Marca-llihuay, 33

Marop. A pestle, 131

Masnu-yauri. A term unexplained by Avila (see *Yauri*), 122

Massuma. A festival in Huarochiri, 122

†*May.* Who, where, 29, 33, 91. *G. de la Vega,* i, p. 198

Maypin. Where is it? 33, 79

Maypini-canqui (see *Canqui*), 28

Maycanmi. Which of them, 79

Maycanmi-canqui. *Canqui,* art thou, 86

Maymana. Where, 32

Mayñic. Whether, 81

Maymantapas. Whence, 81

†*Mayu-cuna.* Rivers, 89

Michtachic. Avarice, 30

†*Michec* (see *llama*)

Micuy. To eat, 31, 32

Micuynin. To eat, 33

Micuncancachun. To eat much, 30

Mirachun. Mirani, I multiply, increase, 29

Miruna (corrupt?), 30

†*Mitanta.* Turn, time, 31

Mitaysanay. Turn, 115

†*Mitimaes.* Colonists, 4, 22, 23, 95, 97, 113, 161

Mojocati. A sacrifice; perhaps *Mosoc,* new, 50

†*Molli.* Trees, 90

Moro-urco. A house near the temple of the Sun, where a great cable was kept; *Muru,* a coloured spot; *Urco,* a hill, 48

Moronpassa tarpuyquilla. July; *Tarpuy-quilla,* "the sowing month," 19

Moya. Forests, 165

Mucha. Worship, 37, 43, 44, 83, 89, 90, 114

Muchancoyqui. Muchani, I worship, 115

Muchascay, 31

Mucumuchun. Muccu, a joint, knot; *Muchuni,* I suffer, 30

Muchun. Suffering, 30

Muchuspacan. Suffering, 30

Mullu. Shell, 17, 20, 62, 63

†*Munayqui.* Love; *Yqui,* second possessive pronoun, 79. See *G. de la Vega,* i, p. 523; ii, p. 239

Musac. Perhaps *Munac,* loved, 28, 32

Mutca. A mortar, 131

Nacasca. Beheaded, 32

†*Nanaclla.* Suffering, 45

Napa. Salutation, 19, 39, 47

Napahuay. Salutation

Ñaui. Eye, 86

Ñeca. Towards, 79

Ñicocupa. To ask for another, 32

Nicpa-carichun. To say anything importunately, 30

Nicpunchac. Nec, towards; for *punchau,* day, 56

Nihuay. Near, 32

†*Ninacta.* Fire, 31

Niocmin (corrupt?), 32

Nipacachun, 71

Ñis, 28

Ñis-caca. Nisca, a particle, denoting one who has the reputation for any quality, 115. *Holguin,* p. 257

Ñiscayqui, 30

Ñispa. A particle, 31

Ñispac, 30, 56

Ñispachucapac, 31

Ñispacamacpa, 86

Ñispacamacatu, 32

Ñispachurascay, 30

Ñispallutac, 33

Nispañicusun, 89

Nisunqui, 81

Niyhuan. Niy, a saying, 115

Ñuca, I, 90

Ñuñu. Bosom, 68, 78, 79, 87

†*Ñusta-calli-sapa.* "A princess unrivalled for courage;" *Ñusta,* a princess ; *Calli,* courage ; *Sapa,* unequalled, 37, 41, 42

†*Ocllo* (see *Palla*)

†*Oscollo.* A wild cat, 141. *G. de la Vega,* ii, p. 116

Pac, 91

Pacamascayqui. Pacani, to hide, 31

†*Paccarisca.* Origin, birth, 38

Paccarimusca. Morning, 78

Paccariscanchic. Born

Pachaccan. Servant, major-domo, 71

†*Pacha* (see *Hurin, Purum, Ocallac,* etc.), 30

Pacha-pucuy. February, 52

Pacha-chacara. Farm, 31

†*Pachacamac.* Creator of the world, 7, 88, 93, 94, 98, 108, 114, 127. *G. de la Vega,* i, p. 106 ; ii, p. 38

Pachachulla, 32

Pachacunaripis, 89

Paclla. Bald, barren, bleak, empty, 32

Pacnipaccarichun, 56

†*Paco* (see *Llama*)

Pacopa, 86

Pacta. Equal, fair, just, 79

Pacu-aclla. Chosen women for chiefs and lords, 82

†*Pahuay.* Flight, 91

†*Palla-sillu.* A female figure; *Palla*, princess, 19

——— †*ocllo. Ocllo*, a woman of the blood royal, who had taken a vow of celibacy, but was not secluded in a convent, 25. *G. de la Vega*, i, iv, cap. 7

Pallcaymantam. A branch; *Manta*, from, 115

Pallarac. Collected, 28

†*Pancurcu.* A torch, 23

†*Papa.* Potato, 29, 159, 162. *G. de la Vega*, ii, pp. 5, 17, 213, 359

Papa-çara. Potato and maize (*sara*), 30

Papi. Injured, damaged, 79

Passa. Pacsa, the moon in the Colla dialect, 37

Paucar-huara. March, time of many flowers, 52

——— *camayoc.* One in charge of royal insignia, 99

——— *paco* (see *llama*), 16

——— *quintu.* Bunch of fruit, 19

——— *runcu.* Small plate of gold, 19

——— *suntur.* Head-dress of the Ynca, 6, 19, 39, 41

Paycaptin. Pay, he; *Captin*, subjunctive of *Cani*, I am, 31

Payllanquitacmi. Payllani, I reward, 79

Pialco. A bird, for *Pilcu*, 25

Pichiu. A bird, 46

Pihucupi (corrupt), 29

Pihuana. Perhaps *Pihiña*, brave

Pilco-camayoc. One who has charge of plumes of a bird, 99

——— *casa.* Garland, 26, 44

——— *pichiu.* A bird, 46

——— *yacu*, 25

——— *luncu-paucar-uncu.* Beautiful head-dress of plumes, 51

Pimicuchun. Perhaps *Pincachun*, jump, 30

Pincanqui. You bound, jump, 86, 91

Pirca. A wall, 96

Piscapapas. Pisca, a large partridge, 29

Picaspapas, 33

Pitispa. Pitini, to break, 30

Pitusiray-sanasiray. One person fastened on the top of another; *Pitu,* equal, a pair; *Siray,* sewn together; *Sana,* perhaps for *Sama,* rest, 75

Pocoyca. Ripe, 79

Puca-caychu-unca. Red tunics; *Puca,* red, 45

†*Pucara.* Fortress

Pucay-urco. A ceremonial dress; *Urco* should probably be *uncu,* a tunic, 49

Pucu-pucu. A bird, 73

Pullao. A tree, 142

Punari. Desert, 31

†*Punchau-Ynca.* The Sun Idol, 16

——————— *Apu.* The Sun Idol, 56

——————— *Huayna.* The Sun Idol

——————— *Churi.* Son of the day, 30

Punchaoca. Of the day. Archaic form of genitive, 79

Purichic. To walk, 30

Purichuruna, 56

Purin. He walks, 79

Puris. He walks, 29

Pusupichu (corrupt), 28

Puracahua. A dress or ornament, 97

Purapura. Pura, both. Ornaments on each side, 90, 106

Purunpacha. Purun, savage; *Pacha,* time, 70, 135

——————— *racyaptin. Racya,* before; *Nntin,* plural of multitude, 70, 135

†*Pururaucas.* Stones turned to men, 154. *Acosta; G. de la Vega,* ii, p. 57

Pururunas. False men, 152. *G. de la Vega,* ii, p. 57

Puti. A trunk, 110

Putu. A large calabash, 143

Qualpay, 31

Quarpas, 31

Queru. A cup, 103

Quespilla. Crystal, 28

Quicta; 30

Quictacamascay, 30

Quichu. A song, 99

Quicusiquispu. A bezoar stone, 31

Quicuchica, 53, 80

Quicuna, 78

Quiuanpas, 89

†*Quillaca.* Moon, 79, 109

Quillari, 30, 36

Quillarincanpas, 56

Quillpunchichpi, 79

Quimampichun, 79

Quinrayñin-pichun. Broad, 79

†*Quinua. Chenopodium Quinoa, L,* 159. *G. de la Vega,* ii, pp. 5, 7, 213, 357, 367

Quipasiyun. Quipani, to cover, 79

†*Quipus.* Knot records, 10, 51, 169

† —— *camayoc.* Keeper of the records, 55, 58

†*Quirau.* Cradle, 53. *G. de la Vega,* ii, p. 531

Quisaruna. Quiso, the birds for sacrifice (*Acosta*), 30

Quiscuar. Tree, 90

Quistacmi, 79

Quispi. July, 20

Quispicta. Clear, bright, 56

—— *pilla,* 30, 33, 56

Quispi-casica, 32

—— *llacta.* Bright village, 30, 31, 56

—— *sutic.* Bright name, 87

Quita. Savage, 30

Rallcapacpalhacan. (*Corrupt*), 79

Rañuptiy, 79

Rañotayri, 79

†*Raurana.* To burn, 41, 42, 43. *G. de la Vega,* ii, p. 531

Raurac. Burnt, 89

Raimicachun. Be at the *Raymi,* 79

†*Raymi Ccapac.* The great festival, 35, 36, 47, 83, 84, 85, 95, 100, 108, 166

Raymi Napa, 39, 41, 42

Raypancanqueña, 79

Recsichillaran. To make to know

Riacllahuay. (*Corrupt*), 89

Riaiytam, 79

Ricaptiy, 79

Ricsi, 79

Riculla, 79

Ricunanquim. To look, 79

†*Rimachun.* Speak, 86

Rimasu, 90

Rimayñi. To speak, 86

Rochocallasun, 89

†*Runa.* A man, 31

—— *yachachachachun.* A teacher, 29

—— *yanani.* Servant, 56

—— *cay.* This man, 30

—— *scay*, 30

—— *rallac*, 79

—— *hualpac.* Good workman, 81, 89

†*Rurac.* Maker, 28, 33. *G. de la Vega*, i, p. 109

Rurascayquicta tacancharin, 56

Rutichico. The cutting of hair, 53

Sacaca. A comet, 95

Sacapac. Castanets, 32

Saccocachun, 31

Sanca-sonco-quila pionco. A dress, 49

Sancu. Sacrificial pudding, 24, 27, 32, 33, 81

†*Sapa.* Only one ; unequal, 37

Sarampion. (*Corrupt*). A disease, 110

†*Sara-colli.* Different kinds of maize, 163

—— *cuma*

—— *paro*

Sasca. Sacsa, ragged; *Sauca*, joy, 31

Sasicuspa, 81

Saycaptiy. To stand. Subjunctive, 79

† *Saycoyñicaypitac.* To tire. Subjunctive, 79

Secsec. Thorn bush, 96. *Mossi*, No. 278

Sihuicas. *Sihui*, a thorn, 96. *Mossi*, No. 235

Simi. Mouth, 86

†*Sinchi-ñaui-yocpa.* Strong eye, 86

† *Situa.* Festival, 20, 32, 34. *G. de la Vega*, i, p. 179

Soncoapa chinacoc huacca chinacoc. Small stones used as love producers, 81

Sulluya. Bastard. *Sullu*, premature, 118

Sunquichay, 81

Suntur-paucar. Royal head-dress, 6, 17, 39, 41, 44, 106, 111, 120

Supa-yacolla. White mantles, 36

Suntinrammica. *Suntuni*, to heap up, 86

†*Suri.* Ostrich, 78. *G. de la Vega*, ii, pp. 31, 394

Suruc-chuqui. A lance with long tassels, 95

Sutic-toco. A window at Paccari-tampu. *Sutic*, name; *Toco*, window, 77

†*Suyu.* Province, 58, 163

†*Suyuntuy.* Turkey buzzard, 88, 101. *G. de la Vega*, ii, p. 390

Tacamachic. A black duck, 30

Tacancuna. *Tacana*, a hammer, 29

Tachca. (*Corrupt*), 89

Taquacaycha. Probably *Taquiani*, I fix, am constant, 29

Taqui. Music, 18, 26, 32, 39, 42, 44, 48

—— *Huallina.* A song, 18

—— *Alançitua saqui.* A song at the Situa festival, 26

—— *Ayma.* Song, 89

—— *Cayo.* Song, 89

—— *Chapay quenalo.* Song, 50

—— *Chupay huayllu.* Song, 51

—— *Huallina mayuriscca.* Song, 89

—— *Haylli.* Song, 89

—— *Cachra*, 89

—— *Quichu*, 99

—— *Uucu*, 59

—— *Torca*, 89

Tarayac, 79

Tarichasquihuay. Tarini, to find, 33

Tarpuntay. Priest; *Tarpuni* is to show, 17, 18, 38, 41, 52

†*Tasqui.* A girl, 80. *G. de la Vega*, i, p. 197

Tayna. Perhaps *Tauna*, a stick, 32

Tayta. Father, 101

Tica-tica. Music, 26

Tica. Brick, or if *Ttica*, a flower

†*Tiya; Tiyana.* Seat, 90, 99

Tiyancay. To sit

Titu. Difficult, 29

†*Toco.* Window, 77. *G. de la Vega*, ii, p. 238

Tocto. Honey; a bird, 47, 49

Tocuya, 86

Topapo. Tupu, a measure, 29

Torca (see *Taqui*)

†*Ttahuantin-suyu.* The four provinces or divisions of the empire, 68, 76, 87, 103, 107, 111

Ttopayaricta. Tupani, to rend, 79

Tupac-huanacu. Royal huanacu, 41

—— *pichuc llantu.* Royal fringe of feathers, 88

—— *usi*, 74, 88

—— *yauri.* Royal sceptre, 41, 74, 75, 88, 91, 97, 106, 111

†‡*Tupu.* Measure, 79, 169. *G. de la Vega*, ii, p. 9; *Cieza de Leon*, p. 146

Turumanya. Rainbow, 75

†*Tuta.* Night, 30. *G. de la Vega*, i, p. 182

Tutaca, 79

Tutacachannas

Tutayac-pacha. Time of night; dark ages, 70

Ucu-pichu. Ucu, deep; *Pichu*, a bird, 28, 33

†*Uchulla. Uchu*, pepper, 32

†*Ucumari.* A bear, 111

Uicchay-camayoc. A preacher. *Huichay* (not *Uicchay*) up, 71

Uhiscayquita. (*Uichccani*) to shut, 30

Uma-chucu. Head dress, 106

Umuchun, 78

Umacta. Head (accusative), 32

Uma-Raymi. September, 34

†*Uma.* Priest, 83, 89, 98, 114

Umiña. Emerald, 94

Unacchuylla. To prolong, 111

Unachayamoran. (*Corrupt*), 75

Unanchaptiy, 79

Unancha. Standard, 91, 105, 106, 120

Unanchascam, 79

Uncancampac, 30

†*Uncu.* Mantle, 37. *G. de la Vega,* i, p. 296

—— *umisca*

Uncallu, 40

†*Unu.* Water, 87. *G. de la Vega,* i, p. 198

Upiachun. Drink (imperative), 30

Upatari. Upallani? to be silent, 102, 104

Uqui-paco (see llama)

Uracahua. A deep place, 106

Uracarpaña. Sacrifice, 85

†*Urpi.* Dove, 129. *G. de la Vega,* ii, p. 393

Usachun. To accomplish, 31

Uscata. Sorcerer, 89

Usnayqui. Usnu, tribunal, landmark, 79

Usnu. Landmark, 107

Usuta. Shoe, 36, 40

†*Uturuncu.* Jaquar, 96. *G. de la Vega,* ii, p. 385

Uyari. To hear, 81

Uyarihua. Hearing, 33

Uyarillaray. To listen, 79

Vallavicas (see *Hualla-huicos*)

Varoytiypas (*corrupt*)

Vatica (see *Huatica*)

Vicuña, 79. *G. de la Vega,* ii, pp. 117, 378, 383, 384

Vilca. Sacred, 63, 93, 107. *G. de la Vega,* ii, pp. 255, 416

—— *camayoc.* One in charge of sacred things, 58

Vilcay-cunapac, 115

Viñaypas. Increase, 81

Y. Possessive particle, 3rd person, 29

Yacachun. Follow, 31

†*Yacha.* A school, 79. *G. de la Vega,* i, p. 335 ; ii, p. 247

Yachachun. Let him learn, 30

Yachaptiy. Subjunctive form, 79

Yacharanquira, 79

Yachipachan, 71

†*Yacolla.* A cloak, 36, 44.   *G. de la Vega,* i, p. 296

Yacarcaes. Wizards, 86

Yacarcay. Invocation, 14

†*Yahuar-sancu.* Sacrificial bread, smeared with blood, 27,
    28, 32

Yahuayra. Festival, 19, 48

Yaichichuruay. (*Corrupt*), 30

Yampac, 56

†*Yana.* Black, 30, 91

Yana-aclla. Wives for the common people, 82, 146

Yanaussi, 79

Yana-caca. Black rock, 146

Yana-namca. (*Obscure*), 123

Yananya. Servant, 31

Yana-yana. Sacrifice

Yaravi. An elegy, 52

Yatalliymay. (*Corrupt*), 29

Yauirca. A thick cable, 95

Yauri. Sceptre, 26, 40, 41, 42, 92

Yayacarui. Rainbow, 75

†*Yayay.* Father, 31.   *G. de la Vega,* ii, p. 353

Ychastalpas. Perhaps, 81

†*Ychma.* Vermilion.   *G. de la Vega,* ii, p. 413

Ychu. Grass, 40, 41.   *G. de la Vega,* i, p. 254

Yllarichun. To shine (*imperative*), 30, 56

Ymay. What, 33

Ymay-pacha. What time, 31

Ymay-pachama, 28

Ynihuay, 28, 33

Ynca-uillu. Female figure, 19

—— *ocllo.* Woman of the blood royal, 25

Ynca-runa-yanami. Royal servant, 30

—— *churi.* Son of the Ynca, 31

—— *ranti.* Viceroy, 112

†*Ynti.* Sun, 31, 90, 101, 112

†*Yntip-Raymi.* Festival in May, 16

Yntic. Genitive (archaic form), 49, 79

Yñimcampac, 30

Yochaycaymayoc, 32

Yocllamunqui, 81

Yquicauras. Perhaps *Yquicayani,* to cut up, 30

Yquicta. Positive particle, 2nd person, accusative, 30, 56

Yurac-aclla. Chosen virgin of medium beauty (*Ramos,* cap. 9), 82

Yuya. Thought, memory, 89

Yuyayronayta. A wise man; a cautious man, 79

IV.—NAMES OF GODS AND HUACAS.

Those with † also occur in Garcilasso de la Vega; those with ‡, in Cieza de Leon.

Achacalla (see *Hapi-ñuñu*)

Anta-puca. A Huaca, 83

Atapymapuranutapya. (*Corrupt*). A Huaca worshipped by the Huancas, 88

Cacha-Uiracocha. The idol in the Temple at Cacha, 18. *G. de la Vega,* i, p. 159; ii, p. 69; *Cieza de Leon,* p. 356

Cacha-huaca (see *Ccapa-cocha*)

Cana-chuap Yaurica. A demon exposed by Ccapac Yupanqui, 86

Canacuay. A huaca, 96. See *G. de la Vega,* i, p. 330

Caprichay. Creator; called also *Tica-ccapac,* 83

Carayucho-Huayallo, or *Huallallo Caruicho.* A huaca of the Huarochiris, 123, 142

Cavillaca. A goddess of the Huarochiris, 125, 127

Chellcascayu. A Huarochiri idol, 122

Chinchay-cocha. A huaca from, 83, 93

Choque suso. A god of the Huarochiris, 145

Chumpi-casico, or *Huanacauri,* 36

Chuqui yllallapa. Huaca of thunder and lightning, 16, 20, 21

Chuquilla, 26, 56, 155, 167

Chuquipillu. A huaca, 83

Chuqui-racra. A huaca found by the Ynca at¹ Villcas.
    Racra, split. Literally " a forked dart" or lightning,
    83, 93

Chuspi-huaca, 94

Coniraya. A god of the Huarochiris, 124, 134

Conopas. Household gods of the Huarochiris, 122

Coropuna. A huaca ; a mountain peak, 83. *G. de la Vega,*
    i, p. 232

Guacamayos. Macaws, ancestors of the Cañaris, 9

Huallallo Caruincho. A God of the Huarochiris, 123

—————— *Chuqui-racra.* (See *Chuqui-racra*), 83, 93

†*Huanacauri.* Huaca of a brother of Manco Ccapac, 13,
    17, 25, 26, 35, 38, 52, 57, 75, 80. See *G. de la Vega,*
    i, pp. 65, 66 ; ii, pp. 169, 230

‡*Huarivilca.* The huaca at Xauxa, 7, 87. *Cieza de Leon,*
    p. 300

Huathiacuri. A sort of demi-god in Huarochiri, 135

Pacha-mama. The earth goddess, 56, 155, 166, 167

†‡*Pachacamac.* "Creator of the world", 29, 31, 33, 60.
    See *G. de la Vega,* i, p. 106 ; ii, p. 38 ; *Cieza de Leon,*
    pp. 251, 253, 254

†*Pachayachachic.* "Teacher of the world". The Creator.
    The Creator, 6 ; Temple to, 11, 106 ; Existence of, 11 ;
    Idol of, 16 ; Prayer to, 16, 20 ; Festival of, 82, 85, 90,
    107, 108, 115, 119, 154, 167. See *G. de la Vega,* i, p.
    109 ; ii, p. 56

Pariacaca. A god of the Huarochiris, 87, 93, 128, 138,
    139, 142

Passa-mama. An idol of the moon, 37

Punchau. The idol of the sun, 16, 30, 56. See *G. de la Vega*, i, p. 182

Rurucachi. A huaca, 88

†‡*Supay.* A devil, 115. See *G. de la Vega*, i, p. 108 ; ii, p. 397 ; *Cieza de Leon*, p. 224

Tarapaca (see *Uiracocha, Tonapa*), 31, 71, 79, 115
†*Tecsi*, or *Ticci Ocapac* (see *Caprichay, Uiracocha*), 6, 81, 83. See *G. de la Vega*, i, p. 109; ii, p. 38
Tocapo Uiracocha, 6, 28, 33
Tonapa (see *Tarapaca*). A legendary prophet or demi-god, apparently in the Collao, 71, 72, 74, 79, 87, 88, 115

Uncuraya. A jar with the figure of a devil so-called, among the Huarochiris, 122
Uiracocha (see *Viracocha*). See *G. de la Vega*, ii, p. 66
Urpi-huachac. Wife of Pachacamac ; a legend in Huarochiri, 129

†*Viracocha* (see *Tecsi, Tocapo, Pachayachachic*)
———— *Tecsi*, 6, 28, 29, 30, 33
———— *Tocapo*, 6, 28
———— *Coniraya*, God of the Huarochiris, 124
———— *Ya*, 29
———— *Chanca*, God of the Chancas, 29
———— *Hatun*, (Great), 29
———— *Apstin*, (Chief), 29
———— *Urusayna*, 29
———— *Chuqui-chanca*, 29
———— *Tarapaca*, 31
———— *Tonapa*, 69, 70, 71, 72
———— *mparaca* (at Huaruc), 88
———— *Ynti*, 112

Yanacauri (see *Huanacauri*)
Ymaymana (*Uirococha*), 6, 30, 32
†*Ynti.* Sun God of the Collas, 112

V.—NAMES OF INDIAN MEN, WOMEN, *AYLLUS* OR LINEAGES, AND TRIBES.

Those with † also occur in Garcilasso de la Vega ; those with ‡, in Cieza de Leon.

Amaru Yupanqui Ynca. Eldest son of Pachacuti Ynca, 95, 96, 99, 104

†*Anahuarqui Mama* (see *Mama*), 98

†‡*Anco-Allu* (*Hanco-Allu*). Chief of the Chancas, 91, 92, 94. *Hanco-hualla* of *G. de la Vega*, i, pp. 242, 324, 326 ; ii, p. 58. *Cieza de Leon*, p. 280

Anco, Don Carlos, 67

Apu-cama. A minister of the temple, 100

Apu- or *Auqui-challcu Yupanqui.* A minister of the temple, 100, 106

Apu-Hualpaya. Governor or Regent of Huayna Ccapac, 104

Apu-Quiricanqui, Don Gaspar, 165

Apu-Tampu-Pacha. Father of Manco Ccapac, 74, 77

Apu-Urco-Huaman-Ynti-Cunti-Mayta. Son of Mayta Ccapac, 85

Arequi Ruca. Ynca general on the march along the coast, 98

†*Asto Huaraca.* Chief of the Chancas, 92. *G. de la Vega*, i, p. 347

†‡*Atahualpa Ynca.* Birth, 107 ; at Quito, 111 ; message to his brother, 112 ; Viceroy, 112 ; war of, 113 ; taken prisoner by Pizarro, 118

‡*Atoc* (see *Huaminca Atoc*)

Aucaylli Ayllu. Lineage which carried the cries to Chita, on the Anti-suyu road, 23

†*Ayar Cachi.* One of the four brothers who came out of the cave of Tampu ; brother of Manco Ccapac, 57, 74

†*Ayar Racca.* Brother of Manco Ccapac, 74. Garcilasso gives the name Ayar *Sauca* (i, p. 73).

†*Ayar Uchu.* Brother of Manco Ccapac, 74

Ayllu. Lineage

—— *Aucaylli*, 23

—— *Chamin Cuzco*, 22

Ayllu †*Ccapac.* The blood royal, 22. See *G. de la Vega,* ii, p. 531

—— †*China Panaca,* 23, 78. See *G. de la Vega,* ii, p. 531

——– *Copara,* 144

—— *Hatun,* 22

——– †*Huañayñin,* 85. *Huahuanina* of *G. de la Vega,* ii, p. 531

—— *Masca Panaca,* 23

—— *Marasaylla,* 22

——– *Quesco,* 23

—— *Tarpuntay.* The priest caste, 23

—— *Sañu,* 23

—— †*Usca Mayta,* 22. See *G. de la Vega,* ii, p. 531

—— *Usca Panaca,* 23

—— †*Vica-quirau,* 22. See *G. de la Veya,* ii, p. 531

—— *Yaura Panaca,* 23

—— *Yapomayu,* 22

—— *Yahuaymin Sutic,* 22

—— *Yaraycu,* 22

Cacya-quivi, Don Baltasor de, 67

†‡*Canas.* A tribe south of Cuzco, on the borders of the Collao, 67, 102, 152

†‡*Cañaris.* Origin, 8 ; Huaca of, 83, 93 ; Conquest of, 49, 98, 111 ; Chief of (see *Urco-calla*), 112 ; Punished by Athahualpa, 113, 116

†‡*Canches.* A tribe bordering on the Canas, 67, 152. *Cieza de Leon,* pp. 355, 358

Capacuyos. A tribe which conspired against Ynca Pacha-cutec, 96

†‡*Caviñas.* A tribe south of Cuzco, 91, 96. *Cieza de Leon,* p. 354

†*Cayaucachis.* An aboriginal tribe of Cuzco, 76. See *G. de la Vega,* ii, p. 239

†*Ccapac Yupanqui.* Ynca, 85, 88

†‡*Chachapuyas.* A tribe in Chincha-suyu, 22, 27, 54, 103

†‡*Challcuchima.* A general of Atahuallpa, 111, 115, 118

Chamin Cuzco Ayllu. A lineage which carried the cries down the Chincha-suyu road, 22

Chana Coricoca. A valiant widow in the war with the Chancas, 92

†‡*Chancas.* A tribe of great power, west of Cuzco, 29, 91, 92, 152. See *Cieza de Leon,* p. 280, 315, 316

Chauca-chiipta. The name of the Indians in Huarochiri, who were found by Dr. Avila, in new shirts called *Musnu yauri,* and *Carhua yelli,* 122

†*Chillquis.* Vanguard of the Ynca army. Tribe near Cuzco, in district now called Paruro, 102, 116

†*China-Panaca Ayllu.* A lineage which carried the cries down the Cunti-suyu road. Descendants of the Ynca Sinchi Ruca, 23, 78

†*Chollques,* 96. Probably *Chillqui* of *G. de la Vega,* i, p. 80

†‡*Chumpivillcas,* 96, 168. See *G. de la Vega,* i, p. 229

Chuqui-huy-pachuquipa. Sister and wife of Ynca Huascar, 111

†*Colla-Ccapac.* Chief of the Collas, 90, 91

Condorcanqui, Don Felipe de, 67

Copara Ayllu. A lineage in Huarochiri, 144

†*Cuys Manco.* A great chief at Cuzco; chief of the valley of the Rimac, 105. See *G. de la Vega,* ii, pp. 185, 190, 192, 194

Haca-roca. Husband of the Princess Mama Ruca, 107

Hanco-Allo (see *Anco-Allu*)

Hatun-Collas. Chief of the Collas, 90

Hatun-Ayllu. A lineage which carried the cries down the Chincha-suyu road, 22

‡*Huaminca Atoc.* General sent against Atahualpa, 112, 113. See *Cieza de Leon,* pp. 167, 273

†*Huañaynin Ayllu.* Descendants of Mayta Ccapac, 85

Huanca Auqui. General of the blood royal, employed against Atahualpa, 113, 115, 117

Huayrotari, Maria de, 67

Huasco Tornay Rimac. Chief of the Chancas, 92

†‡*Huayna Ccapac*, 1 ; born, 98, 99 ; accession, 104 ; coronation, 106 ; wars, 108, 110 ; death, 110

†*Lloque Yupanqui* Ynca, 82

†*Mama-huaca.* Wife of Manco Ccapac, 52, 75, 76
——— *achi.* Mother of Manco Ccapac, 74
——— †*Anahuarqui.* Wife of Tupac Ynca Yupanqui, 98
——— *Chimpu-cuca* or *Tancarayacchi.* Wife of Lloque Yupanqui, 82
——— †*Corillpay cahua.* Wife of Ccapac Yupanqui, 87
——— *Ccoya chuqui huypa chuquipa.* Wife of Huascar Ynca, 111
——— †*Chuqui-checya.* Wife of Ynca Yahuar-huaccac, 90
——— *Chimpu-runtucay.* Wife of Huayna Ccapac, 108
——— *Cuca.* Second sister of Huayna Ccapac, 107
——— *Cusirimay.* First wife of Huayna Ccapac, 105, 107
——— †*Mamicay Chimpu.* Wife of Ynca Ruca, 89
——— †*Runtu-cay.* Wife of Ynca Uira-ccocha, 90
†‡*Manco Ccapac.* Deluge, 4 ; call from the Sun, 5 ; issues from Paccari-tampu, 6 ; brother of Huanacauri, 35, 44, 52 ; birth, 74 ; marriage, 76 ; enemy of Huaca, 76 ; prayers of, 79 ; ceremony ordered by, 80
Manco-Churin-Cuzco. The *élite* of the Ynca's army, 116
†‡*Manco Ynca*, 108, 119
Marasaylla Cuynissa Ayllu, 22
Masca-Panaca-Ayllu, 23
Mayhua, Juan Apu Ynca, 67
†*Mayta Ccapac* Ynca, 83
†*Mayus.* Tribe near Cuzco. Ynca's body-guard, 110, 116
Mihicnaca Mayta. General in army of Huayna Ccapac, 108, 110

Ninancuyochi. A son of Huayna Ccapac, 107

†*Pachacuti Ynca Yupanqui.* Takes the name of Yamqui Pachacutec, 93, 94, 95, 99
†‡*Paullu Ynca*, 23

†*Pinao Ccapac, Tocay Ccapac.* Conquered by Manco Ccapac, 76. Garcilasso has *Pinahua* (i, p. 71)

Pisar Ccapac. Chief of Cassamarca, 94

Quesco Ayllu, 23

†*Quichuas,* 100, 116

†*Quis-quis.* A general of Atahualpa, 111, 114, 115, 116, 117, 120

†*Rahua Ocllo.* Mother of Huascar Ynca, 107, 111

†*Ruca Ynca,* 87, 88, 89

†*Rumi-ñaui.* A general of Atahualpa, 111

Sañu Ayllu

Santa Cruz, Pachacuti Yamqui Salcamayhua, Juan de. Author of "Antiquities of Peru," 67

†*Sinchi Ruca.* The second Ynca, 44, 78, 80, 81

Tarpuntay Ayllu, 23

Tintaya, Gonzalo Pizarro de, 67

†*Tocay Ccapac.* A great idolater conquered by Manco Ccapac, 77, 90. Garcilasso has Tocay (i, p. 71)

Tocto Oclla Cuca. Mother of Atahualpa, 107

Tomay-Huaraca. Chief of the Chancas, 92

†*Tupac Ynca Yupanqui,* 96, 97, 101, 104, 152

Tupac Ranchiri Ynca. A priest of the Ccuri-cancha, 92

†*Uira-ccocha Ynca* (see *Viracocha*), 12, 90, 92, 95

Urcu-huaranca. Son of Mayta Ccapac, 85

Urcu-Ynca. Son of Ynca Uira-ccocha. Slain by the Chief Yamqui Pachacutec, 91, 93

Urcu-Culla. Chief of the Cañaris, 112

Urcuni, Bernabe Apu Hilas, 67

†*Usca-Mayta Ayllu,* 23

Uturuncu Achachi, An Ynca general, 99, 102, 103

†*Vicaquirau Ayllu,* 22

Vilcaquiri. A brave Ynca captain, 92

†*Viracocha Ynca* (see *Uiraccocha*), 12, 90, 92, 95

†*Yahuar-huaccac Ynca,* 89

Yahuaymin Ayllu Sutic, 22

Yamqui huanacu, Francisco de, 67

Yamqui Pachacutec. Chief of Huayra Cancha. Defeats and kills Ynca Urcu. Submits to Ynca Yupanqui, who takes his name, 91, 93

Yaraycu Ayllu, 22

Yauru Panaca Ayllu, 23

Yapo-mayu Ayllu, 22

†‡*Yupanqui Ynca* (see *Pachacutec* and *Yamqui*), 10, 11, 12, 33, 54, 91, 92, 93, 96, 100, 154

VI.—NAMES OF SPANIARDS.

Artaun, Don Sebastian de, Bishop of Cuzco. Treatise on the fables and rites of the Yncas addressed to, 3

Avila, Dr. Francisco de. Author of a narrative of the errors of the Indians of Huarochiri, etc., 121

Barco, Pedro del, 118

Benalcazar, Sebastian de, 169

Bobadilla, Doña Isabel de, 21

Candia, Pedro de, 118

Cañete, Viceroy Marquis of, 164

Castro, Licentiate, 62

Guzman, Diego Artiz de, 11

Lartaun (see *Artaun*)

Molina, Cristoval de. Author of " Fables and Rites of the Yncas", 3

Olivera, Luis de, 59, 62

Ondegardo, Polo de. Report by, 149. *Cieza de Leon,* p. 387; *G. de la Vega,* i, p. 273; ii, p. 91

Pizarro, Francisco de, 118

Segovia, Hernan Lopez de, 11

Toledo, Viceroy Francisco de, 60
Toro, Friar Pedro de, 62

Valverde, Fray Vicente de, 119

THE END.

T. RICHARDS, PRINTER, 37, GREAT QUEEN STREET.